The Direct Marketer's Legal Adviser

ROBERT J. POSCH, Jr.

MCGRAW-HILL BOOK COMPANY

New York   St. Louis   San Francisco   Auckland
Bogotá   Hamburg   Johannesburg   London
Madrid   Mexico   Montreal   New Delhi
Panama   Paris   Tokyo   Toronto
São Paulo   Singapore   Sydney

Library of Congress Cataloging in Publication Data

Posch, Robert J.
  The direct marketer's legal adviser.

  Includes index.
  1. Direct selling—Law and legislation—United States.   I. Title.
KF2026.5.P67   343.73′088   82-7153
ISBN 0-07-050559-4   347.30388   AACR2

1234567890   MUMU   898765432

ISBN 0-07-050559-4

The editors for this book were William Newton and Christine Ulwick, the designer
was Naomi Auerbach, and the production supervisor was Paul A. Malchow.
It was set in Souvenir Light by University Graphics, Inc.

Printed and bound by The Murray Printing Company.

JAMES T. McGRATH
(1934-1980)

A life spent worthily
should be measured
by deeds, not years.
—SHERIDAN

Contents

Preface

This book costs less than $30, which may well be deductible. Yet it may help you avoid hundreds of thousands of dollars in fines, which are not deductible. This book is written for all direct marketers who do not want to see the government feasting on their firms' profits or otherwise interfering in their business operations.

If you are a committed professional in this field (and not merely working at a job), this book will fill a void in your library. As evidenced by the continued volume of consent orders (both in quantity and in fines administered) and a review of the literature on point, there is a definite scarcity of guidebooks which elucidate compliance and contract protection for the direct marketer.

In light of the foreseen business climate of the 1980s, direct marketing will continue to be highly visible to government. The successful marketer will, therefore, be a marketer who successfully reaches his or her targeted audience with the least intrusion from governmental regulatory bodies. Merely creating and fulfilling promotions will not suffice if it is done at the cost of excessive fines, legal defense fees, bad publicity, and government-dictated consent agreements affecting future policy. To avoid this pitfall, the marketer cannot dwell in uncertainty concerning the regulatory environment.

This guide will go far to eliminate such uncertainty in the areas reviewed. It discusses the law and offers feasible solutions to potential problems. It directly addresses the fundamental compliance issues facing the direct marketer in the areas of the list, pricing, free gifts, sweepstakes, discounting, geographic credit testing, celebrity endorsements, and telephone solicitations, as well as the compliance issues affecting other elements you can test and standardize in direct marketing.

Of course, this is not intended as an all-purpose legal service. Any professional in one field knows that there is a need for expertise from specialists in other fields, and so you'll want to review individual promotions with your counsel. However, a careful reading of this book will give you a necessary understanding of the compliance issues involved in the promotions discussed. You will not approach your promotions in a legal vacuum. You will be better prepared to eliminate obvious problems from your copy (and thus save initial counsel time and costs) and to refine and define questions for your counsel concerning specific legal problems. Simply by understanding the issues involved and making sure they are reviewed, you will become a better client for your counsel.

While this book has been written in lay English specifically for the direct marketer, it also is a valuable tool for attorneys providing legal counsel in this field. The notes in the References section alone represent a wealth of research—time-consuming research needed by anyone in this field who provides legal advice.

So, use this book with the knowledge that to succeed in business today you must be three-dimensional. One dimension is knowing your business and how it makes its profits. The second dimension is anticipating and planning in advance to avoid the impact of government regulations on your bottom line. The third dimension is understanding the legal environment in which you are doing business. Beyond luck or nepotism you'll need to be three-dimensional to reach the top today. If you've read this far, you're already two pages into the other two dimensions.

Acknowledgments

This book bears the imprint of many persons, and it goes without saying that it is impossible to list acknowledgments to all those whose influence makes itself felt. However, since this text reflects much of my work, education, and overall lifestyle, I'd like to note special thanks to those individuals who, since I left Hofstra Law School, contributed decisively to my integration of law and direct marketing.

Passing the New York State Bar can be a major hurdle, but it needn't be if one is fortunate enough to make the acquaintance of J. Gardiner Pieper, Esq. As a teacher, mentor, and all-around individual, he represents the antithesis of any adverse comment ever made concerning attorneys.

At Doubleday I received significant assistance from many colleagues and supervisors. Direct-marketing law is not taught in school but is self-taught. I was fortunate as I began my career to be in a work environment which supported mature growth. While dozens assisted me in the formative stages, I'm most indebted to Tony Garramone, Alex Hoffman, George Larie, Clarence O'Connor, Gerard Toner, Esq., and James T. McGrath, Esq., to whom this book is dedicated. Much of the positive impact this book has upon the profession reflects the contribution of those individuals through me to you.

In the evenings I took advantage of an outstanding M.B.A. program at Hofstra University, where the professors encouraged me to incorporate my career knowledge within the curriculum. I am particularly indebted to the Marketing Department, especially to Dr. Joel Evans, Dr. Dorothy Cohen, and Dr. Saul Sands, for encouraging a multidisciplined approach.

In 1981, Hoke Communications, Inc., offered me a forum in *Direct Marketing* through the monthly column "Legal Outlook." I wish to extend a special note of thanks to Henry Hoke, Jr., John McIlquham, and Kevin Hanley.

Specific editorial input came from many and varied sources. Of particular note were the incisive legal comments by George Shively, Esq., and the overall administrative support and physical preparation of the manuscript performed by Eileen DeMilt. Her good humor and skills are highly valued by me.

My overriding debt is to my wife, Mary Lou, who worked through the entire book to eliminate legalese and humanize the content. The personal support given to anyone attempting a major effort is even more important than the professional support. We had a limited amount of time from contract to deadline to complete the manuscript, and simultaneously we were moving into our first house. The sun has never set on an unhappy day with Mary Lou in the 9 years we've known each other. Her patience and that of my children, Judith and Robert III, were greatly appreciated. To extol the merits of Mary Lou is to say the same about her parents, Vernon and Mary Collins. Finally, I acknowledge the contributions of my parents, Robert and Maryrose Posch, who at great personal and financial sacrifice assisted me through the B.A., J.D., and M.B.A.

I am grateful to all those mentioned above in ways that can never be adequately expressed.

ROBERT J. POSCH, JR.

About the Author

ROBERT J. POSCH, JR. has the ideal credentials to write about the diverse and growing channel which will dominate marketing in this decade. He has been employed in the legal department of Doubleday & Company, Inc. for seven years where his duties include monitoring several aspects of compliance with government regulation. He received his MBA from Hofstra University, and he was elected to the National Honor Societies in Business and Marketing.

Other writing credits include the column "Legal Outlook," in *Direct Marketing* magazine, which reviews and clarifies contemporary legal issues affecting the direct marketer. He is also a contributor to *The Direct Marketing Handbook,* edited by Edward Nash and has been published in *The Journal of Marketing.*

Introduction

Direct marketing offers all Americans those novel product lines once available only in specialty stores in select, large urban areas or, conversely, in out-of-the-way rural areas. It is a national boutique, and when viewed in the aggregate, this channel proves capable of serving almost any need currently served by the retail trade.

Further, in an era of increased need for results, this channel, especially mail, offers instant measurable results. For example, every mail-order promotion has a coupon (usually coded) to measure individual results.

Finally, every demographic and social trend favors direct marketing's continued growth vis-à-vis retail. There are obvious reasons: an aging population, the cost of gasoline, or the increased number of women in the work force. More subtle but just as real is the fact that downtowns are often simply unsafe, and retail store shopping is often an unpleasant experience. To cite a personal example, my wife, Mary Lou, and I took our two children (Judith, 5, and Robert, 9 months) shopping July 4th weekend, 1981. We had just bought a home and were stocking it (as your census tracts say our demographic segment should). The unsynchronized traffic lights along Hempstead Turnpike almost halted traffic. After an hour to go 4 miles (and feeding a parking meter), we found that most "sales" were rain checks or in some instances just bait-and-switch ruses, a topic you'll read about later in the book. In one store we could not purchase a picnic table, as the personnel refused to sell it—they were too busy setting up displays! As we went from store to store, either Mary Lou or I was immobilized with a stroller. Then there is that sense of fatigue produced from seeing virtually the same goods, colors, and textures in store after store (especially in the malls). Why bother?

We were very happy for the "cold calls" from telephone sales personnel and purchased a few items. Our oil service resulted from mail, phone, and then personal sales. Much of our furniture will be purchased from a mail-order seller in New Hampshire (no sales tax in that state). Some of our appliances were purchased from Ted Turner's Cable News Network demonstrations. No rain, rude salespersons, or wasted carfare. Better yet, we didn't settle for just anything—we purchased selectively.

I want this channel to succeed. The product lines are usually good, and direct marketing provides diversity and convenience for a heterogeneous American population. The direct-marketing industry is learning that its success is contingent on "keeping its nose clean"— namely, by operating in accordance with the laws and regulations affecting the industry.

How does a direct marketer go about staying within the law? There are two factors necessary to do this. One is to learn the fine points involved and discussed herein. The second is simply to follow your own decent gut reaction to a potential legal problem. Posch's rule of regulatory compliance is simple: If you would not like to be treated this way (copy wording unclear, hard sell, bait and switch, and so on), then someone else wouldn't either. One of those someone elses probably has a law or regulation[1] on point. This ethical and decent gut feeling approach does not replace counsel's advice on a particular law, but it does create the customer-first atmosphere necessary to make you want to comply with the law.

Channel Compliance

Before 1970, the direct marketer was concerned mainly with postal regulations and costs and with physical distribution management. Recently, four major areas of compliance have arisen: the 30-day rules, unordered-merchandise statutes, merchandise substitution, and negative option rules. Each will be reviewed in detail, and I would suggest that every direct marketer become familiar with these four topics, all of which have had a major impact on the industry.

The Mail-Order (or 30-Day) Rules

With increases in costs for almost all aspects of direct marketing (e.g., postage, printing, and the goods themselves), most firms have sought to cut back on inventories. As a result, they can't always fill incoming orders promptly. Some marginal companies caught in the vise of inflation have sought to obtain interest-free loans on the "float," namely, holding their cash flow by delaying fulfillment of the order for as long as possible. Further, there have been occasional abuses involving "dry testing"—that is, marketing a nonexistent product to see if it will be profitable to produce.

   To protect the consumer, the FTC[1] and many states have enacted 30-day rules and laws. The various rules and laws enacted by the particular state(s) in which business is transacted must of course be consulted. Note 5 of the FTC's Rule specifically states that the FTC does not wish to preempt consistent but *narrower* state laws on point; therefore, certain firms will find that they must comply with a narrower state law. One such law is New York's. Since New York is a major impact state for direct marketers, we shall discuss and contrast both the FTC's Rule and the narrower New York State law. It should be noted that by complying with the New York State law, a firm will always be in compliance with the FTC Rule. The reverse is not necessarily the case, as we shall soon see.

A Review of the FTC's Rule

The marketer may not solicit an order for any product or service through the mail unless at the time of solicitation the seller has a reasonable basis for believing that the merchandise can be shipped within the time period clearly and conspicuously stated or, if no statement is made, 30 days after the receipt of a properly completed order from the buyer. This reasonable basis varies because of trade, product, and marketplace considerations. You must maintain internal records to validate your expectations. Three defenses to keep in mind are the following:

1. For purposes of compliance, the 30-day period (or the period stated in the advertisement) does not begin until a *properly* completed order arrives (i.e., receipt of full or partial payment with an order in which the buyer supplies all the required information requested by the seller). If all the information necessary to complete the order hasn't been supplied, the buyer should be notified accordingly. Until the order is complete, you would be wise to retain a copy of the incomplete order and to refrain from cashing any checks received, as the latter may indicate acceptance.

2. You can insulate yourself from the provisions of the rule by stating at the outset a date you can live with. For example, if it may take 90 days, state "90 days from receipt of order." The trade-off here (in any medium) may be a loss in "spontaneity," thereby discouraging orders.

3. The FTC Rule regulates only cash orders received inhouse (cash, check, money order, or electronic funds transfer). You can avoid the straightjacket of the FTC's 30 Day Rule, then, if you bill by credit card or internal credit adjustments, but bill neither type of account until shipment of the goods.

Besides studying the above legal points, you should review your internal procedures.

1. Are you letting orders sit until the checks clear? Is this delay resulting in 30-day shipment problems? If so, does the subsequent improvement in bad debt offset the 30-day problems?

2. To cut down on *potential* complaints because of delays in the mail, try testing the available post offices. The closest may not be the most timely for your needs. Further, investigate the volume flow at your post office. You may gain a few hours or even a day by shipping an hour earlier—particularly before 3 P.M. Every day gained may mean fewer complaints which produce investigations, particularly around the holidays, when a customer may be especially anxious. Again, this recommendation is for goodwill purposes—your only legal requirement is to prove shipment within 30 days. How long delivery takes is in the hands of the post office.

"First-Delay" Situation

When an unanticipated delay of shipment does occur, the seller must cancel the agreement or, alternatively, offer the buyer either the right to cancel the order and receive a prompt refund or the option of awaiting shipment at a specified definite date. The buyer may agree to the refund or the extension. If the buyer does nothing, there is a legal consent to an extension. This extension earns the seller an *additional* 30 days' grace unless the seller informed the buyer that it is not possible to make an accurate representation regarding the length of the delay. A marketer lax in following this policy should be aware of the recent consent order, *United States v. Haband Company, Inc.*[2] The consent order is an excellent overview of the trade regulation rule in general. The violations of interest are as follows:

1. The defendant's notice of delayed shipment failed to provide the buyer with a *definite* revised shipping date and did not clearly and conspicuously inform the customer of the right to cancel the order and receive a prompt refund.

2. The delay notices in question were not accompanied by a pre-paid business reply device (postcard or letter) enabling the buyer to respond. A response vehicle must be provided at the seller's expense. Buyers must *not* have to exercise their rights at the penalty of even a first-class stamp!

"Multiple-Delay" Situations

In general, the seller may obtain as much as 60 days for a grace period in fulfilling an order unless the buyer returns the postage-paid notice requesting a refund. The buyer's silence is construed as an acceptance of the delay. If after 60 days there remains some unanticipated delay (e.g., because of a strike), the FTC Rule will allow further delays in certain limited circumstances.

The seller must notify the buyer of the additional delay. The seller may request the buyer's permission to ship at a certain specified date or even ask for acceptance of an indefinite delay. The buyer may then cancel or may *affirmatively* agree to extend the time for delivery.

In the extended-delay situation, the buyer's silence (failure to return the card) is *not* acceptance but mandates a "prompt refund" by the seller (to be fulfilled approximately 69 days from the initial receipt of the order). The seller must also notify the buyer that even if he or she consents to an indefinite delay, the order may be canceled at any subsequent time by notifying the seller prior to the actual shipment.

The terms of a prompt refund will vary depending upon what payment option was employed. If the buyer sent cash or a check, the refund must be made within 7 business days of the date on which the buyer's right to a refund begins. If a credit card or some other form of credit adjustment is required, the seller is allowed a full billing cycle from the date on which the buyer's right to a refund began. All refunds are to be sent by first-class mail, and they should be in the form in which payment was received, where practical. For example, if cash was received, a return check would be permissible and prudent. Under no circumstances are mere credit vouchers permitted.

Further Points of Note

1. The Rule stresses the need for adequate systems and procedures to create a presumption that there is a good-faith effort to promptly satisfy customer complaints and inquiries and establish that there was an adequate basis upon which to solicit the initial order or request a delay.

2. The Rule does not apply to the "negative option" form of selling (book, record, and other sales).[3] It also does not apply to magazine subscription sales after the first shipment, orders for seeds and growing plants, and COD orders.[4]

New York Law Distinguished

All firms doing business in New York State are advised to be aware of this law and carefully review their 30-day-rule procedures with their counsel.[5]

New York law allows a maximum of 65 days (no mention of "working days," but it is logical to assume this). There is no "multiple-delay" or "extended-delay" provision available to the seller. If the buyer consents to the "first delay," the seller must complete the order or refund the money within a 35-day period after mailing the "delay notice" to the buyer. Section (1)(i) of the law should be reviewed. The seller has the option of offering substituted merchandise, but such merchandise must be described in detail so that the buyer knows how it differs from the goods previously ordered. If done correctly and ethically, this is not a bait-and-switch tactic but an honest attempt to accommodate the buyer.

This is a flat 30/65-day law. The entire order must be shipped or the payment refunded within a maximum period of 65 days. There is no definition of "prompt refund" in the New York State law, but compliance with the FTC Rule's definition would appear adequate.

Finally, the exclusions found in notes 1 to 4 of the FTC's Rule are not found in New York State's law, implying that New York's law *may* apply to negative option sales, magazine subscription sales after the first shipment, orders for seeds and growing plants, and COD orders.

Unordered Merchandise

The federal law[6] regarding the mailing of unordered merchandise is short and should be read by all direct-mail marketing managers. This law forbids not just the blatant sending of unordered merchandise but also the sending of merchandise "on approval" without a customer's *prior* permission. The FTC specifically warned the mail-order stamp industry of this in 1979.[7]

Only two kinds of merchandise may be sent through the mails without prior consent: free samples, which must be labeled as such, and merchandise mailed by charitable organizations. However, even merchandise mailed by charitable organizations is sent "on approval" and need not be paid for. The customer may return it or keep it but need not pay for it. The best strategy is that when in doubt, don't dun. If an innocent error is made (e.g., computer mislabeling), write off the order. The customer won't complain unless an effort is made to compel payment.

The penalties for both firms and individuals are up to $10,000 per violation for engaging in practices after they know such practices are unlawful.[8]

Merchandise Substitution

It should be noted that the unordered-merchandise law defines "unordered merchandise"[9] as "merchandise mailed without the prior expressed request or consent of the recipient." This refers to a situation where there is an absence of a prior agreement between the parties.

Certain states, including New York,[10] permit the seller to substitute merchandise of equivalent or superior quality in very limited circumstances. Where you have received an express order for an item, you may substitute, again so long as the substitution involves merchandise of equivalent or superior quality. Such substitution should be reviewed with counsel (both as to legal availability of the option and whether the particular substitution is permissible). Where a valid substitution is offered, the customer must be afforded the opportunity to return the item at no postal expense.

Even where substitution is permissible, certain products are never of "equivalent or superior quality." For example, each piece of artistic property such as a book or painting is unique. There is no "artistic equivalence," and no artistic property may be substituted.

FTC Negative Option Rule[11]

Most users of negative option plans employ their clubs as a retail channel; therefore, this topic properly falls under this section. In the 1920s, Maxwell Sackheim invented negative option for the Book-of-the-Month Club (now a part of Time Inc.). Under this plan, members' books are shipped automatically unless a member has given prior notification that he or she does not wish to purchase the particular selection.

While at times certain self-appointed consumer activists receive publicity disparaging the plan (and the FTC considered abolishing it in 1970), negative option is socially useful, and that is why this channel of distribution has prospered for so long and is in fact growing.

Negative option makes possible greater control over inventories. This reduces costs, as does the economy of scale achieved through large, mass-produced label runs. In a competitive marketplace of over 150 varied clubs, there is an incentive to pass along much of the savings to the member.

Then there are social utilities. A "guaranteed" minimum market may permit occasional gambles on "unknown" authors. This enhances the free flow of ideas and opinion in our nation. This diversity would be diminished if negative option were curtailed or positive option required, as firms could only bet on sure sellers. I stress diversity here, as we're discussing not just artistic clubs (records, books, graphics) but crafts, vitamins, and so on.

Book clubs are highly accessible (and it is good for society that they are), whereas bookshops are not quite so accessible. There are approximately 39,500 five-digit zip codes in the United States, yet less than 15 percent of these areas have anything approximating a quality bookstore! Book clubs bring literature to all through the mailbox. Further, even where a quality bookstore exists, its floor space is limited, and this places a physical constraint on the number of volumes which may be offered at any one time—a constraint less likely to affect a book club's offerings. A book club, therefore, might have broader fulfillment.

Finally, if negative option clubs were not wanted, they would not be profitable. The ultimate consumer democracy is the freedom for the consumer to choose how he or she elects to spend discretionary income. Nine million people every year participate in book clubs alone. Enough said on the value of these plans—now let's see how to operate them within the confines of the law.

The Rule

Just as the FTC has demonstrated its distaste for marketers who depart from the straight and narrow when it comes to complying with its 30 Day Rule (a lesson learned by at least one direct marketer the hard way), the FTC has little tolerance for *any* changes in literal compliance with the Negative Option Rule. Literal compliance with the Rule's wording is mandated, as a few firms discovered to their detriment in 1978.[12]

A direct marketer employing negative option plans would do well to commit to memory the mandatory disclosures and practices or, better yet, devise a compliance checklist against which all copy is reviewed in advance. The checklist would include all mandatory disclosures. They are as follows.

All promotional material must clearly and conspicuously state the material terms of the plan, including:

1. That a negative option plan is being used.

2. The full obligation to purchase a minimum amount of merchandise.

3. That the member may cancel his or her membership any time after completion of the agreement to purchase the minimum amount of merchandise specified.

4. Whether billing charges include postage and handling. It should be noted that the FTC negative option proceeding considered the advance disclosure of the specific amount of the member's shipping and handling charges. However, the FTC decided not to require specific charges—you may merely indicate up front that such charges exist. However, you must be aware that the FTC has stated on record that shipping and handling charges may *not* include an element of profit to the seller.[13]

5. That the member will be given 10 days to notify the seller that the selected merchandise is not desired or that he or she wishes to order alternative merchandise being offered. If the member receives less than 10 days, the account will be credited for returned merchandise. The seller must give full credit and pay the return postage for merchandise sent to members who have not been sent a proper form or who have not been given the required time to respond.

6. The frequency with which the advance announcement or merchandise will be sent to the member (i.e., the maximum received in a 12-month period).

7. A statement to the effect that introductory, bonus, and/or premium merchandise must be shipped within 4 weeks of the order, unless otherwise disclosed.

8. A form contained in or accompanying the announcement clearly and conspicuously disclosing the procedure required to reject the selection.

Further (while not implicitly required by the Rule), a statement up front that sales tax will be charged enchances full disclosure of all pertinent charges. Since a mail-order house will not have physical presence or situs in most states, a statement to the effect that "sales tax will be added where applicable" is sufficient.

With regard to book clubs, you have no doubt often seen the phrase "Book Club Edition" on book jackets; this is not required by the FTC. It is a matter of negotiation between the book club and licensing publisher.

The Rule should be followed verbatim. No discretion is permissible even if you don't think it is applicable to your particular plan or product. Any direct marketer utilizing or planning on utilizing negative option would be wise to review the various "how to complain"[14] publications to keep abreast of and to anticipate the growth of consumer awareness and activism in this area. It always helps to know what the opposition's strategy is!

Beyond all the legal jargon is the question of practical, everyday application. Throughout I have stressed the need for literal compliance with the FTC's rules. While you may not feel that your own situation warrants literal compliance, a supplier of cases of other firms have proven that less than strict compliance can be devastating to your bottom line.

Help on the Horizon?

On October 21, 1980, the "equal access to justice" bill was signed into law. This act, which took effect October 1, 1981, now permits a private individual or *small* business[15] to recover legal fees from federal agencies in certain administrative and court proceedings where it is found that the action was not substantially justified. Prior to this, an agency with or without justification could conduct a fishing expedition at the general taxpayers' expense against any business. If a business "won," it only had the dubious satisfaction of winning an oftentimes Pyrrhic victory, as the business was out all costs and attorney fees incurred in defending itself, and it lost goodwill through resulting bad publicity. This act will lessen the governmental burden on qualifying parties.

On November 4, 1980, Ronald Reagan was elected in a landslide with 44 states endorsing his slogan of "Getting the Government off the Backs of Legitimate Business." His first Executive Orders, signed 30 minutes after the inauguration, were true to form. The page volume of the *Federal Register* was reduced 40 percent, compared with the volume of the preceding year.

So some trends indicate that you may have fewer problems with government in the 1980s than you did during the preceding decade. However, there are laws on the books already, and more are inevitable. What should you do to best protect your firm's interests?

The safest course for any direct marketer is to comply literally with any law or regulation at any level of government. (A .275 average in baseball might earn you a comfortable free-agent salary, but in the FTC's game, you must bat 1.000.) How can this most efficiently be done?

1. Set up and maintain an internal profit preservation center. This in-house system should monitor all legislation and regulations impacting your profit and cost centers. The center should coordinate its market intelligence and insights about long-term trends with the strategic planners and work with line planners to assure that all current policies are in compliance with existing laws and regulations. *Most importantly,* policies should be updated as the legal dynamics of the marketplace change with new laws and regulations.

2. You should also supplement an effective in-house system by retaining and utilizing the resources of independent specialists in your particular field(s) of direct marketing. I've listed some proven specialists with exemplary problem-solving records in the References section of this chapter.[16]

3. Make sure all present and future direct-marketing decision makers in your firm as well as counsel have read this book and that it becomes a consulted text in your reference library.

Will a profit preservation center help in dealing with the FTC? Most definitely. On April 29, 1981, I formally addressed this question to James Sneed, Director of the FTC's Bureau of Consumer Protection (DMMA Washington symposium, 1981). He was very candid and replied that such a formal and functioning in-house center would be viewed favorably by the FTC and might affect its subsequent follow-through. Adequate systems and procedures were required in the text of the FTC's 30 Day Rule[17] as well as in the laws of certain states.[18] Maintaining your own will save you dollars and headaches. Then with an expert covering your legal flank, you can securely press forward with the ultimate goal of your business: *selling your product profitably.*

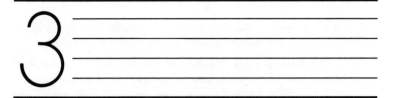

Comparative Pricing

The "sale" is one of the most effective tools available to the marketer, and therefore one of the most popular. Before you forge ahead enthusiastically, let me assure you that the FTC has its finger in this pie too. It has established guides[1] which set forth explicit identifying information and material terms which should be disclosed when comparative pricing claims are used. The FTC emphasizes that the advertiser should not make such claims unless they can be substantiated by objective evidence. First of all, what are material terms and what is objective evidence?

"Material terms" are facts which influence a decision to undertake an action. For the marketer in this situation, the material terms are those facts disclosed in the advertisement which will influence the decision to purchase or not to purchase the product. "Objective evidence" is documentary evidence such as invoices or sales records.

The FTC has stated that the application of these guides will be governed by the following principle: Since price is an important criterion in consumer purchasing decisions, the advertiser who does more than state the asking price must tell the truth in such a way that it cannot be misunderstood.

Highlights are as follows:

1. No comparisons should be made or implied between the price at which an article is offered for sale and some other reference price unless the nature of the reference price is explicitly identified and the advertiser has a reasonable basis for substantiating its accuracy.

2. When former-price comparisons are made, bona fide sales must have been made by the advertiser at the advertised former price in the recent past. If the article was offered for sale but no sales were made at that price or any other price in the recent past, that fact must be disclosed in connection with any mention of the former price. This test is important. The seller must be able to demonstrate that the product was openly and actively offered for sale, for a reasonably substantial period of time, in the regular course of business, honestly and in good faith. Again, sales records, checks, invoices, and even correspondence will be helpful here.

3. The guidelines concerning "sales" noted above must be geographically comparable over the entire marketplace and not merely isolated or unrepresentative geographic comparisons (see the discussion of the Kroger Company, below).

Two recent FTC decisions indicate that the guidelines will be construed narrowly and strictly enforced.

Home Centers[2] is a chain of appliance stores which allegedly represented price reductions and potential savings to consumers without reasonable basis. "Reasonable basis" refers to both the veracity of a claim and the documentary evidence to substantiate it. Home Centers was unable to demonstrate comparative geographic savings or actual sales made at the reference price. The reader should note that the recent FTC penalties include the FTC's right to examine your records—specifically, in this case, all records relevant to sales, pricing, and advertising substantiation for a period of usually 3 or more years.

Perhaps the most comprehensive discussion of these guidelines to date is found in *In the Matter of the Kroger Company*.[3] This firm at the time was the third largest retail food seller (measured by sales) in the nation. The FTC challenged, among other things, the comparative claims made by the company's "Price Patrol."

A key theme[4] running throughout the decision is that the items compared must be "identical or substantially similar." All comparisons must be made upon a reasonable basis (i.e., specific, objective documentary evidence). The reasonable-basis requirement "questions both the reasonableness of an advertiser's actions and the adequacy of evidence upon which such action is based." The reader should note that increasingly "reasonable" no longer refers to the historical "reasonable person" test. A lower common denominator could be considered the norm, namely "the ignorant, gullible, and the credulous."[5]

The FTC will review and consider the following five factors:[6]

1. Type and specificity of the claim made

2. Type of goods sold

3. Possible consequences to the public of a false or misleading claim

4. Degree of reliance upon the claim by reasonable consumers

5. Type and accessibility of evidence adequate to form a reasonable basis for the particular claim

The Kroger decision noted that a price survey or comparison "must be based on sound price survey procedures as recognized by experts trained and experienced in the science of survey methodology. . . . If Kroger is not willing to expend the necessary time and financial resources, it should simply forego comparative price claims."[7]

What constitutes "comparability" for competitive comparison purposes may be neatly summarized in a five-point checklist.

1. The items you're comparing must be identical or substantially similar.

2. When meats are being compared, they must be identical in cut and grade.

3. You must account for geographic changes in pricing or provide a disclaimer stating that the comparison prices do not mean that the consumer will always save by purchasing the item being advertised. Otherwise the FTC considers the comparative-price claims misleading, deceptive, and unfair.

4. If an identical or substantially similar item is unavailable, you must exclude the item from all surveys.

5. Competitors to be surveyed must be selected in such a way as to provide a valid basis for any generalizations to be made from the results.

Conclusion

When you are advertising a sale, the key point to remember is that "overall" price comparisons are judged to determine whether the items compared are identical or substantially similar. This determination is based on a methodology of comparison, the quality of the goods compared, whether the overall price comparison is valid in all 50 states simultaneously, and whether the comparison may be affected by such variables as shipping and handling charges.

Then, assuming that you can meet the threshold validity tests above, the comparison *must* be substantiated by documentary evidence.

Copy Headliners

The objective of the direct marketer in any medium is to design promotions which will obtain the viewers' interest immediately. Recently my wife and I received a circular from a furniture store addressed to its "preferred" customers. The circular aroused our interest for three reasons: it advertised the store's semiannual *sale,* offered a 20-percent *discount* to preferred customers during the 2-day promotion, and also promised a *free* bottle of wine just for stopping by. Judging by the thriving business the store did the evening we went, one could say that the promotion was obviously successful.

The promotion piece is usually designed to catch the viewer's eye with respect to both aesthetics and a simple dollars-and-cents bargain. The aesthetic value is primarily the work of the creative team, though care must be taken that all visual depictions convey a correct impression of the size and identity of the product. The major compliance issues arise when a certain kind of wording is used either orally or in print to capture the reader's interest. A thorough knowledge of the subtleties of the words "sale," "free," "new," and "discount" and of words of similar impact will greatly help the marketer reach the goal of maximizing reader interest while minimizing negative involvement by unfair and deceptive advertising.

"Sale"

There is something almost magical about the word "sale."[1] The first section many customers turn to in the Sunday paper is the sales circular; people vie with each other in overcrowded stores to get a $7 item for $3.50, and folks will buy items which they never would have purchased at the regular price.

From time to time, therefore, the marketer will wish to make its customers special offers. The ad copy may at times refer to the promotion as a "sale," "savings," or "price reduction." Three questions I'm most frequently asked about a sale are the following:

1. What is a sale?

2. What discount reduction from our former prices is sufficient to constitute a sale?

3. Does every item featured in the promotion piece need to be on sale?

What Is a Sale?

A "sale" is a reduction from the advertiser's own former price for an article. The former price must be the actual, bona fide price at which the article was offered and *sold* to the public on a regular basis for a reasonably substantial period of time; it provides a legitimate basis for price comparison. I emphasize "sold," as this sales test is a necessary hurdle which must be overcome with (what else?) objective evidence. Such evidence must establish significant previous sales of the same product in the same geographic marketplace to discourage the entry of an overpriced article into the market. With an overpriced article, few, if any, sales are made, and the article is then "reduced" to its realistic market price and offered as a "sale" item.

What Discount Should Be Offered?

The advertiser must take care that the amount of reduction is not so insignificant as to be meaningless. Because it influences the purchase decision, the discount should be sufficiently large so that the consumer will believe that a genuine bargain or saving is being offered. A nominal reduction—for example, less than 5 percent—is unacceptable. Depending on the market, ticket price, and trade practices, 10 percent or more would be a safe *starting* point. It should be noted that the alert customer may well be suspicious of a promotion claiming a large reduction or discount but not stating the actual discount percentage.

Must Every Item in a Sales Promotion Be Reduced to Satisfy Compliance?

Every item advertised in the sales promotion should represent a reduction from a former price that was openly and actively offered for a reasonable period of time in the regular course of business.

An item not reduced from a former price at which the *same* (not similar) product was openly and actively offered for sale, for a reasonably substantial period of time, in the recent regular course of business,[2] honestly and in good faith, has no business being offered in a sales promotion. Furthermore, you should not use language such as "formerly sold at $10" unless substantial sales at that price were actually made. Also, if you state "at our lowest price ever," *all* merchandise included in the description must be at its lowest price ever.

Therefore, the use of expressions such as "annual sale," "Fall Sale," and "Super Savings" in catalogs, advertising or other promotional pieces containing nonsale items is an unfair and deceptive trade practice if it is not revealed in immediate conjunction with such representations that nonsale items are contained therein and if the nonsale items are not distinctively identified. While there is the opportunity to distinctively label nonsale items as such, the marketer should clearly weigh the risks of confusion and where possible only present valid sales items in a sales promotion.

When it comes to price reductions, "puffery" is not permitted. For example, in 1977 *New York Magazine*[3] guaranteed its charter subscribers "the lowest possible renewal rate." An irate customer complained to the New York City Department of Consumer Affairs that this "lowest rate was $3 more than the general Christmas offering. As a result, the magazine had to refund $3 to the 3432 subscribers who were overcharged as well as pay New York City for all costs incurred by the department to process the complaint.

The obvious conclusion must be drawn: Carefully monitor your sales, or an agency will. The latter's public investigation may leave a sour taste in the public's mouth—more than negating any short-term profits derived from the "sale."

Using the following checklist to monitor your sale will help assure that you don't wind up "donating" your profits from the sale to some local, state, or federal agency.

1. Be sure the sales price is a reasonable and honest statement of the valid former market price which is now reduced.

2. All the items advertised as "sale" items in the promotion should represent an honest reduction.

3. You should be prepared to substantiate your claim that every item in the sale was *sold* in the marketplace (and was not just "offered") previously.

4. Items not on sale in the sales promotion must be distinctively identified and distinguished.

5. Finally, it should go without saying that if quantities are limited, you should disclose the limitation up front.

"New"

This is a relatively straightforward term. Merchandise may not be offered as "new" if it has been used or refurbished. This means returned merchandise may not be cleaned or "improved" in any way and then returned to inventory. Unless there is a statement indicating different circumstances, merchandise offered for sale must be new and may not have been used during a trial period or otherwise (see the discussion of trial versus examination in this chapter).

The word "new" is also used to promote a product which has not yet been introduced into the marketplace or which has been "improved," enabling the marketer to advertise the item as "new and improved." There is no particular usage period for an offer, but FTC[4] Advisory Opinion 120 has indicated 6 months as a tentative outer limit. This suggestion is subject to certain variables. A new product should be the latest model in a particular line and certainly not have been widely marketed elsewhere. However, in a bona fide test marketing of a new product which does not cover more than 15 percent of the population and does not exceed 6 months in duration, the 6-month rule does not apply until the test period has ended. Certain states[5] have very exact disclosure requirements. As always, the reader must consult the various state laws and not merely be content with understanding the FTC's position.

"Free"

One word which the marketer knows will always prompt a second glance is "free." From free checking to free panty hose to free TVs, the word "free" has permeated our society, enticing people through every imaginable medium. It follows the cardinal rule of any promotion: An ad must start off immediately holding the customer's attention. One way to do this is to open with your highest card, namely, whatever is of most significant benefit to the customer, especially if that benefit appeals to the self-interest of your reader or listener. Not many people wouldn't like to receive something for nothing; the beauty of the simple word "free," therefore, is that it inspires self-interest and helps get the product into the prospect's hands, where it can then sell itself. Caveat vendor ("seller beware" in plain English) is an appropriate admonition here, however; because "free" has the ability to highlight and enhance the promotion piece, it is a highly regulated term of art as to both definition and disclosure. The following discussion will guide the marketer though the regulatory thicket.

What Is a Free Item?

The word "free" indicates that a person is paying nothing for the article advertised as free and no more than the regular price for the article to be purchased. Thus a purchaser has a right to believe that the seller will not directly and immediately recover, in whole or in part, the cost of the free merchandise by marking up the price of the article.[6] Finally, shipping and handling charges cannot be built into or added to a free item. For example, if a package is sent to a customer for a "free 15-day examination," the cost of returning the article must not be borne by the customer—a prepaid mailing label must be provided, *or* some other device must be used to guarantee no postage costs, such as refunding the cost of the postage or crediting the customer's account for the expense incurred. The use of an item during a trial or examination period is not considered free if the recipient must pay the cost of returning the item, should returning it be his or her desire. A good marketer is not thinking return costs anyway, because the key is to get the product into the home and then bet on human inertia to keep it there.

You should be aware that playing games with semantics won't get you off the hook when it comes to *free* offers. Words of similar connotation such as "gift," "no cost or obligation," "at no extra cost," "given without charge," "bonus," and the like "which tend to convey the impression to the consuming public that an article of merchandise is Free"[7] are held to the same standard. So, if you are looking to obtain the promotional response benefits of a "free offer," or if you believe that a reasonable customer would construe your offer as free, your best bet is to comply with the "free rule" and keep the FTC happy.

What Conditions Must Be Disclosed?

Any and all terms, conditions, and obligations you are imposing, such as credit limitations or qualifications and prepayment requirements, should appear in close conjunction—that is, physically adjacent so that the elements are naturally read together with the offer of "free" merchandise. If you don't set forth your limitations, the item is free to all, even to those individuals who have a definite history of credit delinquency. Any limitations you are imposing must conform to the following criteria.

1. The type size must be at least half as large as the largest type size in the introductory offer copy, exclusive of numerals. (This is the rule in several states as well as in New York City.)

2. The minimum type size must be 8 points.

3. The qualification terms must be stated together in the same location of the ad, not separated by copy or graphics.

4. Disclosing the terms of the offer in a footnote in the advertisement to which reference is made with an asterisk or similar symbol does *not* constitute disclosure at the outset and will result in noncompliance.

Once you've set forth all your limitations in close conjunction with the free offer, you're home "free." You are then able to use "free" or any words of similar impact (such as "no cost") as often as you wish without any further qualifications in every paragraph of your print or oral presentation, if you so wish. You may even use it again in the all-important postscript paragraph. This last paragraph is almost always read, particularly in direct mail, and by featuring the word "free" here, you will tie it in well with your initial headline.

To Sum Up

"Free" may be used if the product is an unconditional gift or, when a purchase is required, all the conditions, limitations, or other criteria which modify the offer of the free product are clearly and conspicuously stated in immediate conjunction with the first use of the word "free," leaving no reasonable probability that the terms of the offer will be misunderstood. No "hidden" requirements are permitted. Ambiguity is no asset. Language which might be construed in favor of a free ad will be so construed against the creator of the ad.

To avoid copy clutter and redundancy, the marketer should regard each promotion piece as constituting *one* component offer. To meet the "clearly and conspicuously" test, the qualifications merely need to be stated at the outset after the first use of the word "free." Thereafter, the term "free" may be used as often per offer as is thought advisable regardless of how many items are being offered for sale by the material.

Some Practical Marketing Hints Which Will Save You Dollars When Designing Your Free Promotion

Use of Currency   You should know that certain highlights of a free offer may be prohibited. For example, you may not show a ten-dollar bill to highlight a free $10 value. Printed illustrations of paper money, checks, negotiable instruments, and other obligations and securities of the United States are not permitted for advertising purposes. The reproduction of coins *is* allowed—for example, a reproduction of a penny could be used to highlight a 1¢ sale. (For your overall compliance program, it should be noted that all states as well as the District of Columbia have statutes prohibiting the use in advertising of their own flag as well as the U.S. flag.)

Tax Pointer   You should review the laws of the respective states in which your promotion is being run. In some states[8] an out-of-state seller is not subject to sales-and-use tax on free promotional materials because there is no sale or taxable use of such materials.

Trial Versus Examination   Trial or examination—is there a difference? And which term should you use? These terms are important and distinguishable, yet if you review the various advertisements you receive each day, you'll observe that marketers use them interchangeably. Use of the term "trial" may cost you dollars and/or regulatory harassment and fines.

Substitution of a used product for a new one without disclosing the fact that the item is used is unlawful, even if a qualitative equivalence is shown. Merchandise which has been previously used on a "trial" basis (for example, "15-day home trial") and then returned may not be offered for resale as anything but a used product. The FTC, in an investigation, will review your inventory records and study the disposition of returned merchandise.

The FTC distinguishes between the practice of a "trial" (implying a sustained use) and that of "inspection" or "examination" (indicating a mere looking at but not "use"). You should too. You should also be aware that if your firm enters a joint promotion with another firm, it is co-equally liable for the deceptive-practice penalties incurred for offering used merchandise as new. So, too, is a credit card organization promoting the sale of merchandise through its lists.

I was once asked this question in a discussion on this topic: Why not always say "examination" and avoid the problem altogether? Sorry, the FTC won't let you off the hook that easily. Use of the term "examination" will not insulate you from a deceptive-practice charge if it is apparent that the products have been used and not merely inspected. Also, the legal result of the use of "trial" is never mitigated by a policy of visual inspection which eliminates the obviously used products. *All* products are presumed tried and therefore used.

Finally, if you do elect to use either "trial" or "examination" and the trial or examination period is "free" to credit-qualified members only, the fact must be stated clearly and conspicuously.

Timing The following are little-known points concerning the whens and how oftens of free promotions. You would be wise to incorporate them into your compliance program.

1. A single size of a product should not be advertised with a "free" offer for more than 6 months in any 12-month period.

2. At least 30 days should elapse before another such offer is promoted.

3. No more than three such offers should be made in any 12-month period.

4. In this period, your sales of the product in the size promoted should not exceed 50 percent of the total volume of your sales of the product, in the same size.

Conclusion The direct marketer must strictly comply with the FTC guidelines on point and not rely on any "general trade custom." There are many abuses of the word "free," such as "free checking." A sign for free checking catches your eye, but upon further inquiry within the bank you learn that "free" checking may require that a minimum balance be retained, or that there is a limit on checks, or that the purchase of other services is required, and so on. The lack of clear and conspicuous disclosure of the costs and conditions of services such as consumer banking services is no defense to the direct marketer (though as a consumer of banking services, you are free to complain). Your test is that the word "free" is prohibited unless the item is truly without cost or undisclosed obligation.[9]

Warranty Disclosures

A warranty or guarantee is a solid consumer benefit and a business opportunity which belongs in a benefit-grabbing headline. Naturally, if it sells, it's regulated. The warranty is considered part of the product you sell, and the customer should have the opportunity to examine the whole package before a purchase decision is made. The Magnuson-Moss Warranty Act[10] is now a way of compliance life for business. This act was originally dubbed "Lemonaide" because of consumer complaints that so many products being sold were "lemons." This law requires that warranties on consumer products costing more than $15 must be available for the consumer to review before the purchase. Generally, direct marketers have few warranty disclosure obligations, but certain matters should be understood.

First, the obvious. No matter what direct-marketing medium is employed to obtain the sale, the mail is probably the response vehicle. Therefore, your product must be mailable—that is, not too brittle, too perishable, or too heavy, making shipping and handling charges prohibitive.

Second, the law. The Magnuson-Moss Warranty Act applies only to *written* warranties extended to consumers. Oral express warranties continue to be covered by Section 2-213 of the Uniform Commercial Code. Now let's review the direct marketer's obligations.

The direct-marketing firm can insulate itself from warranty disclosure requirements for products it promotes and bills for but does not manufacture. The principal and supplier should agree in their contract that:

1. No warranties will be offered in advertising.

2. The supplier will not provide a written warranty with the product (even though the same product as sold through other channels may include a warranty).

3. The written warranty may not require the consumer to use a branded or trademarked product service to service the warranted product.

If a warranty is involved, the direct marketer should seek protection contractually by stating that the warrantor will provide the seller with supplies of the warranties, which must disclose all conditions:

1. Clearly and conspicuously

2. In a single document

3. In simple and readily understood plain English

Direct Mail

There are specific warranty requirements for catalog and mail-order sellers. First, what constitutes a catalog or mail-order sale?

> Catalogue or Mail Order Sale means any offer for sale or any solicitation for an order for a consumer product with a written warranty, which includes instructions for ordering the product which do not require a personal visit to the seller's establishment.[11]

Catalog and mail-order sellers must include in the catalog or solicitation either the full text of the written warranty *or* the fact that the warranty can be obtained free upon specific written request. The address to which the request may be sent must be included, and if this option is elected, the seller must promptly provide the requested copy for the consumer. The text of the warranty or the statement that the warranty will be provided upon request must appear in close conjunction with the description of the warranted product or in an information section of the catalog or solicitation — clearly referenced, including a page number. "Close conjunction" here means on the same page as the description of the product or on the facing page.

However, even if the marketer did not mention the warranty a supplier provided, the supplier alone, and not the marketer, would be liable for any defect in the warranty or in performance under it. This is the result of Section 700.4 regarding cowarrantor requirements. The direct marketer, however, would probably be in violation of the presale availability disclosure rule.

Note: Here as elsewhere the marketer is not afforded the luxury of merely reviewing federal law. All states of impact must be consulted.[12] Consider, for example, New York State's law concerning disclosures in advertisements for the sale of unassembled goods. While not strictly a "warranty" law, it requires your catalog to clearly and conspicuously disclose in close proximity to any items needing assembly:

1. The need for such assembly
2. Whether any specific tools are needed
3. If other parts are not supplied and must be obtained separately

The instructions for assembly should be on or within the package. The purchaser should not have to write away separately for them.

This law does not apply to unassembled kits and toy and hobby products, the primary purpose of which is assembly by the consumer as a recreational activity.

While issuing no formal guidelines to date, the FTC would also expect some clear, up-front language (not buried in the copy text) indicating that the product requires assembly.

Door-to-Door Sales

Those direct marketers involved in door-to-door sales should be aware of the following warranty provision directly impacting their operations:

> Any seller who offers for sale to consumers consumer products with written warranties by means of door-to-door sales shall, prior to the consummation of the sale, disclose the fact that the sales represen-

tative has copies of the warranties for the warranted products being offered for sale, which may be inspected by the prospective buyer at any time during the sales presentation. Such disclosure shall be made orally and shall be included in any written materials shown to prospective buyers.[13]

Other pointers for the direct marketer in warranty compliance are as follows:

1. The terminology, "guarantee" or "warranty," is essentially interchangeable for consumer purposes.

2. For individual warranty complaints, the customer should be reimbursed for shipping and handling costs incurred for returns.

3. The nature of the warranties offered (e.g., limited or full) should be spelled out in contracts signed with vendors.

4. State laws and regulations as well as the Uniform Commercial Code (UCC) and FTC consent agreements should be reviewed for your compliance audit.[14]

Conclusion

The warranty is the manufacturer's. You are in marketing. However, you should review every warranty you do advertise—not just for legal compliance but because a warranty problem affects your goodwill even if you can legally avoid the issue.

Magnuson-Moss is a truth-in-warranty law. It mandates that all warranties be written so as to be understandable to the average lay customer. If you can't understand a warranty, your customer probably can't, and therefore the customer may not buy the product. So review it as to who is protected and what parts of the product are covered, and know whether the warranty is full or limited, as well as its effective date (and total life). Also, does the warrantor attempt to disclaim any implied warranty? This is illegal. Finally, review the steps the buyer must take in the event the product is defective. Is notification of the seller (you) involved? If so, you should have established procedures to deal with such contingencies.

Discounts

Discounts, like two of the headliners already discussed ("sale" and "free"), can generate a great deal of consumer interest and goodwill.

Discounts may be offered to the general public, as when you advertise "10 percent off our already low prices," or to segmented audiences, such as the employees of a firm in your neighborhood or members of an association. I am using the term "discount" here to mean a percentage reduction in order to distinguish between discounts and *coupons*—a headliner which will be discussed next. I might also mention that a discount differs from a rebate in that the discount involves an up-front price reduction, whereas the rebate involves an "after-the-fact" price reduction. A rebate is primarily a creation of federal interference in the marketplace. Firms which fear price controls will not reduce or discount prices but will instead offer a "rebate" to meet competition. That way the price remains "high." Rebates are counterproductive in two ways: they are not an up-front benefit, and they do not have the same impact as reduced prices. Further, they distort the consumer price index, since they are not included; thus they create the appearance that prices are higher than they actually are in the marketplace.

When offering a discount, if you are imposing limitations such as credit restrictions, you must state the limitations in your advertisement just as you would for a "free" offer. *However,* you may use an asterisk to direct the consumer to another part of the text to read the limitations. In other words, unless the discount offer is used in conjunction with a free promotion (in which case the "free" rules apply), you do *not* have to set forth your limitations "clearly and conspicuously" in close conjunction with the discount offer.

If you are offering comparison discounts involving a competitor's product, it must be provable by objective criteria acceptable in the trade that:

1. The competitor's merchandise is comparable to yours, namely, of like grade and quality. (You might wish to review the chapter on comparative pricing for a more detailed discussion of this area.)

2. The other merchandise is not only essentially similar in quality but also in fact obtainable in the market area so as to provide realistic savings for the consumer.

One type of discount which you may not want to offer but which you could be forced to offer in the future is the cash discount. The direct marketer must be vigilant in the legislative and regulatory marketplace to thwart continuing efforts to promote an involuntary discount or "cash discount" in lieu of a credit card purchase (see the chapter on credit policy and the influence of the Truth-in-Lending Act). Widespread passage of laws concerning cash discounts is to the direct marketer's disadvantage for two reasons:

1. If a credit card payment option is offered, any customer (cardholder or not) could elect the cash discount — so in effect an involuntary discount is being offered to the public.

2. To forestall such a discount drain, the marketer might cease offering the credit payment option. The result of this might be lost sales and possibly a higher bad debt ratio.

Naturally, offering a cash discount is perfectly legitimate if you choose to make it part of your marketing policy; however, on an involuntary basis, its effect on the industry would be negative indeed.

Conclusion

A discount is a type of sale and may resemble a free offer, so both rules must be consulted. Then the unique "discount questions" related above must be considered in drafting copy that is adequate to meet regulatory compliance.

Coupon Promotions

Ads with coupons generally can pull 10 percent or more inquiries than the same ads without coupons. According to government estimates, approximately 76 percent of all American households are redeeming cents-off coupons. Even better news, regulations affecting coupons rarely present a problem for the direct marketer. Nevertheless, a review of this area should be undertaken when a bonus coupon or a dollar-off certificate or a similar promotional device is considered to avoid a trading stamp regulatory problem.

Less than half the states have specific regulations on point. Of the states that do, Tennessee's recently enacted Coupon Sales Promotion Act of 1980 is fairly representative:

> SECTION 2. For the purpose of this chapter, the following terms shall have the following meanings except where the context requires otherwise:

(a) "Coupon" means any writing, form, ticket, certificate, token or similar device designed or intended to be sold or offered for sale which is represented as entitling the purchaser or holder to purchase or procure goods or services at a reduced price or free of charge upon presentation thereof to the seller or supplier of such goods or services. The term "coupon" includes "coupon book." It does not include:

(1) Coupons sold or offered for sale directly by the coupon sponsor where all proceeds from the sale are returned to the sponsor;

(2) Coupons redeemable only for motor vehicle parking or urban mass transit privileges;

(3) Coupons published by or distributed through newspapers or other periodicals, in advertisements other than their own;

(4) Coupons within, attached to, or a part of any package or container as packed by the original manufacturer and which are redeemed by such manufacturer;

(5) Trading stamps;

(6) Cents-off or free coupons authorized by the original manufacturer or retailer and distributed in any fashion.[15]

Conclusion

Most coupon promotions will be excluded from the stringent regulations. However, a review of the coupon promotion with counsel is advisable, since even the excluded categories may require, among other things, that a cash value be placed on the face of the promotional device.

Trademarks

We have reviewed the law as to promotional eye-grabbing headliners. Let it never be forgotten, however, that if a firm does not have a favorable reputation, no promised benefits will sell well. Therefore, prior to any important direct-marketing campaign, it is important to see to it that your firm gets good publicity. Such publicity reflects on your key communications headliner. If your firm enjoys a good reputation and your product's name is associated with high quality, by all means *use that name.* Like the old saying goes, if you've got it, flaunt it. But like the new saying goes, if you've got it, protect it! A trademark can be an incredibly useful device, so long as you're vigilant and don't allow your competitor to abscond with it while your guard is down.

Protect It

What is a trademark and why should you protect it? The term "trademark" refers to any word, symbol, letter, number, design, picture, or combination thereof which is used to designate a product or service identity. The designation must be *affixed, adopted, and used* for the purpose of denominating the good or service. Your trademark is a distinctive mark of authenticity through which your brand may be distinguished from your competitor's. Once you have a brand identity, it assists you in designing your advertising along one line so the consumer will recognize, distinguish, and buy your brand.

Many people are unclear about the difference between a trademark and a trade name. The key is that the trade name need not be affixed to the product; it has been used long and intensely enough so that the public associates it with the product. In any event, a trademark or a trade name can be a valuable asset in your communication strategy.

A trademark communicates information about your product; it provides consumers with a handy reference point which summarizes their past experience and information obtained about brands using the same mark. It acquires meaning over a period of time through associations formed in the minds of consumers; consumers will come to identify certain quality standards with the mark. Repeat purchases eventually build up a positive reputation for your brand; consumers come to associate it with satisfaction of their needs.

Finally, a low-cost consumer product sold nationally is the very kind of product for which trademark protection is most necessary. Since this is the typical market and product for most direct marketers, you'll want to register.

Registration

A few would-be advisers stress that registration with the U.S. Patent and Trademark Office is expensive (it is) and not worth the investment in counsel (very foolish). Further, this is not a procedure for a storefront lawyer—see a specialist.

First, counsel will recommend whether the mark is generic (more later) or descriptive (*see* below) or whether it infringes on another (read on).

Second, if you have a nonregisterable or weak mark (i.e., a word having a dictionary meaning[16] — a *strong* mark is not a dictionary word), a good counsel will get involved in strategy. For example:

1. Registering a joint mark of the design and name together will enhance the strength of the mark.

2. Certain marks may be too descriptive (terms describing quality or function) of the product. Counsel could suggest alternate registration. Supplemental registration is the appropriate procedure for registering marks which are not inherently distinctive (e.g., too descriptive) but are capable of acquiring trademark significance in the *future* through exclusive use by the registrant.

Note: The *Supplemental Register* is also the *only* proper place for registering marks which are not truly in the nature of marks but are more like slogans. Your counsel can and should distinguish and provide recommendations.

Third, counsel will carefully explain the advantages of formal registration. Use helps (your rights arise through the use of the mark, not the registration), but it's not preferable to registration.

Consider the case of another firm (not necessarily a competitor) introducing a mark identical or similar to yours. This duplication or similarity would give rise to the likelihood of public confusion as to the source of goods or services. Prior registration of your descriptive mark with the U.S. Patent and Trademark Office will enable you to obtain the following advantages:

1. Other firms receive actual notice of your right to use the mark. With registration, notice to the world is presumed in *your favor*. Without the protection of registration, you must (in defending your mark against infringement) successfully prove that the other party had actual knowledge or notice that you were using your mark. If you could not prove this, the other party would have concurrent rights to use what was formerly your own property.

2. Registration gives you the right to sue in a federal court rather than a state court. The former tends to be more sophisticated in these matters and also more inclined to stop the infringement than a state court, which might favor a local interest.

3. The notice discourages a good-faith firm from "accidentally" infringing. Even where there is no intention to infringe, it still costs money and time to alert and stop the infringer. Further, you've lost exclusive use of your mark, even if only for a short period of time.

4. Finally, aside from an infringement situation, registration asserts and increases distinctiveness. A trademark, which can otherwise be protected, could conceivably lose its distinctiveness if the owner is not careful in asserting it. If you don't protect and the improper use is continued, the mark could become generic, that is, understood as a name for a kind of product rather than the name of one brand of that product. You're probably aware that Du Pont lost the mark "cellophane" in 1936[17] and that Bayer lost "aspirin" in 1921.[18] Sanka and Xerox spend millions each year to publicize their marks. Formal registration and *identification* of a mark enhances distinctiveness.

What is formal identification? The procedure is to use ™ (or ᔆᴹ for a service mark) on all material where the mark is used (such as stationery, business forms, and advertising) while the registration procedure is pending. Once the product or service mark is obtained, the mark is followed by the letter "R" enclosed within a circle; thus ® indicates a *registered* trademark.

Once you're registered:

1. Don't let your company's trademark cross the line from a unique product designation to a common descriptive saying for all products of that type. You'll lose your exclusive use. Protect such exclusivity and distinctiveness by taking these precautions:

    a. At least once in each ad, and preferably near the beginning, use your mark in conjunction with the generic names for your product.

        (1) Always spell your trademark in exactly the same manner.

        (2) Have the trademark appear in the style of printing in which it is registered (whenever possible).

        (3) Use the symbols ® or ™.

2. Fight infringement immediately. The test is whether the other mark would confuse or deceive the normal purchaser.

3. Be concerned with how your mark is used on products. If a pornographic magazine adopts your emblem, there may be no confusion or deception per se, but the use may reflect adversely on your image.

4. Be careful if you cease to use your mark, even temporarily. While a short period of nonuse may be permissible, nonuse for 2 years or more may result in the presumption of abandonment.[19]

Still Not Convinced About the Need to Register?

The name "Book-of-the-Month Club" is almost synonymous with "Book Club." The Book-of-the-Month Club was the first book club, and it remains a dominant market force in the book club channels. Its name is a distinctive competitive asset based upon years of goodwill, solid service, and fine selections.

Some years ago, a competitor registered the name and legally established the right to use it as its own in western Australia and Tasmania. Neither firm was currently using the mark in Australia (Australia at that time permitted registration prior to use), but one firm pursued registration, while the other sat on its rights.[20]

Register and protect your mark. Otherwise your competitors will whittle away at your best asset and copy headliner — your good name.

Conclusion

Developing a working knowledge of the terminology and compliance issues involved with common promotional words (such as "sale," "new," "free," "warranty," "discount," and "coupon") and understanding the market value of a trademark will assist the direct marketer in creating a sales promotion piece which will not incur the wrath of a state or federal agency or the Attorney General's office. The information in this chapter will enable the marketer to ask the proper questions and to create copy which will easily pass a final compliance review by counsel.

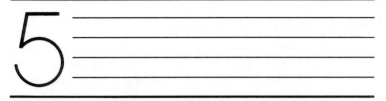

5

Key Specific Promotions

The limits of promotional devices and channels to distribute them are bounded solely by the marketer's imagination, creativity, and budget. Commenting on all of these is impossible within the confines of this text.

However, certain promotions should be illustrated to demonstrate legal problems inherent in each. I chose four common ones in everyday experience which have proved successful in a rollout.

1. Endorsements—excellent for mail promotions, door-to-door sales, telephone promotions, and especially media such as cable.

2. Customer referrals—logically follows "endorsements," as your best endorsement is a current satisfied customer. This form of promotion works well in all media, especially mail.

3. Sweepstakes—excellent in most media, particularly mail.

4. Simulated checks—in eclipse since the *Reader's Digest* decision, but they remain a viable device for mail contact, especially when complemented by a follow-up telephone call or a visit from a member of your sales force.

After you've reviewed this section, you'll be prepared to handle the legal challenges of the above; in addition, you'll be more conscious of the legal dimension in any similar promotion.

Planning an Endorsement Promotion

Direct marketers are increasingly examining the celebrity endorsement or testimonial[1] and employing it in their promotion pieces.
Because of the importance of endorsements to direct marketers, we
shall review this area itself as well as all its myriad compliance requirements. Before we begin this review, it should be noted that while there
are subtle differences in meaning between endorsements and testimonials, the FTC treats both types of promotions identically for
enforcement purposes. I use the two terms interchangeably in the
ensuing discussion.

The FTC staff has consistently taken the position that when an
advertisement contains a reference to a source of authority, consumers are particularly likely to believe the claims, especially when
such claims are directed to or involve the central attributes of the
advertiser's product or service. Thus high standards of truthfulness
and substantiation are applied in the guidelines themselves and in follow-up enforcement.

Endorsements and Testimonials as Effective Promotional Devices

What does the use of a person's (particularly a celebrity's) status contribute to an advertisement?

It attracts attention. Any name—or, more particularly, any picture—of a person attracts attention to an advertising message or, if
used at the point of purchase, to a product or service. Attracting the
potential customer's attention to a product is the first step in selling
the product, and to the extent that the use of a likeness attracts attention to a product, that use benefits an advertiser.

Names and pictures do more than merely attract attention to an
advertisement or a product. They suggest endorsement and otherwise
influence decisions to purchase. They give the advertisement or product credibility that the advertiser's own statements about the product
or organization may lack.

The bulk testimonial of satisfied customers capitalizes on human
nature's tendency to believe the words of "one of their own," who
has nothing to gain, rather than the words of the seller, who has a
pecuniary interest in the product. One or two sincere and believable
sentences from varied ethnic names and geographic regions may cre-

ate a satisfaction bandwagon effect. However, please omit the full address, for you may antagonize your endorsers if they begin to be barraged with requests for verification. Other points to remember are these:

1. *Do* get a signed release permitting the use of the endorser's name, all comments, photographs, illustrations, and so on.

2. *Don't* solicit particular comments.

3. *Don't* relate the comments out of context or distort the opinion expressed.

4. *Don't* pay the people. (However, see page 47, "Contractual Notes," for further clarification.)

5. *Don't* use endorsements from persons no longer using your product or service.

6. *Don't* attribute any particular experience, competence, or expertise to the person's comments.

7. *Don't* use fictitious people.

8. *Don't* feature "actual consumers" when you are using actors or models.

If the advertisement is designed to show ordinary consumers engaged in the process of demonstrating the "ordinary consumer experience," actual consumers must be used. If professional actors or models are used to represent such consumers, this fact must be disclosed in the advertisement.

However, nothing beats the shorthand communication device of a correctly chosen celebrity or expert (and the legal discussion will now focus on these two categories). What do we mean by "correctly chosen"? It means that the celebrity's or expert's image must match the image you wish to project for your product through the selling proposition. A good example of this was Firestone's choice of Jimmy Stewart as an endorser a few years back after the company had been besieged by adverse publicity concerning the Firestone 500's defect. Jimmy Stewart was the perfect antidote to this bad publicity, since he is perceived by the public to be as scrupulously honest and credible as Abe Lincoln. Billy Carter wouldn't have been as desirable in this spot!

Therefore, the marketer must solicit endorsements from people especially respected for integrity or achievement. Those who plan the promotional campaign must pay attention to sex, geography, and other special audience and product-image factors in selecting the endorsement or testimonial. Naturally, if the targeted audience doesn't respect or admire the celebrity chosen to endorse the product, chances are the promotion will be an abysmal failure! Obviously, the most effective testimonials are those which relate the benefits which the celebrity received from the product or service.

Finally, a celebrity's endorsement gives the consumer an opportunity to associate himself or herself with a public figure, however fleetingly and remotely. Many, perhaps most, consumers value this association, at least unconsciously.

The FTC as Government Regulator of Advertising

Understanding the compliance issues affecting endorsements and testimonials is facilitated by an understanding of the FTC's attitude toward advertising regulations. In general, the FTC, under its broad Section 5, has a mandate to root out "unfair methods of competition in or affecting commerce, and unfair or deceptive acts or practices in or affecting commerce."[2] It may act against materially deceptive speech (i.e., that speech which may influence the consumer's purchasing decision) when the injury is either to the consumer or to the advertiser's competitor.[3] The FTC has jurisdicition over violations "in or affecting commerce."[4]

Throughout its history, the FTC has attempted to follow the ideal that its regulation would serve two objectives: to provide truthful data and to maintain effective competition.

To ascertain the meaning of an advertisement, the FTC consistently employs the following standards:

1. Advertisements will be considered in their entirety—the advertisement's total *net impression* governs.

2. Literal truth will not save an advertisement if it is misleading when read in the context of the entire advertisement.

3. The advertisement is false if any one of two possible meanings is false.

4. Expressions of subjective opinion (puffery) are not actionable (that is, the FTC won't come after you!) unless they convey the impression of factual representations or relate to material terms.

5. An advertisement is generally tested by the impression it is likely to have upon the "general populace," the "ordinary purchaser," or an "appreciable segment of the public" (though advertisements directed at special audience groups will be interpreted on the basis of their meaning to that group).

Particular Factors Involved in FTC Consumer Endorsement[5] Regulation

In designing this form of promotion, all the above factors concerning advertising in general must be considered as well as the following points unique to endorsements—particularly the endorsement of experts.

1. The endorser must make reasonable inquiry into the truthfulness of the claim.

2. Any endorsement must be typical of the ordinary consumer experience, or the advertisement must "clearly and conspicuously" disclose either the performance that can actually be expected or that the endorsement has limited applicability.

3. The endorsement must be based upon a true belief in the properties of the product and not upon a mere exchange of compensation. Simply stated, the endorser must be and remain a bona fide user. The advertiser must have "good reason to believe" that the endorser still uses the product. Such good reason to believe must be established through regular inquiries at "reasonable intervals." However, a "reasonable interval" is not sufficient when a product previously endorsed by an expert is reformulated (e.g., "New Crest"). All endorsement promotions must cease until the endorser determines if the product change affects his or her views of the product's performance. It may or may not be obvious, but when notice of the *death* of an endorser is received, all his or her endorsement promotions are immediately terminated.

4. The endorser must be qualified by education or experience to make the statement.

5. All proprietary interests of the endorser must be disclosed.

" . . . Make Reasonable Inquiry"

The "supplementary information" provided by the FTC is emphatic in stating that the Commission wishes to modify the examples in 16 C.F.R. 255.0 to clearly distinguish an endorser from a mere "spokesperson."

> The modifications have sharpened the distinction between the use of a celebrity as a "spokesperson" and as an endorser by making clear that in an endorsement the party appearing must purport to express his or her real, personal views about the product based presumably, but not necessarily, upon personal experience with it. Unless the party appearing is represented as a source of information about the product independent from the advertiser, there is no endorsement.[6]

As noted above, a spokesperson is not an endorser. When the person in the advertisement speaks in the place of or on behalf of the advertiser rather than on the basis of his or her own opinion or personal experience, that person is a spokesperson — *not* an endorser.

As stated above, an endorsement must generally relate direct personal experience with the product. When this personal experience is lacking, the endorser must make a "reasonable" objective inquiry into the truthfulness of his or her claim. This is particularly true in the case of an expert's endorsement, as the total impression created on the targeted audience rests on the expert's endorsing a product from his or her experience as an expert in the field *and* as a personal user.

The pitfalls of ignoring or haphazardly approaching such inquiry are illustrated in the recent *Coogo Moogo decision*.[7] This was a landmark case, since for the first time in the history of the FTC an endorser of a product agreed to be personally accountable for representations he made in an advertisement.

Mr. Pat Boone was prominently featured in a television and magazine advertising campaign to promote an acne remedy. The remedy failed to live up to the claims made for it.

Mr. Boone agreed to personally pay a percentage of any restitution ordered against the manufacturer. He also agreed to make reasonable inquiry into the truthfulness of any products he endorses in the future. In a statement about the agreement, Albert H. Kramer, Director of the FTC Bureau of Consumer Protection, stated that while the pact did not set a binding legal precedent, it would stand for the principle that an endorser must verify the claims made for the advertised product before the first commercial goes on the air or appears in print, or risk FTC action. As to the means of verification, Kramer explained that if the endorser is not himself an expert, he must look to independent and reliable sources to check out claims, tests, or studies supplied for him by the advertiser. Kramer cautioned that the agreement with Pat Boone may only be a first step in the evolution of FTC policy toward endorsers.

"Typical of Ordinary Consumer Experience"

> . . . because the endorsement of product performance by a consumer or group of consumers may imply that the average person can expect to obtain comparable performance, advertisers should possess substantiation for this implicit claim or clearly and conspicuously inform consumers of the limited applicability of the endorsed performance.[8]

This area was discussed at length in *In the Matter of Porter & Dietsch, Inc.,*[9] which concerned the promotion of a diet aid. Several of the advertisements included testimonials reciting weight reduction and/or figure improvement purportedly attained by lay users of the preparation X-11.

As indicated on the ad copy, the testimonials of ordinary consumers were presented and accompanied by statements such as "from Georgia to Nebraska to California." The net impression implied the general nationwide success of the users of X-11. Such results (as to amount of weight lost) were not an accurate reflection of the typical or ordinary experience of consumers who used X-11 under circumstances similar to those depicted in the advertisements. The advertisements did not disclose or identify this difference.

Thus a material fact (i.e., a fact likely to affect the purchase decision) was not disclosed in the advertisements. The ads were found to be false and misleading. The decision not only held the firm liable but maintained that any retailer who runs an ad prepared by a supplier is legally liable for the truthfulness of everything in it.

Another variation of the "typical and ordinary" theme was found in a case concerning the Ford Motor Company.[10] Here the company advertised mileage test results for five small cars. There was an implied "you" in the mileage claims for driving performance—that is, "you" the purchaser would have a similar result if you drove the company's cars.

Here it was found that evidence of actual deception is not necessarily essential to a finding that an advertisement is unfair and deceptive. The capacity to deceive is important. Even if people submitting a testimonial honestly believe they obtained the results or that "you" will obtain similar results, consumers as a group are subject to too many variables that affect gas mileage, such as how fast they start and stop and actual driving conditions. Ford ceased advertising mileage claims which could be construed, with reference to the Environmental Protection Agency (EPA) mileage standards, as implying the success of a typical driver. Such problems have been alleviated by the federal EPA mileage standards.

A final case on point is that of National Dynamics Corporation.[11] Here, "endorsements" were published which stated the history of select and highly successful performance incomes of users of this particular service.

While all statements were true, many were no longer current, and few releases had been obtained in writing. In the future, the firm's endorsements must be current, and each person must have given permission in a signed document.

The Commission's experiences in the above related cases suggest that the more specific the endorsed experience is, the more likely the representation will be considered a claim that the average consumer can expect similar results.

Need for Personal Belief

In general, so long as an endorsement concerns only points of taste and individual preference, neither the fact of compensation nor the amount needs to be revealed.[12]

A case illustrating this point[13] concerned the endorsement of Milk Duds by various athletes and the Major League Baseball Players Association. In the case cited, Lou Brock was filmed stealing second and then stating that he gets his energy for his speed from Milk Duds.

The impression left is that this athlete and the association (also mentioned in the promotion) would be regarded as "experts" in the field of athletic energy nutrition because the average viewer would expect them to rely upon nutritious foods as part of their business needs.

The complaint accurately alleged that no nutritional benefit was received by the athlete. The endorsements were based upon a monetary relationship only. This type of relationship would have to be dislcosed, and the endorsement as it stood was expressly prohibited for future use.

When Sandy Duncan strolls through wheat fields expounding on her attraction to Wheat Thins, she is expressing only her personal taste and individual preference; consequently, no mention needs to be made of any financial remuneration which she may receive.

The advertiser must be careful so as not to present the endorsement out of context. Also, the advertiser must be vigilant so that he or she can determine whether the endorser continues to subscribe to the views presented. Once the endorser ceases to be a bona fide user of the product, the advertisement must be discontinued.

Endorser Must Be Qualified

This is similar to but distinguishable from the factors related above. A leading case on point[14] concerned certain toy products aimed at children. In this specific area of endorsements, the FTC prohibits endorsements of the worth, value, or desirability of a particular toy to a child by famous celebrities unless they also have the experience, special competence, or expertise to form the judgment expressed in the endorsement.

Contractual Notes

In obtaining an endorsement, the marketer must be careful to note whether the person endorsing the product or service is an "actual" person and not merely a pen name or some other fictitious personality. If the person is the latter, a specific clause should be placed in the contract whereby a real and accountable person stands behind the fictional name.

In any event, signed releases should be obtained for any and all names, photographs, and the like, that are obtained. It is also wise and proper to obtain an affidavit executed by the endorser attesting to the validity of all claims being made. The affidavit should relate the full text of the endorser's comments so as to prevent any ambiguity.

Such proper documentation will insulate a firm in the event of regulatory scrutiny. A minor consideration given in exchange for a release would not involve any Section 255.5 disclosure violations (see References, number 12).

Conclusion

Endorsements and testimonial advertising remain an area in flux. Nevertheless, in view of the published guides and the FTC's decisions to date, a marketer should consider the following questions:

1. Have we reviewed with counsel whether this situation is one of an endorser or one of a spokesperson? It is important that all these promotions be reviewed individually and specifically with counsel. If the former:

2. How was the endorser selected, and how was the contract prepared?

3. Was the endorser a user of the product or service prior to this promotion? Is he or she still a satisfied user?

4. Has this person ever been employed by the promoting firm, or has this person in any other way possessed a personal pecuniary interest in the success of the firm or product?

5. Is this person a professional performer? an "average" customer?

6. If performance claims are made, what competency or expertise or lack of same does the endorser have in evaluating this particular product?

7. Is the total impression that this promotion creates on the targeted audience one of an endorser endorsing a product from his or her experience (as an expert?) in the field and/or as a user?

8. Has a release been obtained?

9. Has an affidavit been obtained—one that is signed by the endorser and that attests to the truthfulness of his or her endorsement?

It is inescapable that endorsements will be carefully scrutinized by the FTC in the 1980s. All such promotions should be reviewed with counsel. This is particularly important as to the drafting of the necessary releases or with regard to the overall context of the contract itself if you are employing an outside firm or agency to manage your promotion.

Customer Referrals

Either through a book club, a food service, an oil company, or any number of business operations, you may at one time or another have received a promotion piece offering a "reward" (cash or merchandise) for getting your friends to try the product or service.

This is because the marketer knows that a satisfied referral is the *best* recommendation for any product. The personal relationship factor is all-important. Many smart firms have established plans which encourage customers to recruit other customers.

This may be done by word of mouth, or a customer may pass along your catalog to a friend. However, offering recruitment incentives may spur this along. These can vary from promotional kits to the offer of free merchandise to the recruiter.

Sounds good. Sounds easy. Is there a potential legal problem? You bet.

First the obvious. Check your contract. If you are giving away books, records, prints, and so on, make sure such promotional giveaways are permissible. Further, in drafting the initial agreement, make every effort to eliminate royalties on all promotional giveaways.

The subtle problem inherent in this plan is that you must avoid creating a chain referral, pyramid-type scheme. The key law is that no free, discount, bonus, or other incentive may be made *contingent* upon the *acceptance* of the referral. In other words, you are liable to pay the referral fee or "gift" if the referred customer signs up for the product or service, *regardless* of whether or not your firm decides to accept the referral or whether or not the customer subsequently decides not to receive the product or service after the required "no cost or obligation" examination period. The customer must not be obliged to invest any consideration in order to participate in the recruitment plan. Most states prohibit any schemes in which participants invest money in order to obtain the right to recruit other participants and to receive commissions for such recruiting.

Therefore, if you offer a free record for recruiting a new member for your record club, you must give the recruiter the free record even if you don't accept the applicant because of credit reasons (e.g., a deadbeat on file) or the applicant decides not to remain in your club after completing the "10-day examination," for example. The recruiter may not be penalized in any way, and if a free offer or an offer of similar import is involved, then you may *not* bill for shipping and handling with the free promotion.

Note: It is a good idea to have a signature line on your order card for these promotions. The signature requirement discourages forgery by the "recruiter" and emphasizes for the applicant that he or she is entering a potential business relationship and not merely "helping out a friend." Finally, if your club is a juvenile club, you should have a parent or guardian cosign. This will discourage lark entries by those who know or may be told by the recruiter that their contractual obligations are generally voidable at their initiative.

The Sweepstakes Promotion

You've no doubt received a chain letter in the mail at some time or another requesting you to send a dollar (or more) to one or more of the persons whose names appear in the letter and then to send copies of the letter with your name at the top of the list to a certain number of friends. Naturally, the financial remuneration you're promised is tremendous if "the chain is not broken." Fun and games? The government doesn't think so.

First of all, if you "played," you probably lost your dollar. Secondly, the use of the U.S. Postal Service to send chain letters involving money can result in civil or criminal penalties. Why? This scheme violates the lottery laws which make illegal any promotion which has *all* the following elements: prize, chance, and consideration.

If you understand the legal concept behind the chain letters, sweepstakes compliance will be fairly easy for you.

Market Impact of Sweepstakes

Sweepstakes account for more magazine subscriptions, record and book club memberships, and catalog sales than all other mail-order sales promotions combined. They test well, and they roll out well. One authority specifically recommends them for negative option programs.[15] The magic of a sweepstakes is in its economics. The total cost of prizes is significantly lower than would be necessary for premiums, cash reductions, or free goods to generate the same response. Also, it is a compelling form of promotion to consumers. Here the envelope is selling before the prospect has even looked at your copy. It is much harder to throw away an unopened envelope bearing the message "you may already have won $50,000" than to throw away an envelope that features price discounts or a free premium.[16] You're getting a strong attention-grabbing headline benefit on your envelope which appeals to self-interest and just basic human curiosity. You can amplify your benefit with an "early bird" limited offer. A reader is less likely to file away the mailing piece if it is necessary to make up one's mind immediately. This impulse for action may result in a sale on the spot.

Any advertisement must first attract and then hold attention. The sole function of "sweepstakes" is to sufficiently capture the prospective customer's interest so that the customer will read the part of the promotion piece which presents a product or service. However, since the sweepstakes component accompanies the product-advertising portion of the promotion piece, it must enhance — not impair — consumer goodwill. The fact that one is being offered a chance to get something for nothing does not necessarily preclude the possibility that the manner in which it is done may leave one with a feeling that there is something improper or unfair about the promotion.

Advertising in general and chance promotions in particular are subject to increasing government regulation and restriction. And the consumer movement inspires a critical reaction to even technical departures from existing legal restrictions. Resulting consumer and official complaints, with attendant publicity, can go far to nullify the goodwill that is expected to be generated by an otherwise promising promotion. Therefore, successful planning for sweepstakes requires careful observance of applicable federal and state legal requirements as well as drafted contractual clauses negotiated with any independent agencies assisting your promotion.[17]

This chapter will systematically guide the reader through the legal and contractual pitfalls present in planning and promoting a contest of chance.

Compliance Review Key: Clear and Conspicuous Disclosure of Rules

If members of the public are to feel that they have been dealt with fairly, it is essential that the rules of the sweepstakes and all conditions and terms which will govern the awarding of its prizes be stated thoroughly and in an understandable manner. This should be done at the time they are invited to take the first step necessary toward receiving a prize. In that way they will be spared undertaking "any effort" if they don't like the rules of the game. *Note:* "Any effort" beyond returning a first-class envelope should be reviewed by counsel. Many "efforts" will result in being classified as "consideration" and fall within the lottery laws.

It is not feasible to derive a definite and precise formula for describing the term "clear and conspicuous." In principle, however, terminology should be simple, nontechnical, and unambiguous. The size, style, and location of typeset matter should be such that one can view the promotion piece at a glance and see that the rules and conditions are there to be read if one chooses to do so and that the reading can be easily done. It is to the sponsor's advantage to undertake a separate compliance review (e.g., through an in-house checklist) so as to have all copy reviewed from an impartial viewpoint.

The following are practical points to consider in drafting the rules and promotional material. These elements[18] are common to most sweepstakes and should be disclosed, in addition to any others which may be peculiar to a particular promotion.

The Promotion Piece

A marketer's first exposure to possible governmental and consumer complaints about a sweepstakes occurs upon the publication of the offer and its rules for participation. Therefore, every effort should be made to state clearly, fully, and accurately the terms and conditions for participation and to avoid any misrepresentation. Ambiguity in the rules will be construed against the sponsor who drafted them and in favor of the participant. If you are employing an independent sweepstakes firm for assistance, make that firm warrant protection and recovery for you in the contract's indemnification clause.

There are five categories which should be examined during your compliance review: the entry blank itself, the description of prizes offered, the official rules, recordkeeping, and the contract with a professional sweepstakes firm if one is used. Each of these topics will be discussed in detail.

Entry Blank

1. May a facsimile of the entry blank be used?

a. If a facsimile may be used, a potential lottery violation is removed if the facsimile is made acceptable in lieu of an official entry blank, if obtaining the official entry blank would require a purchase. (Remember, the elements of prize, chance, and consideration must *all* be present for the promotion to be considered a lottery.) The rules should clearly indicate what the facsimile is to state or reproduce.

b. If a facsimile may not be used, the rules must specifically say so—that is, "Only official entry blanks will be accepted. No facsimiles permitted."

2. Is a simulated check being used with the promotion piece? Simulated checks may not be used unless they have value independent of the promotion and impose no obligation upon the recipient. Recipients must be able to cash them, redeem them, or exchange them for U.S. currency. (See the discussion in detail concerning simulated-check promotions in the next major section.)

3. Is a signature line available in the portion specified for name and address? While there is no legal requirement for a signature on the entry blank, it may be legally advantageous for you to obtain the signature of the sweepstakes subscriber. The signature is a specific manifestation of the customer's assent to the terms of the sweepstakes promotion. It helps to remove any ambiguity as to whether or not all terms and rules were definitely understood and agreed upon, including such issues as sales tax liability and any limitations concerning the recipient (for example, no minors).

4. Is a "lucky number" used? If so, it must be directly relevant to the awarding of a prize.

Prizes Offered

1. Is a complete list of all prizes by category set forth in detail as to their exact nature and the number to be awarded?

2. Are all visual depictions of the prizes accurate (e.g., in correct size proportion)?

Especially with sweepstakes promotions, you should be aware that photographs or printed illustrations of U.S. coins may be used for advertising purposes. However, printed illustrations of paper money, checks, and so on, are not permitted in connection with this form of advertising.[19]

3. Is a clear specification of value set forth? No award may be described as a prize unless it has a retail value greater than $1. No prize may be described, directly or by implication, as having substantial monetary value if it is of only nominal intrinsic worth. The "value test" must be substantiated by written records (e.g., prize purchase receipts); mere opinion is not permissible.

4. Have all enumerated prizes been purchased prior to the commencement of the promotion? You must be able to verify this with dated receipts. All prizes are then set aside until utilized for the specific awards.

5. Are you placing any restrictions or limitations on the prize? Remember, you are offering a *free* prize. *All* the free-rule requirements discussed earlier in the text must be complied with. For each prize that is offered, any qualifications must be stated immediately at the outset of the offer. Such qualifications must be set forth clearly and conspicuously so as to leave no reasonable probability that the offer might be misunderstood.

For example, a free trip for two persons anywhere in the United States or to Tahiti, for example, is a prize that is wide open. Words like "first-class" or "travel in style" will be interpreted literally. There is "no rule of reason test." Therefore, the marketer is best advised to use language such as "total package cost," "limited to," and "the trip will cover...." You must disclose any qualification immediately. Using an asterisk to indicate that the qualifications are specified elsewhere or setting them forth in the rules only will fail the contingency test and be disallowed.

A clause negating liability for the recipient's personal negligence, liability, or property loss while on the trip is also advisable.

Official Rules

After the entry blank has been designed and the promotion piece presenting the prize offerings has been created, the rules of the sweepstakes must be set forth in an area of the copy easily accessible to the reader. The type size must be the same as (or larger than) the type size used in the main body of the advertisement. The following areas should be addressed:

1. Whether purchase of the advertised product is required in order to win a prize (if it is, there is a lottery problem). The "No" and "Yes" boxes must be equally conspicuous.

Note: It's very foolish to risk major fines by discouraging in any way a "No" response. Besides the fact that it is illegal to discourage negative responses, you may find that the "No—names" are very valuable. These are people who retained your piece, opened it, read the rules, and acted upon them. Save all your "No—names" for future testing. They are direct-mail customers; they may not have made a purchase this time, but maybe they will be your buyers next time.

These names are valuable. If a primary or secondary objective of your promotion is to build a mailing list for future use, you should consult your counsel to confirm that such solicitation and compilation is not consideration for the purposes of the lottery laws. In general, it is not, but counsel must review the specifics of *your* promotion.

2. Whether a facsimile of the entry blank and/or proof of purchase (if applicable) is permitted. Again, remember that requiring an official entry blank or proof of purchase necessitating a purchase may constitute consideration and create a possible lottery violation.

3. The commencement date and termination date for eligibility and whether the latter is the date of mailing or the date on which the entry is received.

4. The total number of prizes to be awarded and the method or manner of selecting the winners (e.g., "random drawings from all entries received").

5. A statement that all prizes will be awarded.

6. A statement describing the disposition of unclaimed prizes.

7. The odds of winning. Statements such as "the odds of winning depend upon the number of entries received" or "we anticipate the odds to be . . ." may be sufficient for a direct-mail promotion. (The specific details and procedures of your promotion may require different wording, and so a review of these with your counsel is advised.)

8. Qualifications statements:

a. Are substitutions permitted? If not, say so.

b. Age restrictions. Certain age restrictions are patently obvious (when a promotion involves alcoholic beverages, tobacco, etc.). More subtle issues relate to the enjoyment of the prize (e.g., automobiles or vacations). In such situations, you might wish to disqualify minors or restrict delivery to a parent or guardian.

c. Whether entry is restricted to one application per family or address or whether the consumer may enter as often as he or she wishes, "but only one entry per envelope." Another good idea might be "one person per entry." This obviates the need to "divide a prize" between two or more winners on a single entry. I personally don't like the restriction of one entry per family or address, but since it is often found in promotions, let's review it. I believe that "one entry per person" and "one person per entry" are the only limitations possible. "One entry per address" would complicate your promotion because of various living-together arrangements, from male/female to college dorms. The same issue is raised by "one entry per family." Can you really bar the entry of a 21-year-old son simply because the mother also entered? What about spouses living apart in legal separation? Any limitation but "one entry per person (18 or over)" could present potential legal problems as well as create the potential for the loss of your goodwill.

d. Exclusions based on employment—that is, any member of the sponsoring firm and his or her family.

e. A voiding clause: for example, "void wherever prohibited by law." *Note:* This is a fluid area, and the state legislatures must be carefully monitored. Prior to December 1978, sweepstakes were effectively banned in Missouri by action of the state's attorney general. This was altered by a popular vote; a constitutional amendment ratified on November 7, 1978, redefined "consideration" (people *like* and *want* sweepstakes promotions).[20] Utah at one time held that payment for a first-class stamp was consideration enough for the promotion to be considered a lottery. This rule was overturned by the state's Supreme Court (September 1979). Things are always in flux with the varied state laws.

Careful consideration should be given to North Carolina law. A negative law was enacted in 1979 but positively altered in 1981. This state (like all others) bears watching.[21]

f. Endorsement. If you are planning to use the winner's name or picture for future publicity and promotions, notice must be set forth in the rules, especially if no further compensation is planned.

g. Any geographic limitations (e.g., continental United States).

h. A disqualification policy for entries which do not substantially conform to the rules of the promotional offer. A record of any disqualifications should be maintained for 30 days after the cessation of the promotion.

9. Taxes. State sales taxes apply not to the prize winners but to the sale of prize items to the sponsor.

The sponsor will be insulated from *income* tax liability by a statement such as "taxes are the responsibility of the winner."

Note: Particular attention must be paid to the tax implications of a joint venture with another firm. Such cosponsoring of a sweepstakes might expose the firm to "doing business in the state" where the coventurer is doing business. The tax issue is another reason to review all promotions in this sensitive area with your counsel.

10. A provision stating that all federal, state, and local laws and regulations apply. When running a sweepstakes promotion in any state, you should obviously comply with the rules of the particular state. For example, the New York General Business Law requires that a game-of-chance bond be obtained and that formal registration of the promotion be filed with the secretary of state. Florida[22] currently requires a similar bond with certain qualifications.

11. The identity and address of a specific addressee to whom inquiries concerning the sweepstakes (for example, obtaining a list of winners) may be directed. Usually this is the independent judging organization you have retained to assist in the promotion. It is permissible to require the customer to send a self-addressed, stamped envelope to obtain the list of winners.

12. Method by which winners will be notified. If by mail, obtaining a signed affidavit of identity and acceptance is advisable — particularly for the larger-dollar-value prizes.

The promotion must be conducted strictly according to its published rules. If an unforeseen development mandates a change, timely notice must be given.

Record Keeping

You are required to maintain the following data in your records for 3 years after the published termination date for entries. The data must be submitted upon FTC request.

1. The approximate number of entry blanks distributed

2. The total number of prizes advertised in each category

3. The approximate number of participants

4. The name and address of each winner of a prize having an approximate retail value in excess of $10, together with a description and the approximate retail value of the prize given to each

5. The method by which winners were determined

The FTC's games-of-chance rule has recently been modified to reduce the amount of information about winners that must be posted and the length of time between games deemed necessary to avoid confusing the public. The practical effect upon direct marketers is as follows: The first amendment made to the rule will limit the length of time between games to 30 days or the duration of the previous game, whichever is less. Previously, any new game was prohibited without a break in time equal to the duration of the previous game. The second amendment affects posting and reporting provisions. A retail outlet is now permitted to post a list of only those winners who redeemed their game chance in that store. Also, the requirement that a list of all winners must be forwarded to the FTC has been eliminated. However, this information must be retained for *3 years,* and it must be available to the FTC upon request.

Contractual Pointers

Most firms enlist the aid of an independent professional sweepstakes firm (see References, number 17, for four candidates). This firm provides advice and assistance with regard to all elements of the promotion. It is not merely an independent judgment body. The firm will present you with a "standard" contract outlining its services. Make sure you do the following:

1. Include language to retain your right to final written approval of all creative copy and promotion wording.

2. Have the agency specifically warrant competent legal and compliance review. Words such as "practical knowledge" are vague. Have all warranties included in your indemnification clause. This clause should specifically:

 a. Indemnify against class actions. (Your recipients are a "built-in" class, and poor administration of the promotion could expose you to high dollar and goodwill costs.)

 b. Indemnify against any action undertaken against you by a regulatory authority (federal, state, or local), as this form of adverse action is much more likely than private action.

 c. Add language that "the foregoing representations, warranties and indemnities shall survive termination of the Agreement."

3. Include a paragraph barring assignment without the mutual consent of both parties.

4. Include a paragraph identifying and protecting the trademark if you're engaged in a joint venture with another firm.

5. Specify if you want the firm to handle and receive all mailings and prize purchases, set up escrow accounts, deal with state bonding requirements, and so on.

6. Retain certain controls, such as right to receive entry counts at specified periodic intervals. Another control involves sending all important mail certified, return receipt requested.

7. Draft a tight confidentiality clause, particularly if the firm is to have access to your mailing lists.

None of the above points are designed to reflect adversely in any way upon any independent service. They are designed to make you think self-protection before you sign any form contract that the firm devises. Few form contracts are in your interest.

Conclusion

If the above guidelines are mastered, you will have exhausted the problems that are apparent in today's state of the art. You will be insulated from adverse actions by public regulatory bodies, private actions, or the negligence of an independent agency retained for various aspects of the promotion. If you design your sweepstakes promotion in compliance with these guidelines, you can have the confidence of knowing that your successful promotion won't be negated by fines or consent agreements.

The Simulated-Check Promotion

The direct-mail marketer (this is one of the few topics which are logically not applicable to other media) knows that the envelope is a key variable affecting the success of a test or rollout. The contact envelope is the first reflection of your image. A stamped reply envelope always increases the response (more so, by the way, than a neutral envelope). Better even than a plain first-class stamp is a commemorative stamp on either the introductory envelope or the response envelope because it lends greater "warmth and personality."

Pull tabs can be useful; also, a multiwindow envelope has a distinctive look. The latter has been used as a "hot" item in the last few years; it has been designed to resemble a check envelope. The object is to create an instant image of *implied* financial benefits. However, if the benefits are only implied, the promotion may be illegal.

In 1980, a major direct-marketing periodical endorsed this type of promotion without qualification. The same month, Chief Judge James L. Latchun of the U.S. District Court of Delaware imposed a $1.75 million civil penalty on Reader's Digest Association, Inc. This was the highest penalty ever awarded in a case concerning deceptive advertising and promotion. What had Reader's Digest done to receive such a punitive penalty (plus attorneys' fees, various costs, and so on)?

The Digest violated a 1972 consent order by mailing to consumers 13,898,521 Travel Checks and 4,042,000 Cash-Convertible Bonds as part of a promotional campaign.

The above-mentioned periodical did not responsibly present this particular marketing option; it did not qualify its idea with reference to the legal environment. Never depend on the trade literature alone—even the more reputable literature—to cover all the bases for you. Trade literature helps you sell your product—which is fine—but you should always consult with counsel before any new or innovative promotion is undertaken. *Prevention* through legal compliance of a loss of profits is just as important as your making profits through marketing strategy. Because of this decision's importance to direct marketers, we shall review it here.

United States v. Reader's Digest Association, Inc.[23]

On January 15, 1972, a consent order was finalized against the Reader's Digest. It prohibited the Digest from "using or distributing simulated checks, currency, new car certificates or using or distributing any confusingly simulated items of value."[24]

The Digest allegedly proceeded to violate the order the following year and also compounded the violation by continuing the mailing even though it was specifically advised by the FTC in writing that such mailings were in violation of the consent order.

The Digest argued that the government hadn't proved that individuals were confused or deceived by the promotional materials. That, said the judge, was beside the point. He argued:

> The principal purpose of a cease and desist order is to prevent material having a capacity to confuse and deceive from reaching the public. Thus, whenever such promotional items reach the public, that in and of itself, causes harm and injury. . . .[25]

Thus the court held that violating the provisions of the consent decree establishes liability without any further proof of deception being demonstrated.

In determining the size of the penalty, the court was influenced by:

1. The good or bad faith of the defendant
2. The extent of public injury
3. The financial resources of the defendant
4. The desire to eliminate any benefits derived from the violation
5. The necessity of vindicating the authority of the FTC[26]

Here the court viewed each individual promotion piece as a separate and distinct offense. Thus the fine came to approximately 10 cents for each of the 17,940,521 violations alleged. The direct marketer should note the ominous implications of this ruling. A fine per *individual envelope* (as opposed to each total mailing) could decimate a small firm. Further, *each day* that a firm fails to obey a final consent order of the Commission constitutes a *separate* offense.

Simulated-Check Promotions After Reader's Digest

The simulated-check promotion is not dead. The key is to offer a bona fide check as part of the promotion. Otherwise, you must avoid employing any promotion piece which could be interpreted to be a "confusingly simulated item of value." What could be interpreted as "confusingly simulated"?

The direct marketer should avoid:

1. Check-style paper (e.g., coloration, watermark)

2. "Traditional" check-style borders

3. Wording which might create an air of authenticity pertaining to a final document

4. A traditional check-size or check-style envelope

5. Other items normally found on checks (e.g., reference to negotiability or even the lack of same)

Further, the above items to avoid are cumulative. Obviously, the more items of avoidance actually included, the more you have increased your exposure to marketplace confusion.

The direct marketer can employ a check promotion using a negotiable document. The promotion may be qualified so long as the check itself is *not* in the final analysis.

For example, AMOCO Motor Club (1979) and the Credit Card Services Bureau, Inc., (1980) employed check-promotion devices whereby a customer might receive $2 or $3 off a trial membership in the club or service. If the customer elected to remain a member after 30 days, the check was credited to his or her account. However, if the customer did not elect to continue in the club or with the service, he or she could retain the full amount of the check as personal income. The check had value apart from its value as a reduction of the cost of membership.

Note: This is not an issue against which a firm can indemnify itself contractually. It is against public policy. If an outside creative firm creates your piece, you (as well as the firm) are responsible for all public FTC decisions. Printing a decision in an FTC newsletter constitutes actual notice.

Tax note: This form of penalty is *not* a deductible business expense: it comes right off your bottom line.

Conclusion

To employ a check-simulation promotion after Reader's Digest, the direct marketer must be sure the negotiation of the instrument is a separate action—apart from and not solely contingent upon the promotion (i.e., the check has value apart from its reduction of the cost or fee).

If the check doesn't have a separate value, an alternative may be to create a discount coupon, but avoid any instrument which could lend itself to being classified as a confusingly simulated item of value.

Finally, ask yourself an ethical and practical question. Are you fairly seeking to attract business with an honest, negotiable promotion device, or are you deviously *implying* a financial benefit? If it is the latter, you might get your letter opened, but when the customer realizes that there is no benefit, your goodwill suffers. If the customer unwittingly participates in the promotion and is taken, make sure this is a one-shot situation, because your firm may lose the customer forever. So, too, may the whole direct-mail channel.[27]

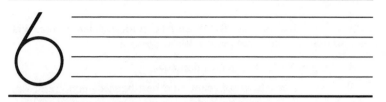

Implications of the Credit Disclosure Laws for the Direct Marketer

In today's business environment, it would be a dubious policy for the direct marketer to assume that consumer credit laws are solely the province of financial institutions. Many of the payment options now offered are considered "credit." The consequences of a violation in this area can be very serious indeed.

The FTC has major enforcement responsibilities in the area of credit regulations that may affect you and your business. The regulations involved have an increasing impact on situations and practices far removed from those which are generally thought to involve either consumers or credit.

For example, Montgomery Ward[1] established a credit-scoring system based upon various factors. Upon being denied credit (including the right to defer payment), the customer would receive notice that credit was denied. The customer could then inquire into the specifics of the denial. Often the reasons given in response were incorrect. Certain specific reasons for denial—such as the geographic area in which the applicant lived, determined by zip code (a principle reason for taking adverse action against an applicant)—were *never* disclosed. The FTC alleged that Montgomery Ward violated the Equal Credit Opportunity Act. The civil penalty payment provided for by the resulting consent order was the largest to date to involve either the

Equal Credit Opportunity Act or an FTC trade regulation rule. While not admitting guilt, Montgomery Ward agreed:

1. To pay $175,000 in civil damages.

2. To contact *every* applicant who had been denied credit since March 23, 1977, and who had inquired as to the rejection. These applicants were informed that Montgomery Ward may have failed to comply with the Equal Credit Opportunity Act. Also, they were given an FTC pamphlet informing them of their rights under the act, and they were invited to resubmit an application for credit.

3. To provide all applicants denied credit in the future with *specific* reasons for credit denial (e.g., age, number of dependents, rent).

4. To make available to the FTC *all* credit-scoring records for the next 10 years.

5. *Not* to consider zip codes or any other geographic unit in evaluating future credit applications. The wording in the consent agreement is of particular interest to direct marketers. Specifically:

> The defendant is enjoined from using zip code or any other geographic unit, as a characteristic in any of its credit scoring systems on or after the passage of one hundred eighty days from the date this Consent Judgment is entered.[2]

In light of the increasing complexity of the credit laws and the potential impact upon the direct marketer, a summary of these laws is presented in this chapter. The essence of these acts is notice and disclosure. This summary will detail the threshold requirements governed by the respective acts and alert you to potential problems. It is impossible within the scope of this book to provide an explanation of all the intricate details of the act which may affect your business. The text should, however, arm you with enough information to enable you to know when a particular law affects your business. You can and should then obtain specific advice from your legal counsel.

The Truth-in-Lending Act—Regulation Z[3]

One of the most comprehensive federal regulations affecting direct marketers began as the Consumer Credit Protection Act of 1968. This regulation launched Truth-in-Lending.

The basic purpose of the Truth-in-Lending Act is to ensure that your customers are provided with an accurate disclosure of the costs of consumer credit. The act requires that the full purchase price and other financial information be disclosed to the purchaser without consideration of the economic bargaining power of the purchaser. The consumer then will be able to compare more readily the various credit terms available and avoid the uninformed use of credit. To accomplish this fundamental objective, the act imposes an extremely complex and technical set of rules. These rules contain many pitfalls for the unwary. Further, the cast of administrative enforcers is legion.

The act assigns the administrative enforcement of its requirements to the following agencies: Federal Trade Commission, Federal Reserve Board, Comptroller of the Currency, Federal Deposit Insurance Corporation, Federal Home Loan Bank Board, Bureau of Federal Credit Unions, Civil Aeronautics Board, Department of Agriculture, and Farm Credit Administration!

The entire legal text of the Truth-in-Lending Act can be found in the Code of Federal Regulations, Title 12, Part 226 (cited in the References as 12 C.F.R. 226).

Must You Comply?

The Truth-in-Lending Act does *not* govern every extension of credit, but it applies to an extension of credit where a finance charge is imposed for the extension. The law likewise applies where there is no finance charge but payments will be made in *more* than four installments. To come within the provisions of the act, a transaction must contain *all* four of the following variables:[4]

1. It must be a credit transaction which is defined as the right to incur debt and defer payment.[5]

2. It must be a consumer credit transaction which involves credit offered or extended to a consumer primarily for personal, family, or household purposes.[6] (The credit must not be for business or commercial purposes.)

3. Payments must be made by written agreement in more than four installments or with a finance charge.[7] If payment is made in more than four installments, you must state clearly and conspicuously that "the cost of credit is included in the price quoted for the goods and services" *even* when there is no separate finance charge. Further, you must advise the buyer (separately and distinctly) of the (*a*) cash price, (*b*) deferred-payment price, and (*c*) total payment. Again, this is mandated even if these are all the same dollar amount! If a finance charge[8] is involved, you must state:

    a. The "annual percentage rate"

    b. Whether or not a down payment is required and, if so, its specific amount

    c. The cash price

    d. The number, amount, and period of payments

    e. The total of *all* payments made

4. It must involve a creditor,[9] that is, one who regularly extends or arranges for the extension of credit. Note this: To be a creditor you need not extend credit; you may merely "regularly arrange for the extension of credit." "Regularly" means extending credit more than 25 times in the preceding calendar year.

If not all the preceding criteria are met, the federal act does not cover you; however, it is advisable to consult state law, because Regulation Z will defer to substantially similar state laws.[10] An important example is the California "Unruh Act,"[11] which applies to extensions of credit involving *four or more* installments. This requirement is significantly narrower than the "more than four" requirement of the Truth-in-Lending Act. As a national direct marketer you may believe you are in compliance with a four-installment plan without finance charges, but you may have a potential problem if you are doing business in California. Review your policy with your counsel, or you may have to review your policy with the attorney general—and bring your checkbook!

One subtlety that is not readily apparent from the third requirement above is that to be a creditor, you need not charge any finance charges, late fees, or other premiums so long as the product is to be offered for a price payable in more than four installments (even if such installments include no extra charges, which in our inflationary era would give the customer a "float" advantage in delayed payment).

Watch your late-payment policy.[12] If you demand a fee for a late payment and you want to avoid this act, make sure the fee is not a finance charge. This is accomplished by making sure it is imposed only for an actual, *unanticipated* late payment. You should state your payment policy up front, for example, "Payment Due Upon Receipt." Then state a penalty which may be imposed after a reasonable period of time. I wouldn't stress the grace period, as this term may dilute the immediacy of your payment demand. You want no inference made that you are giving your customers any right to *defer* payment. You expect it now, and you are demanding it *now*.

Then there is the issue of credit cards. Regulation Z imposes minimal compliance[13] on those who merely honor a credit card where no finance charge is imposed at the time of the transaction.

If your business practices are not within the realm of the above definitions and interpretations, the Truth-in-Lending Act does not directly affect you. If you are included or think you might be, counsel must be consulted. This is not an area where you can cross your fingers and "hope for the best"; most judges will demand literal compliance. Areas such as specific disclosures or even how such disclosures are placed on the copy become issues. For example, you may be required to use only one side of each piece of paper in order to avoid the problem of "hidden" disclosures on the back.[14]

Before we move on, it goes without saying that with the Truth-in-Lending Act and all credit requirements discussed hereafter, the more protective state statutes and regulations are usually permitted. In addition, the legislative and judicial dynamics at the federal and state levels are such that these laws are constantly in flux through legislative amendment and court rulings.

The Fair Credit Reporting Act

Title VI of the Consumer Credit Protection Act (added by Public Law 91-508) is known as the Fair Credit Reporting Act[15] (FCRA for short). It is one of the few federal acts to regulate the collection and use of personal information (including lists) in the private sector. Because of its impact on lists and other information, I have detailed this act as lucidly as possible so that when you have reviewed this section, you'll have gained a basic understanding of the FCRA.

Before we proceed, it should be understood that the credit industry provided solid input for this act. The law is straightforward and sets forth due process protections for the subjects of credit reports. Some of these rights include:

1. Notification to the subject upon denial of credit[16]

2. Disclosure of specific reasons for the denial

3. The subject's right to dispute the information and compel possible reinvestigation[17]

4. Failing correction of the subject's file, the subject's right to have his or her story included in the file[18]

The most relevant provisions of this act are included in the References and/or Appendix. However, there are three key definitions essential to your understanding of the FCRA (emphasis added).

1. The term "consumer reporting agency" means

> any person which, for monetary fees, dues, *or on a cooperative non-profit basis regularly engages in whole or in part* in the practice of assembling or evaluating consumer credit information or other information on consumers for the purpose of *furnishing consumer reports to third parties,* and which uses any means or facility of interstate commerce for the purpose of preparing or furnishing consumer reports.[19]

Note: Whether or not your firm operates for profit and whether or not this reporting constitutes a major part of your business has no bearing on determining whether you may be considered a "consumer reporting agency."

2. The term "consumer report" means

> any written, oral, or other communication of any information by a consumer reporting agency bearing *on a consumer's credit worthiness, credit standing, credit capacity, character, general reputation, personal characteristics, or mode of living* which is used or expected *to be used or collected in whole or in part* for the purpose of serving as a *factor* in establishing the consumer's eligibility for (1) credit or insurance to be used primarily for personal, family, or household purposes, or (2) employment purposes, or (3) other purposes authorized under section 604 (15 USCS 1681b). *The term does not include any report containing information solely as to transactions or experiences between the consumer and the person making the report. . . .*[20]

3. Permissible purposes of reports. A consumer reporting agency may furnish a consumer report under the following circumstances *and no other:*

> To a person which it has reason to believe —
> (a) intends to use the information in connection with a credit trans-action involving the consumer on whom the information is to be furnished and involving the extension of credit to, or review or collection of an account of that consumer's; or
> (b) intends to use the information for employment purposes; or
> (c) intends to use the information in connection with the underwriting of insurance involving the consumer; or
> (d) intends to use the information in connection with a determination of the consumer's eligibility for a license or other benefit granted by a governmental instrumentality required by law to consider an applicant's financial responsibility or status; or
> (e) *otherwise has a legitimate business need for the information in connection with a business transaction involving the consumer.*[21]

Must You Comply?

Almost all direct marketers in the various media use lists, which may be rented or purchased. A consumer's address in and of itself is information bearing not only on creditworthiness but also on credit standing, credit capacity, general reputation, and mode of living. The type of neighborhood in which one lives and one's living status, both discernible from an address, are important factors which influence a credit decision. None of these factors are yet illegal because they're considered positive criteria, though you should keep an eye on the state legislatures.[22]

At present, the sale or rental of *positive* commercial information is permissible with certain qualifications. Further, if your firm keeps its own records about transactions between itself and a consumer, you need not comply with the FCRA so long as the information is being assembled or evaluated for the firm's own use and not for transmittal to third parties. However, once a firm sells, rents, or exchanges *adverse* credit criteria (e.g., a deadbeat list), it may subject itself to compliance with the FCRA.

Getting the Information You Want While Avoiding the FTC

You can eat your cake and have it too. However, you must be careful. You must pass the FTC's "permissible purpose test."[23] The test must be met for *each* name on the list. Essentially, that "test" requires that you demonstrate that you are contemplating the *immediate* extension of credit to (or otherwise have a permissible purpose for obtaining information on) *each* consumer on the list at the time you request or receive the list or information.

Similarly, in response to a request for credit information from a user, you cannot disseminate such a list unless you are satisfied that you have reason to believe that the user has received a request for "credit" from each consumer on the list.

For example, a firm may request, for its own use, information from another business concerning its dealings with a *particular* customer. As long as the business limits the use of the information received from the other business to its own individual application and does not disseminate the information to third parties, it will not become a "consumer reporting agency." The act of seeking credit information from other businesses might appear to be "assembling or evaluating" consumer credit information; however, as long as the information is strictly for the firm's own use, such assembling or evaluating cannot be said to be for the purpose of furnishing consumer reports for "third parties."

If you have been careful to follow procedures for the immediacy and timeliness of a specific report about a particular customer, you will probably have a trade report,[24] that is:

> any report containing information solely as to the transactions or experiences between the consumer and the person making the report.

Congress[25] exempted trade information reports from FCRA regulation because a report based solely on a merchant's personal experience with a consumer is likely to be reliable.

OK, so you've escaped compliance by carefully selecting and disseminating the adverse credit information. It's helping to reduce your bad debt, and you'd like more information—*without* necessitating compliance with the FCRA.

Formal Contractual Protection

Obviously a credit bureau is a good source of information about deadbeats or delinquent payers. However, a firm in your industry or product line (especially a competitor) might be preferable because that firm is more likely to possess the bad file histories you wish to avoid. Set up a formal arrangement to exchange the information.

Whether you employ the services of a credit bureau or exchange information with another firm, you should have a basic contract drawn up by your attorney to protect your interests. Your contract should state that all parties to the contract agree not to homogenize their lists. Otherwise you will no longer be relating your respective experiences; instead, you will have the total experiences accumulated from your own lists and the lists of the other contracting parties.

If you are dealing with a credit bureau, your contract should also have a good indemnification clause. The credit bureau should protect you with the following warranties:

1. No negligence (e.g., not correcting its lists, not recording judgments, removal of stale names). These issues are important. With an inaccurate list your money is wasted on useless names.

a. The time for retaining adverse credit records may vary. The FTC's current position is 7 years, but New York State's is 5.[26] Therefore, you don't want New York State names a day older than 5 years.

b. The time for the removal of stale names varies. New York State[27] requires every consumer reporting agency to clarify its records within 60 days of a proper or partial satisfaction piece.

2. The credit bureau must warrant that it is in compliance with all relevant federal, state, and local laws and regulations *and* that it routinely monitors its system and updates it as ongoing legislative dynamics impose changes. This warranty not only enhances the integrity of the names acquired but follows the FTC's mandate that any firm acquiring credit information must use its best efforts to obtain only accurate information about delinquent debtors.

Compliance With FCRA

We've reviewed creating a trade report and contractual protection. There are two ways to get yourself involved in consumer reports: voluntarily and involuntarily. We'll discuss the latter first, because without due caution, you can easily become involved in reporting consumer credit.

In Re Howard Enterprises, Inc., is a good summary of what is and is not a consumer report. The case involved a firm which furnished merchants (by subscription) with "alert lists" of consumers who allegedly had passed "bad checks." The lists did not pertain to a particular customer a firm was preparing to do business with, but from 30 to 500 names were provided at random.

Howard Enterprises, Inc., did not have an adequate system for either checking the allegations on its lists or deleting the names of those incorrectly placed on the lists. Further, the subscribers did not have a *legitimate business need* for the data. The Commission's ruling was as follows:

> Alert list subscribers have a legitimate business need for information about a particular individual only in the context of a consumer transaction with that individual, such as when the individual offers a check in payment for a purchase . . . subscribers did not have a legitimate business need for information regarding all of the individuals on the list. . . .
>
> By providing subscribers with consumer credit information for which they had no legitimate business need, Respondent Howard violated Section 604 of the FCRA. The Commission has previously indicated that the permissible purpose for furnishing the consumer report must exist at the time the report is distributed; it is not sufficient that the consumer report be distributed in anticipation that a permissible purpose will subsequently arise.[28]

Finally, it is important to note that the Commission felt the violations would not have occurred if a proper coding system existed. Such coding would consist of

> . . . a unique identifier, other than a name, through which the subscriber may identify the consumer and decode the information in connection with a business transaction. Thus the decoded information will become available to the subscriber only at that point when a legitimate business need for the information in connection with a business transaction involving the consumer arises.[29]

If you are unsure about whether or not your firm may be dealing in consumer reports, it would be a good idea to review a few other FTC decisions on this topic[30] and, of course, to consult counsel.

Voluntary Compliance

If, after all the above considerations and options, you still have a business need to involve yourself in the dissemination of consumer reports, then your firm will be considered a consumer reporting agency. The consumer has the right to the following services.

1. When a consumer (alleged debtor) is adversely affected by information contained in a report, the user of the report must notify the consumer of the adverse action and provide him or her with the name and address of the consumer reporting agency that made the report.

2. The consumer may then contact you (or the consumer reporting agency), and upon proper identification, you are required to disclose the "nature and substance of all information in your files on the consumer" at the time the request is made, including the sources of such information. The procedures for correcting disputed information extend to *all* the information in a consumer's file and not just to information included in a consumer report. The term "file," when used in connection with information on any consumer, means all the information on that consumer recorded and retained by a consumer reporting agency regardless of how the information is stored.[31]

3. You must furnish the names of any persons who have received a report on the consumer within the last 6 months.

4. Upon giving a consumer access to his or her file, you are required to provide trained personnel who can explain the contents or use of the file or decode any data.

5. The consumer may have obsolete, inaccurate, or unverifiable information deleted from his or her file.

6. You must reinvestigate the information in the file if its accuracy is disputed by the consumer.

7. If the information remains in dispute, the consumer may file a brief explanatory statement concerning the disputed items. This statement *must* be included on all subsequent consumer reports.

8. All adverse information must be deleted from the consumer's file after 7 years except in certain exceptional situations. State laws may require deletions after a shorter period of time; for example, New York State mandates 5 years.

Further, compliance includes proper encoding to ensure anonymity and not getting involved with the publication of overbroad "protective bulletins" or "alert lists."

Finally, every name reported on must be an ascertainable *individual* person. "Address hits," if they are used (and many firms do use them), must produce specific information which concerns only the person who is the subject of an inquiry. Address hits that report on others at the same address are prohibited by the FTC.[32] In the complaint against Hooper Holmes (a credit reporting agency), the FTC was not impressed with a reporting system based solely on last names and street addresses.

> In a substantial number of instances, using this system respondent has furnished and is furnishing consumer reports on individuals not involved in the extension of credit or other business transaction. Respondent's system uses no identifiers in addition to the last name and street address to ensure that information concerning separate individuals with the same or similar last name at a specific mailing address are not reported and, therefore, respondent has failed to follow reasonable procedures designed to limit the furnishing of consumer reports for the purposes listed under §604 of the Fair Credit Reporting Act and has, therefore, violated §607(a) of that Act. . . .
>
> Respondent uses no system of supplementary identifiers to identify with more specificity items which may relate to neighbors, relatives or spouses of the applicant, and in a substantial number of instances, the information items included in the respondent's reports relate not to the applicant but to neighbors, relatives or spouses of the applicant.[33]

What is required for the individual home is also required for a larger housing complex. The apartment house, because of size alone, presents an infinitely more complex problem. For example, in a 1500-unit apartment house Mary Smith of 1C applies for credit. The credit reporting agency must be careful to make sure that the report you receive concerns only Mary Smith in 1C and says nothing about Mary Smith in 6R.

The FTC also took exception to a "home hit." A credit report requested for the husband might produce information on the wife and children. If a reporting agency in answering a request for credit information on Mr. Oscar Krasner, Sr. also provides information pertaining to Mr. Oscar Krasner, Jr. living in the same abode (or, for that matter, anyone else in the family), it is in violation of the Fair Credit Reporting Act. If there was ever any confusion, the FTC has clarified matters in in the Hooper Holmes decision.

Conclusion

If your firm merely acts upon in-house credit information, the FCRA does not affect you.

If your firm obtains credit histories about specific individuals with the immediate intention of granting or denying credit, there is probably no problem, but such activities should be reviewed with counsel.

If your firm homogenizes outside delinquent lists or sells such lists, then it is probably dealing in consumer reports. Thus it will be considered a consumer reporting agency, and it will be required to comply with the FCRA.

The Fair Credit Billing Act[34]

This act became effective on October 28, 1975, as an amendment to the Truth-in-Lending Act. Since this is an amendment to the act, compliance is predicated upon whether your practices came within the specifications of the Truth-in-Lending Act discussed in the beginning of this chapter. The entire legal text for the Truth-in-Lending Act, including this amendment, can be found in the Code of Federal Regulations, Title 12, Part 226 (cited in the References as 12 C.F.R. 226). The Fair Credit Billing Act was designed to protect consumers against unfair practices of issuers of *open-end* credit. The act requires such credit grantors to inform debtors of their rights and responsibilities in a billing dispute which essentially involves five steps. It also requires creditors to resolve billing disputes within a specific time period (activated by the customer's *written* correspondence—more about this later) by making appropriate account adjustments or explaining why the original bill is believed to have been correct.

Must You Comply?

There are four definitions which determine whether you must comply. You should review the sections in the text of the regulation which define "credit,"[35] "creditor,"[36] and "consumer credit."[37] The definition of "open-end credit" is especially important[38].

If your promotions do not fall within the definition of open-end credit, you are not required to provide with your billing a statement informing the consumer of the right to dispute billing errors. However, if you honor credit cards in a consumer credit transaction, certain sections of the act should be reviewed, specifically those which deal with open-end credit, credit card accounts,[39] and possible exceptions to the general rule.[40] As with all such federal acts, similar state laws should also be reviewed.[41]

If you *are* within the act, you will be required to distribute a notice in the form prescribed[42] informing each customer of his or her rights under the act and the means to implement such rights. You've probably received this type of notice with your credit card bill every few months.

You should acquaint yourself with the general and specific disclosure requirements of the Fair Credit Billing Act.[43] As a creditor, you are required to disclose to the consumer the following customer and creditor obligations under the act:

The customer is required to put the complaint *in writing*. The letter must include the name, the account number, a description of the error, and any other pertinent information, and it must be mailed to the company *within 60 days* of the alleged billing error. A telephone call will not preserve the customer's rights.

You, the creditor, must acknowledge the customer's written inquiry within 30 days of receipt. Within two complete billing cycles after receipt (and in any event in no more than 90 days), you must either correct the error or explain why you believe the bill was correct.

During this interval, neither you nor a collection agency may take any collection action concerning the amount in dispute. Action includes imposing a finance charge or compelling periodic payment of a minimum amount when only that minimum amount is involved. The consumer is, however, obliged to pay all undisputed debts during this interval. Once you have explained the bill in the correct manner, you may then proceed to collect in the normal manner. After compliance you have no further responsibility under this section if the consumer "continues to make substantially the same allegation with respect to such error."[44]

Conclusion

A system should be set up internally to handle billing dispute correspondence. Your specific practices should be reviewed with counsel in light of this act and applicable state laws. If you are not strictly within the definitions set forth, this act's provisions provide a workable model — one the FTC is familiar with and endorses.

The Equal Credit Opportunity Act[45]

The Equal Credit Opportunity Act (also known as Regulation B) was originally passed in 1974 to prohibit credit discrimination on the basis of sex and marital status. It was an amendment to the Truth-in-Lending Act. However, certain important definitions vary, so you should not presume that you can automatically avoid compliance if you've avoided the Truth-in-Lending Act.

The heart of this act is a prohibition against credit discrimination in any aspect of a credit transaction because of the enumerated protective categories (significantly amended in 1976), which include race, color, religion, national origin, sex, marital status, and age (provided the applicant has the capacity to enter into a binding contract), or because all or part of the applicant's income is derived from a public assistance program, or because the applicant has, in good faith, exercised a right under the Consumer Credit Protection Act. The act provides that an aggrieved applicant may sue for actual damages, punitive damages, and equitable and declaratory relief.[46] A successful litigant is also entitled to recover costs and a reasonable attorney's fee.[47]

Effects Test

To implement the prohibition against discrimination, Regulation B deals with the information which may be requested in connection with an application for credit. If you fall into the category of creditor, you should be aware that the test for discrimination is the *use* of information. There is no requirement that the creditor *intends* to discriminate, and applicants do not have to prove that there is any motive to do so. The "effects test," developed in employment discrimination law,[48] is incorporated into this act. This means the use of an otherwise "neutral" criterion may be illegal if it has a discriminatory impact and is not justified by business necessity.

The best way to understand the "effects test" is to review note 48 in the References as well as the following interesting case on point.[49]

A white female typesetter living in a predominantly nonwhite residential area of Atlanta was denied a credit card, in part because of Amoco's previous credit experience in her immediate geographic area. (Amoco's experience was based on its use of zip code criteria.)

The woman argued that she was denied a credit card because of her residence. She alleged that the use of such zip code criteria was the equivalent of racial discrimination because of the segregated pattern of housing in the Atlanta area. Thus her individual right to be evaluated upon the basis of her own merit was denied.

Amoco utilized a complex system to evaluate applications. It took into account 38 predictive and objective factors, including the level of income, occupation, and prior credit experience in the U.S. Postal Service zip code area where the applicant resides.

There was no intent to discriminate. However, did the *effect* of Amoco's credit scoring system result in disproportionate racial discrimination? No, the court held. Amoco demonstrated that the zip code ratings did not tend to adversely affect black applicants disproportionately. No distinct racial pattern was found.

Conclusion: Zip code criteria survived, although Amoco agreed to discontinue the practice of using such criteria (see the section in this chapter on the demographic and geographic frontier for the 1980s). However, the important lesson to learn is that although your in-house system evidences no intent to discriminate, you must carefully monitor *(at least annually)* the quantitative impact or effect with regard to the various prohibited-basis categories set forth in Regulation B.

Must You Comply?

Regulation B requires *full* compliance from all creditors covered by the Truth-in-Lending Act. (See the discussion in the beginning of this chapter to determine if you must comply with Truth-in-Lending.)

Limited compliance (Section 202.3) is required from credit grantors who extend incidental credit to consumers and/or business credit for commercial purposes falling within any of the five categories. This area has been amended from time to time, and so you should update internal compliance with counsel. Creditors who fall within the limitations of Section 202.3 should review carefully the extent to which Regulation B affects them.

The five categories are as follows:[50]

1. Public utility credit[51]

2. Securities credit transactions[52]

3. Credit transactions primarily for business or commercial purposes, including agricultural purposes[53]

4. Extensions of credit to governments or governmental agencies[54]

5. Incidental consumer credit transactions not involving credit card accounts or finance charges and not involving payments in more than four installments[55]

The fifth category, concerning incidental consumer credit, is the one most likely to affect you. If it might, Section 202.3's definitions should be reviewed, specifically the definitions of "consumer credit,"[56] "credit,"[57] "creditor,"[58] and "extend credit."[59]

The above parts of Section 202.3 as well as Section 210(a) and (b) would define your inclusion as an incidental creditor under this act. It is important to note that the definition of "creditor" in this act may be broader than the definition in the Truth-in-Lending Act.[60] It excludes a person who merely honors a credit card but nothing more. It would benefit you to check this out before you exempt yourself from compliance.

If your operations exclude you from compliance, you're home free. If not, you are either an "incidental creditor" or a full creditor under the act.

Incidental-Creditor Compliance

If you fall into the category of an incidental creditor, then you are effectively excluded from the more onerous sections of the act.[61] Essentially all that is left is the general rule prohibiting discrimination,[62] which states that "a creditor shall not discriminate against an applicant on a prohibited basis regarding any aspect of a credit transaction" (i.e., no discrimination on the basis of the categories mentioned above, such as race, color, and religion).

Note: You should watch legislative developments here. There have been various efforts in Congress to amend that act's prohibited-basis criteria to include residence and geographic location. If an amendment is made and you use address hits or zip code qualification criteria, a problem may result.

Further, you may not make the existence of a telephone listing in your applicant's name or a specific telephone number a prerequisite for doing business.[63] Any question like this is a red flag for a consumer agency. However, a telephone number may be requested specifically as an *optional* item (the number may be desired as information for follow-up *telephone marketing*). You may *ask* whether a telephone exists at the applicant's residence.[64]

Finally, Regulation B preempts only inconsistent state laws and only to the extent of the inconsistency. A state law is not inconsistent with Regulation B if it is more protective of the applicant.[65]

Full Compliance

Remember, if your firm meets the criteria for creditors covered by the Truth-in-Lending Act, then Regulation B requires full compliance with the Equal Credit Opportunity Act. Tight compliance is enforced here as to both the civil rights aspects discussed above and Section 704(c),[66] which authorized the FTC to enforce this act as if it were an FTC trade regulation rule. Enforcement to date has resulted in stiff fines and penalties for alleged violations of the act. Three examples are *Aldens, Inc.,*[67] *United States v. Federated Department Stores, Inc.*[68] (fined $50,000), and *United States v. Montgomery Ward & Company, Inc.*[69] (fined $175,000; see the discussion at the beginning of this chapter, as well as note 1 in the References). Besides fines, the paperwork burden is considerable for all violators. All fines are generally the result of alleged violations of the use of the prohibited-basis criteria.

To Avoid an FTC Problem

First, review your application(s) for credit. Remove any references to prohibited categories (race, sex, national origin, color, religion, public assistance, or marital status[70]) and any questions as to whether or not the applicant has previously exercised his or her rights under the act. Age is also a prohibited-basis criterion, except when you must determine whether the applicant is of the age of majority (i.e., old enough to sign contracts that are binding and *not* voidable). Usually this age is 18 or over, but the law of each specific state should be reviewed. Preference to those 62 or over is usually OK.

Second, review all in-house credit criteria. Eliminate the possibility of treating anyone differently (except to benefit—but watch this carefully, too) because of a prohibited-basis criterion. At present, geographic criteria may be used, but watch out for disproportionate racial impact (such as excluding certain zip codes because they represent areas where most of the residents are members of minority groups). Further, read the section in this chapter on the demographic and geographic frontier of the 1980s. Don't build your plans around geographic criteria, or your plans may be built on a sandy foundation.

Third, once you've sanitized you applications and in-house criteria, make sure you answer all applications within 30 days. Then the applicant's rights are similar to the procedure explained in the Fair Credit Billing Act (discussed in a previous section of this chapter). If the applicant requests in writing the specific reasons for denial, you must respond with *specifics* within 60 days, and such specifics must be the real reason(s) why credit was denied. Stress truth and specifics in all your customer relations, and you'll survive FTC scrutiny. Here and elsewhere the FTC is educating consumers as to their rights and, more onerously, how to complain. You should pick up and review the FTC's pamphlet *Equal Credit Opportunity Act.*

Fourth, retain all records for a minimum of 25 months after any notification process.

Fifth, review the laws[71] of the states in which you are doing business. As in most cases, this act preempts only inconsistent state laws and then only to the extent of the inconsistency. A state law is not inconsistent if it is more protective of an applicant.

Conclusion

The Equal Credit Opportunity Act is more understandable than other acts because it is based on "newspaper law," that is, the obvious, straightforward, nonesoteric legal debate you've witnessed unfolding and accelerating since the late 1950s.

Each person is uniquely different and must be considered for and granted credit solely on the basis of his or her individual merit. You may not base your decisions concerning a particular applicant on your general experiences with a race or sex.

Even a firm with the best intentions may blow it if its application for credit is worded in such a way (even innocently) that a particular group is merely *discouraged* from applying. Again, counsel should read all documents that get into the hands of the public as well as all internal criteria for granting credit. The test of equal credit opportunity—at every stage of the process, from application through final notification—revolves around this question: Have the avenues of acceptance been open coequally to all?

Demographic and Geographic Frontier for the 1980s

The discussion of the Equal Credit Opportunity Act briefly touched upon "incidental creditor." Many direct marketers will fall within the parameters of "incidental creditor." For most, it is at present an innocuous provision. Nevertheless, it may be a future powder keg. Many direct marketers do use demographic criteria in accepting applicants, and then once an applicant is accepted, such criteria may determine the credit class the customer is placed in. If residence or geographic area is added to the protected categories, the value of many lists and market segmentation programs will be in jeopardy. Entire internal credit policies may require reworking.

In the past few years, the House Banking Committee has explored this area, and potentially adverse legislation was introduced each year. Fortunately, all such bills have died in committee.[72] While the initial target is redlining, the direction is apparent.

The isolated precedent of Montgomery Ward's being barred from using zip code criteria was discussed at the beginning of this chapter. Many petroleum companies have likewise been asked to refrain from using these criteria.[73] In one case, the FTC filed a complaint against Amoco Oil Company alleging discriminatory impact.[74] Amoco had devised a complicated "point system" for determining credit ratings. The system was based in part on zip codes and placed some weight on a credit card applicant's neighborhood as well as his or her state.

Amoco denied the allegation of discrimination, but again you are dealing with an "effects test" rather than intent. Amoco had no intent to discriminate. One rational argument put forth was that this geographic factor was more difficult to falsify, unlike information about an applicant's income or job.

Eventually, Amoco agreed to settle by discontinuing the use of a zip code or any other geographic unit smaller than the individual's state in determining creditworthiness.

Another FTC action impacting geographic criteria was against Hooper Holmes (discussed previously), which made use of a noncontrolled system of "address hits" impacting apartment houses and other housing units sharing a mailing address.[75] The FTC believed that the use of "address hits" resulted in the denial of credit to some individuals, not on the basis of their own individual merit but because of the credit history of neighbors, relatives, and former residents. This decision does not prevent a firm from compiling a list of valid deadbeats or even reporting them by address if certain safeguards and standards are met. However, if residence is added to the categories, a system of address hits might invite close regulatory scrutiny.

The marketer interested in another detailed review of this area should consult the statement of L. H. Goldfarb of the FTC before the Subcommittee on Government Information and Individual Rights of the House Committee on Government Operations.[76] The testimony also contains an interesting discussion of the nine-digit zip code, which would be used to divide the five-digit zip code areas into much smaller units.

Finally, state laws should be reviewed. Some states have enacted laws on point,[77] while many bills are introduced each year in Congress and various state legislatures.

Conclusion

While most direct marketers will fall into the category of "incidental creditors" only, care should be taken to understand the prohibited basis for discrimination as well as to refrain from putting a request for a telephone number on ad copy unless the ad copy request specifically states "optional" and the answer, if given, does not affect the decision about whether or not to extend credit.

Then the direct marketer should remain vigilant at the state and federal levels to prevent the enactment of zip code or residence restrictions which would adversely affect lists in general and compiled lists in particular.

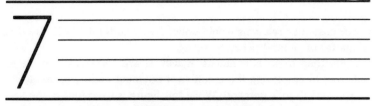

Your Complete Guide to Dunning Compliance

Certain areas of this book attempt to convey the meaning, intent, and enforcement trends of the law. Other areas do all that and attempt to saturate the law on point. This is done when a topic is applicable to all direct marketers employing one or all of the various direct-marketing channels.

No legal experience is more common to all marketers than the bad-debt problem. It may influence your market and the medium you use, segments of the medium, and possibly even the product selection decision itself.

One way to buy "insurance" is to use a standard credit card payment option (approximately 20 percent of all mail-order sales are currently being charged with credit cards). Then American Express, Visa, and the like, absorb your bad debts after they approve the orders. Further, under the 30 Day Rule, the merchant need not even notify a credit card buyer of a delay in shipment unless he or she has already charged the account. Therefore, in a limited-quantity situation, a merchant might ship to other customers and delay shipment to the credit card purchaser. This avoids the burden and cost of notification and the possibility of losing the order. While certainly not recommended as a standard business procedure, this "loophole" has been useful.

Your customer relations would undoubtedly suffer if it were used as a matter of general policy.

Offsetting these advantages, however, are certain disadvantages inherent in employing the credit card payment option, primarily the costly fees (5 to 7 percent). While this figure is fixed (unlike the variable market bad-debt figure), it represents a cost which must be built into the cost of your product and/or taken off the bottom line. Certain states[1] do not even permit a recovery of the sales tax paid on your bad debts, though efforts are being made in some of them[2] to correct this injustice.

The following sections will present an in-depth discussion of Congress's Fair Debt Collection Practices Act. They will also focus on the FTC's enforcement of the act with regard to recalcitrant firms.

Don't let your guard down just because much of the discussion concerns third-party collectors. After reviewing this area, you will find that:

- Many provisions apply to in-house collectors as well.

- The FTC and certain members of Congress have expressed a desire to incorporate all collectors.

- The outside collector your firm retains reflects on your firm's goodwill. You should screen all dunning letters and scripts employed before you pay a retainer and sign a contract. While outside collectors are independent contractors, you certainly have a right to insist that they obey the law. The public will view the outside collector as an extension of your company's judgment. Any adverse actions will reflect badly on you. You will not upset a worthwhile relationship with an independent contractor by merely protecting the good name of your firm.

After reviewing the following sections, you might consider whether collecting your marginal accounts is worth the cost involved as well as the potentially adverse legal and regulatory exposure.

The Fair Debt Collection Practices Act[3]

Title VIII of the Consumer Credit Protection Act is known as the Fair Debt Collection Practices Act. The act covers personal, family, and household debts, precisely the debts that your customers run up with you. Its purpose is to eliminate abusive debt-collection practices by debt collectors. Given the high number of complaints engendered by debt-collection practices, the FTC has tried to enforce this particular law vigorously.

Must You Comply?

The following are specifically excluded from coverage under Section 803(6) of the Fair Debt Collection Practices Act.

(A) any officer or employee of a creditor while, in the name of the creditor, collecting debts for such creditor.

This provision expressly ensures that "in-house" collection is not covered by this act.

(B) any person while acting as a debt collector for another person, both of whom are related by common ownership or affiliated by corporate control, if the person acting as a debt collector does so only for persons to whom it is so related or affiliated and if the principal business of such person is not the collection of debts.

This would exclude from the act an "in-house collection agency" utilized by a creditor to collect the firm's own debts. It exempts from coverage one subsidiary corporation that collects for another subsidiary corporation. However, the exclusion is applicable only if the principal business of the collector is *other than* the collection of debts.

All in-house collection efforts are excluded under 803(6)(B). However, this area is in flux. A few bills have been introduced into Congress to narrow this exclusion, and certain cities (e.g., New York City[4]) already have narrowed the exclusion, as well as certain states (e.g., Pennsylvania law is tighter than the law in most states, but it is not as all-inclusive as New York City's).[5] Further, there is an increasing legislative trend toward making firms more responsible for their outside collection efforts. It is therefore prudent to review your dunning letters and/or telephone scripts (more on this later) with counsel to make sure the independent agencies that you employ and that represent your goodwill are in compliance.

To best review your policy, you should be aware of two themes running throughout collection law.

■ Don't make any statement which is not unmistakably true or imply any action which you don't intend to take.

■ Don't discuss a customer's debt with third parties (except your attorney or a bona fide consumer reporting agency).

Let's take a closer look at these and other topics covered by the Fair Debt Collection Practices Act.

What the Act Requires

The following points highlight the compliance requirements of the Fair Debt Collection Practices Act.

Locating the Debtor   While a debt collector is permitted to contact third parties for the purpose of locating a debtor, Section 804 of this act provides certain guidelines which must be followed:

1. The collector may not tell the third party that the person whose whereabouts are being sought owes a debt. Also, the collector should identify his or her employer (i.e., the debt collection agency) only if specifically requested to by the third party.

2. The collector may not contact the third party more than once unless such contact is necessary to obtain complete or correct information.

3. The collector may not place an indication, mark, or symbol on the outside envelope which identifies the sender as a debt collector. An innocuous firm name or a simple return address is all that is permitted. Obviously, postcards are prohibited.

4. Under Section 804(6), the collector may not contact third parties for any reason once he or she knows that the debtor is represented by an attorney *with regard to the debt* and that he or she can contact the attorney (that is, the collector knows or can readily obtain the attorney's name and address or phone number) *unless* the attorney fails to respond to the debt collector's communication within a reasonable period of time. Fourteen days would be considered reasonable, but whatever your policy is, it should be consistent.

Validating the Debt   Once the debtor has been located, within 5 days of the *initial* communication with the debtor, the debt collector must send the debtor a *written* notice containing the following information:

1. The amount of the debt

2. The name of the creditor to whom the debt is owed

3. A statement that the debt collector will assume that the debt is valid unless the consumer sends a *written* notification with 30 days after receiving the notice that he or she is disputing the debt

4. A statement to the effect that if the consumer does dispute the bill, the debt collector will send the debtor verification of the debt *or* a copy of the judgment against the debtor

5. A statement that the debt collector will provide the identity of the original creditor, if different from the current creditor, if the debtor requests it in writing during the 30-day period

This notice is not required *if* all the above information was included in the initial contact, provided the initial communication was in writing; if it was by telephone, this notice must be sent.

If the debtor does dispute your bill or asks for the identity of the original creditor in writing within 30 days of receiving the notice, the debt collector must stop all efforts to collect the debt or any disputed portion of the debt. However, collection efforts may be resumed when the verification of the bill (or a copy of the judgment) or the name and address of the original creditor is *mailed* to the debtor.

It should be noted that even if a consumer does *not* dispute the debt within the 30-day period, that in itself is not an admission of guilt on the consumer's part.

Also, if a debtor owes more than one debt and makes a payment, the debt collector may not apply the payment toward the disputed debt and must, where applicable, apply the payment according to the debtor's instructions.

Communicating with the Debtor   The debt collector may not contact the debtor in regard to the collection of the debt

1. At a place or time inconvenient to the debtor. A convenient time is assumed to be between 8 A.M. and 9 P.M. at the debtor's location (i.e., taking into account the different time zones). If the debtor has indicated that such hours are *not* convenient (if, for example, the debtor works at night), he or she has the right to be contacted at times which are convenient to him or her. Again, watch for narrower state variations, such as Pennsylvania's.

2. At the debtor's place of employment, if the employer does not allow such calls.

3. If the debt collector knows that the debtor is represented by an attorney with regard to the debt and has or can obtain the attorney's name and address. The debt collector may, under the circumstances, still contact the debtor directly if the attorney doesn't respond within a reasonable period of time (again, 14 days would be considered reasonable) or unless the attorney consents to such direct communication.

There are exceptions to the above prohibitions, namely, if the debtor has given prior permission directly to the debt collector *or* if a court of competent jurisdiction gives express permission.

The debt collector may not threaten the debtor (with physical harm or damage to the person's reputation or property), use obscene or abusive language, or call repeatedly with the purpose of annoying or harassing any person at the called number. Also, it should go without saying that extortion and blackmail are criminal acts which must certainly not be employed.

The collector may not publish a list of consumers who allegedly refuse to pay debts *except* when the list is for a consumer reporting agency or persons meeting the requirements of 603(f) or 604(3) of the Fair Credit Reporting Act (you might wish to review the act in this chapter).

Section 807 states that the collector may not use "any false, deceptive, or misleading representation or means in connection with the collection of any debt." The many subsections cover the whole range of violations; if you have any doubt as to whether you or your collection agency may be in violation here, you should review this section with your counsel.

Telephone dunning will be reviewed in detail later on in the chapter. For the purposes of this act, however, it should be noted that repeated calls (to be safe, don't call more than once every 7 days) and any telephone contacts in which the caller is not identified are specifically prohibited.

Ending Communication The debtor may inform the debt collector *in writing* that he or she refuses to pay the debt or wishes further communication from the debt collector to cease. In this event, the debt collector may not contact the debtor except to advise the debtor that all collection efforts are being terminated and/or to inform the debtor that a certain *specific* action will be taken. This action *must* then actually be carried out.

The above points are included in the checklist presented at the end of this chapter. Comply with these guidelines, and the FTC won't have any complaints with your dunning efforts.

Knowing What Not to Do A classic case concerning what *not* to do under the law is found in *Housh v. Peth.*[6] Here's the story (emphasis my own).

> The record shows that the defendant deliberately planned a systematic campaign of harassment of the plaintiff, not only in numerous telephone calls to the plaintiff herself *every day* for a period of three weeks, some of which were *late at night,* but also calls to her superiors over the telephone, informing them of the debt; that she was called out of the classroom in the public schools where she was employed *three times within 15 minutes;* that she lost a roomer at her rooming house because of the repeated calls, and was threatened with loss of employment unless the telephone calls ceased. The calls to the employer, and the rooming house, were all part of the pattern to harass and humiliate the plaintiff and cause her mental pain and anguish and cause her emotional disturbance for the purpose of coercing her to pay the debt.

The moral of this story is short and sweet: Don't do anything which this particular dun did, and you should be OK.

The above are the don'ts. One positive area to investigate is a national and regional nonprofit service: Consumer Credit Counseling Services.[7] The service charges a percentage fee but is often successful in working out a payment schedule with a debtor. This is a useful social function in times of economic uncertainty when even an individual with the best intentions may suddenly face credit problems because of the unexpected loss of his or her job or a reduction in overtime. If the debt is large and/or the debtor acts in good faith in notifying you of his or her plight, this service can be recommended to help the debtor get back on his or her feet. Also, using this service may help you preserve a good customer, one who will make purchases again when paychecks begin arriving.

The FTC Enforces the Act

This act was passed amid many horror stories from people testifying before Congress and from constituents' correspondence. One story that I heard (but can't confirm) was about a woman walking in the rain supported by crutches. She was stopped on the street by a van. Two men took the crutches and told her she would get them back when she paid her debt!

Section 814(a) with certain exceptions gave enforcement powers to the FTC. The FTC is not an agency which lets the grass grow under its feet, especially when enforcing a popular law. It moved with vigor. It is important to be aware of all the FTC's activities, as they form a body of case law applicable to all. Under Section 5(m)(1)(B) of the Federal Trade Commission Act, the FTC may commence an action for civil penalties against any firm or individual who engages in an act or practice which violates an applicable cease and desist order, *regardless of whether such person or firm is a party to the order,* if the person or firm has knowledge that the practice is unfair or deceptive and violates the FTC Act. While the burden of proving knowledge is greater with a cease and desist order violation than with a rule violation, you would be well advised to place yourself on the FTC's mailing list.[8] After reviewing the following decision, you will have an idea of the FTC's interpretation and enforcement of the Fair Debt Collection Practices Act and how you and your independent collection agencies can avoid the FTC's enforcement powers.

In Re Capax, Inc.[9]

This cease and desist order was entered into after the effective date of the Fair Debt Collection Practices Act (March 20, 1978) but *not* decided under the act. Therefore, it is useful reading as to the FTC's position on dunning before the congressional enactment. All of it remains as FTC "case law."

In its dunning procedures, Capax, Inc., misrepresented its status, activities, and actions as well as the immediacy and urgency of its collection efforts. Specifically:

1. Capax stated that it would initiate legal action when it was not empowered to do so. Wording such as "all possible legal means will be taken to collect" is not permissible unless true. Even the *inference* of legal action is not permitted if not true.

2. Capax stated that it would take action to adversely affect the debtor's credit record when it was not empowered to do so.

3. Capax used simulated telegrams that communicated a false sense of urgency. Those telegrams were therefore not permissible. However, the actual use of a bona fide telegram is allowed.

4. Capax used wording indicating a sense of urgency and immediacy when no such urgency was required. For your own purposes, remember that wording such as "urgent," "imperative," "reply immediately," and "reply within 48 hours" or implications that action will be taken if the debt is "not paid within one week" may not be used unless such statements are true. If a debtor's failure to meet a "deadline" or act "immediately" results in no more than the receipt of the next form letter in the series, there is no urgency to reply.

It is important to note that the test is the *capacity* to deceive. The intent to deceive or actual deception is not necessary.

You might at this time review a few of the collection letters your firm employs. Do they have the capacity to deceive? For example, do you use an attorney's letterhead with a subtle inference of legal action (many bar associations frown on this practice in general) or "urgent wording" in a headline or anywhere within? If so, it is time you examined your in-house review policy for dunning letters.

Beyond Capax

If you reference and read just one decision, read the Capax decision. With the exhaustive analysis presented in Capax and the enforcement powers granted by the Fair Debt Collection Practices Act, the FTC broadened the collector's obligations.

The FTC hardly went into hibernation after the Capax decision. The following case capsules should give you a good idea of the FTC's attitude toward questionable dunning practices. Realize that these decisions are on a case-by-case basis and do not represent universal laws or regulations. They do set precedents, though, and a word to the wise should be sufficient, because the next case decided could be *yours.*

In one complaint following the Capax decision, the FTC demanded the following disclosure in each first-contact letter:

> Federal Law protects you from unfair debt collection practices. If you have any complaints about the way we are collecting this debt, contact the Division of Credit Practices, Federal Trade Commission, Washington, D.C. 20580.

This type of wording is punitive in nature (as the FTC may have intended) and would not improve a firm's collection recovery ratio.

More localized but equally ominous wording in the first-contact letter was demanded in a 1981 consent decree:[10]

> Federal Law protects you from unfair debt collection practices. If you have any complaints about the way we are collecting this debt, contact the Federal Trade Commission, New York Regional Office, 22nd Floor, Federal Building, 26 Federal Plaza, N.Y., N.Y. 10278.

Besides hurting the collection effort, these wording requirements use up expensive letter space!

Another firm[11] not only agreed to use similar language; to avoid the appearance that it is a credit reporting agency, it also agreed to legally amend its name!

Finally, in the ever present bid to be creative, Credit Assistance Programs, Inc.,[12] sent postcards that read, "Please call me collect. . . . Very Important!" The FTC objected that the postcards failed to disclose the fact that the sender was collecting a debt and conveyed a false sense of urgency. However, if a debt had been indicated on the card, sending the card would have been a violation of the Fair Debt Collection Practices Act as well as a multitude of FTC precedents. Don't use postcard dunning in any form.

So far we've reviewed the act on point and prior significant points raised in FTC decisions. We've also seen that in addition to possible fines, costs, and injunctions, the FTC may impose stiff diclosure penalties. Is there more?

Telephone Dunning

Many direct marketers or the agencies they employ dun by telephone. Obviously, you need not be a telephone marketer to dun by phone, though you might build up some ancillary expertise in telephone marketing to use in telephone dunning. The following are points to be aware of in designing your script.

All the previously discussed points (e.g., "urgency") are relevant to telephone dunning, if applicable (i.e., obviously the postcard issue is a moot point here, unless you follow up your calls with a mailing).

If you are doing a *national* dunning campaign, no calls should be made before 9 A.M. or after 9 P.M. (8 P.M. in Pennsylvania and New York City—possibly elsewhere). By calls, I mean all actual discussions terminated *by* 9 P.M. Any calls "under the wire" risk being called a violation. Individual state laws and regulations should be reviewed.

Make sure you ask for the alleged debtor by full name, and say nothing until the debtor answers. Then politely ask if you are speaking to him or her. If the person is not in, you may leave a return number. Here you must not identify the nature of the call (and this will assist in getting a return call). You need only to state your name and the firm you represent. This holds true if you call a home or a place of employment. As to places of employment, you might try to purge these from your file unless they are the only access you have to certain debtors.

Once you are speaking with the debtor, you should identify yourself and the purpose of your call before starting your "pitch."

There are certain public policy issues as to telephone intrusion. Three to ten days may be the norm, but I'd recommend no call interval shorter than one week.

There is no prohibition as to "repeated" dunning if you place your dunning call the same day your dunning letter arrives or the day after. Likewise, you are permitted to follow up on any "promises to pay" with a letter confirming the conversation, the amount, and the date of promised payment. A coordinated policy such as this that is managed with reasonable restraint is not intrusion.

For an exaggerated example of a lack of propriety refer back to a case discussed earlier in this chapter: *Housh v. Peth.*[13]

All dunning calls should be manually dialed unless you have carefully examined the law of the state you are calling into (see the chapter on telephone marketing).

No harassing or abusive calls are permitted. Make all calls in a businesslike manner, and use a subdued tone.

Finally, if you are thinking of taping or otherwise listening in on

employee calls for testing purposes, first review the section on monitoring employee calls in the chapter on telephone marketing.

Contractual Protection

Despite the relation of the FTC problems of a few agencies cited
above, hiring an outside agency for collection expertise may be a wise
investment depending on the size of the debts and the volume of calls
you wish to make or the amount of letters you wish to mail.

Obviously your contract is going to be reviewed by counsel, but
before you begin negotiations with an agency, you might first check
with the FTC and state attorney general's office, the Better Business
Bureau, and the Consumer Affairs Department. There might have
been complaints against the agency, but were they satisfactorily
resolved? If so:

- Make sure your agency is bonded and insured to your satisfaction. A good agency has a professional liability insurance (libel, slan-
der, and other errors and omissions) policy. Obtain a copy, and review
it with counsel in light of your needs.

- Is your agency licensed? If not, have counsel review the applicable law of the state(s). The states have the power to require licensing of debt collectors under the Fair Debt Collection Practices Act
(Section 816).[14] Maryland[15] requires licensing of all agencies collecting
in that state. Connecticut[16] prohibits employing unlicensed agencies.
California[17] makes it a misdemeanor to engage an unlicensed collection agency. You'll probably want a license.

Now to the text of the contract. You'll wish to state a clear relationship between the parties: that is, you'll want to separate yourself
from the independent agency and narrowly draft its duties and
authority. Reserve the right to an overview, however. Examine all letters and scripts in advance, and have your agency *warrant* that it will
use only those letters and scripts which you have approved in
advance. For the protection of all concerned, such approval should
be in writing.

The agency must *warrant* that it is aware of all the complex laws
and regulations on point, that it monitors and stays atop all compliance developments, and that it will abide by the law and professional
ethics (including, at a minimum, that all statements made in commu-

nication with a debtor are true). Be sure you are indemnified against the breach of this and all other warranties. I'd personally recommend that you have your agency *warrant* that it will comply with the Fair Debt Collection Practices Act literally and further that it will require the same standard from each secondary agency it might employ.

You'll want provisions specifying the duration of the relationship, compensation, the conditions for termination, assignability, and the state in which the contract will be interpreted. You'll also want an integration clause.

If you are supplying a list of names, you should get a *warranty* specifying the confidentiality of such names and that such names are at all times your sole property. Your lawyer will write it in such a way that you'll obtain consequential damages. Of course, as a prudent businessperson, you'll *seed the names.*

Conclusion

For all dunning letters and dunning telephone scripts, you'll want to create a checklist for legal compliance or risk the consequences. The checklist will include the following items.

Dunning Checklist

1. If our firm is not collecting on its own, has a proper contract with a licensed, bonded, and insured agency been executed? (If so, then the agency is responsible for the following compliance items, but you should retain the right of prior review and follow this checklist. If not, you are solely responsible for the following compliance items.)

2. If we have to locate the debtor, are we careful not to tell third parties that the person we're looking for owes a debt?

3. Are we contacting third parties more than once in our location efforts only if it is absolutely necessary to get correct and complete information?

4. Are we sure not to contact the debtor directly when we know that he or she is represented by an attorney with regard to the debt?

5. Have we carefully examined all envelopes to make sure there is no reference to a collection effort visible on them? Obviously, only envelopes are considered, as all forms of postcards are prohibited.

6. Do any of our communication pieces misrepresent the nature and urgency of the communication (i.e., no *simulated* telegrams, Mail-grams, or court process documents)?

7. Does any wording such as "urgent," "immediate," or "10 days to reply" have legal significance? If not, it's fraudulent.

8. Does the wording of any communication misrepresent in any way, directly or by implication, the purpose, intent, and procedure of our collection efforts with this debtor?

9. Do any communications threaten any consequence that we do not *routinely* follow through on? For example:

    a. Reporting the debtor to a consumer reporting agency

    b. Taking legal action

    c. Arranging for attachment or garnishment

10. Do we threaten *immediate* action? Even if such action is *eventually* pursued, no likelihood of immediate action can be indicated if no immediate action will take place (e.g., don't say "it must be settled immediately" if such is *not* the case).

11. Does our use of an attorney's letterhead indicate directly or by implication that legal action will result (but in fact legal action won't)? Have we confirmed in-house or with the outside agency that the attorney is a real, living member of the bar and not some fictitious figurehead?

12. Does the first written contact piece include the following items, or are we sending the debtor a notice within 5 days of the first communication that includes the following items?

    a. The name of the creditor owed

    b. Identification of the debt by amount and account number, if applicable

    c. The nature of the default and how it can be cured

    d. The name, mailing address, and (where applicable) telephone number to use for contact to verify the debt

    e. A statement of the right to obtain verification of the debt

    f. The procedure for verification

    g. A statement of the right of the debtor to have the collector cease communication (and a statement of the consequences resulting from the exercise of such right)

13. If the debtor disputes the debt or requests the name of the creditor, are we stopping our collection efforts until we have mailed the verification of the debt or the creditor's name?

14. Is every statement made in each follow-up letter or call true and in compliance?

Note: One good reason to read and review the FTC complaints and consent orders on point is that all problem letters are attached as exhibits. Therefore, you can review specific letters and then proceed to avoid the problems they present.

Telephone

15. Have all our telephone scripts been screened as to compliance?

16. Have all callers been informed in writing of our policy regarding (and the penalties for) obscene or profane language, the use of threats, and so on? All calls should be made in a professional manner, and a subdued tone should be used.

17. Do all our callers properly ask for and obtain the specific person desired?

18. Do they then properly identify themselves and the nature of the call? Within 5 days of the first call, do we send the debtor a *written* notice of the right to verification of the debt, the right to dispute the debt, and the right to end communication?

19. Are all calls reasonably spaced in time and made at a proper hour to avoid harassment?

20. Have we carefully checked time zones to make sure all calls are within the proper hour period?

21. Are our employment testing procedures (if taping is involved) lawful?

22. Finally, have we established written systems and procedures or checklists to demonstrate to an investigating body that any error was accidental—not a matter of policy or negligence?

Remember, the FTC takes a very literal view of the wording of laws on point. You should too. The fact that "other firms are doing it" is no defense as to noncompliance.[18] They just haven't been caught yet. Good luck!

Credit Balances

We shall now go from the problems of bad debts to the possible problem of overpayment. Overpayment a problem? Maybe!

Before we leave the topic of credit, the direct marketer should review his or her policy as to credit balances. Credit balances apply not just to credit card payments but to in-house charges as well (even if no finance charges, late fees, and the like, are involved).

In a nutshell, the FTC requires merchants to provide charge or other credit account customers having a credit balance with periodic statements that set forth the credit balance. The statements must be sent not less than three times in a 6-month period following the creation of the balance. Each statement must notify the customer with the credit balance of his or her right to an immediate cash refund of the balance.

Then after the lapse of a 7-month period, all credit balances over $1 must be refunded to the customers. Credit balances under $1 may be written off. However, you must be prepared to refund within 30 days any credit balance requested within 5 to 6 years of its creation.

What do you do after you make repeated efforts to refund a balance and the check is returned "addressee unknown" or "no forwarding address"? Here the respective state escheat laws must be examined in light of your firm's specific business practices. You need not have all the checks pile up. However, to protect yourself, you should keep a record of your efforts. Both the check and the envelope showing attempted delivery should be microfilmed. Then they should be retained for the applicable period (5 to 6 years). After that, if the check is still unclaimed, it will probably be escheated to the respective state of the "owner." Your consolation is that you had the "float" value of the funds during this interval.

The respective state and federal laws should be reviewed with counsel as to when and how credit balances must automatically be refunded. The FTC strictly enforces the laws in this area.[19]

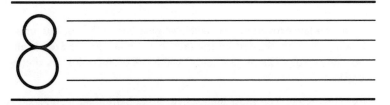

The Future Is Now

Since World War II the United States has been in the vanguard of a new, postindustrial economic era. This new economic order is characterized by rapid development in information handling and telecommunications technology. This "knowledge industry" is built around the sale of services and knowledge with significantly less emphasis on the manufacture of durable goods.

By 1985, more than half of the gross national product (GNP) will be devoted to the production, consumption, and dissemination of knowledge. Further, this "Third Wave"[1] society is still very much in its infancy. This nation is about to go through a major change of vast proportions in the way in which information and goods are advertised and distributed to the general public.

Don't Let the Future Pass You By

Recent and ongoing developments in electronic and telecommunications media are already altering traditional direct marketing (focused on the mail as the primary vehicle). However, the electronic media will increase the utility and use of direct mail in a well-coordinated campaign. Mail, electronics, and telecommunications will be integrated, providing informational and promotional opportunities which are breathtaking.

Has the law arrived in this electronic environment? Yes, but understanding it is complicated by the fact that the law in this area is also evolving rapidly. Chapters 8 and 9 will focus on three key marketing vehicles.

■ *Telephone.* The most interactive direct-marketing technology is already in place in over 99 percent of the American homes as well as in a lower though significant percentage of homes throughout the free world. This vehicle has the capacity presently to make profits roll in 24 hours a day.

■ *Commercial TV and commercial radio.* These vehicles are here. Certain principles or trade guidelines unique to these media will be reviewed.

■ *Cable TV.* This emerging entertainment vehicle, when coupled with computerized interactive devices being tested as well as the available telecommunications, will bring direct marketing to new horizons. Most of the applicable law on point is the same as for commercial television. However, interactive cable presents potential legal problems not involved in commercial television, such as the dormant privacy issue. If the information segmentation possibilities are abused, an aroused public might reexamine the entire spectrum of personalized data accumulation—so vital to all vehicles of direct marketing.

Before you begin these two chapters, you must understand that they cannot be viewed in isolation. These chapters focus on the laws and rules of specific interest to the topics listed above. The legal environment discussed previously affects these topics as well. *Don't forget* the body of the law we have already reviewed. Even if your business is confined solely to electronic direct marketing, don't handicap yourself by being parochial and reading only these two chapters. For example:

1. If you are a negative-option seller, the FTC Rule applies to your telephone or electronic media message as well (review Chapter 2).

2. Any "free" promotion in *any* medium must comply with the Rule discussed in Chapter 3.

3. If you offer installment payment options, you'd better be sure you have read Chapter 6.

Get the point? This book builds. Now let's proceed to build our knowledge of direct-marketing law further.

The Telephone—Opportunities and Legal Pitfalls

Consumer familiarity with the telephone eliminates one barrier to marketing entry: up-front resistance to new technology. The consumer is familiar with certain dial-up services (time, weather, directory assistance, and even Dial-A-Joke).

Payment by phone is meeting with increasing public acceptance. This service allows the consumer to telephone his or her bank and then authorize payments by touching appropriate tabs on a Touch-Tone phone or by recording the authorization through the phone onto an audio tape. Debit cards which can automatically transfer funds from a customer's account to a creditor's account through a point-of-sale terminal will become commonplace in the future.[2] Telephone bill payment is an intermediate step in the direction of automated electronic funds transfer from the home. One delay in acceptance is the simple fact that a consumer lifestyle profile can be created at your financial institution—a profile open to the Internal Revenue Service (IRS). The Howard Ruff school has a good point when it advocates the purchase of personal items as well as other items (e.g., firearms and collectibles) only by cash.

With the in-place technology and increasing ease of payment, it is no wonder that the telephone is the fastest-growing medium in marketing goods and services. Further, this immediate medium enables commercial television, cable television, and radio to function as two-way media (for example, when there is a toll-free number to call), thus opening up huge new marketing opportunities. In the following sections the major types of telephone consumer marketing you can profit from in the 1980s[3] are outlined, and the law affecting each marketing opportunity is discussed.

Getting Started
To begin with, you need to understand the medium's special characteristics. Then you need:

1. A product suitable for this medium

2. A list of the numbers of consumers who have a predetermined interest in your product

3. Trained personnel

The product that is salable through this medium (in general) is fairly inexpensive and nonperishable. Lists are discussed in depth in Chapter 10. However, one point should be stressed: Don't attempt to transfer a direct-mail success to a telephone promotion. Each channel's customers often respond differently.

Personnel

Obviously, you obey the equal opportunity employment laws. Telephone selling can help you meet your affirmative action goals. It is an excellent means of employment for handicapped and functionally older citizens. Further, the 24-hour-a-day 800 numbers will encourage you to hire for irregular shifts, thus opening the doors of employment opportunity to those at home with children during "normal" hours. The social utility of this marketing medium is apparent even before the financial benefit accumulates!

Now you want motivated people who are good in human interaction. Further, as we shall see, you want your staff members to be problem solvers as well as order-takers. Ideally, they are quick and personable: they know the product; and in some instances they are even good with a CRT! Tall order. It will take training and maybe a script.

The telephone solicitor must be able to handle the rapid fatigue rate and have the intestinal fortitude to handle rejection. Further, listening is a skill equal to articulation; in fact, in general it may be more important. One note of optimism is the fact that the telephone, not the letter, is today's primary communications medium. Therefore, just as your customers have and understand the in-house technology, all your staff callers arrive with some experience in operating and talking over a phone.

Depending on the abilities of your staff, you may or may not wish to use a script. In either case, you'll emphasize the soft sell. You may not wish to use your telephone duns in your marketing area, as the skills are different.

Training

Telephone solicitors and order-takers must be able to articulate. This is a skill which often must be acquired through training. A training program without monitoring calls is impossible. But in these days of post-Watergate consciousness, will the law allow a firm to monitor live calls with an outside party? Surprisingly, yes it will.[4] The Wire Interception and Interception of Oral Communications Act in the U.S. Code, 18 U.S.C. 2511, provides, among other things, that it is unlawful for any person to use "any electronic, mechanical, or other device to interpret any oral communication. . . ." For your business needs, an understanding of certain definitions and exemptions in 18 U.S.C. § 2510 is important. Let's review them together.

To violate the act, you must intercept an oral or wire communication. A telephone conversation is a wire communication. However, an interception does *not* occur unless an "electronic, mechanical, or other device" is employed. The definition of these devices specifically excludes a telephone used in the regular course of the subscriber's business. Specifically, 18 U.S.C. 2510 (5)(a)(i) grants an exception to

> (a) any telephone or telegraph instrument, equipment or facility or any component thereof,
>> (i) furnished to the subscriber or user by a communications common carrier in the ordinary course of its business and being used by the subscriber or user in the ordinary course of its business; . . .

If you ask the telephone company to install a monitoring device which will permit you to listen in on telephone conversations between employees and customers, you will come within this exception. It is part of the service rendered by the telephone company on request. This is predicated on the fact that ordinary-course-of-business duties include only lawful and proper activities. If you meet the ordinary-course-of-business exemption, you needn't worry about the ordinary telephone book's discussion (usually under "Telephone Consumer Information") of the "beep tone."

Lawful and Proper Activities

The courts that have reviewed the issue do not want to see evidence of surreptitious monitoring for personal gain or gossip. At all times you should be able to demonstrate that the monitoring was undertaken solely in the interest of the company's business operations. At no time do you wish to appear to have monitored a strictly "private" call. A recent example is as follows.

The Bell system installed monitoring equipment on telephones in a newspaper organization's departments that have direct contact with the public. The business purpose of this monitoring was to assist the employee training program as well as to protect employees from abusive calls. The monitoring was not surreptitious. On the contrary, it was performed with the prior knowledge of management and all affected employees (who were informed in writing). The court held that there was no interception, since the equipment was used in the ordinary course of the employer's business.[5]

All Worries Over?

Of course not—in law the worry never ceases, it just varies. You must note for your training the following points:

1. As always, state and local laws as well as current state legislative and regulatory activity must be reviewed with counsel. The federal law on point permits narrower state standards.[6] This sensitive area remains in flux because of the fact that no notice is given to the outside party in the "ordinary course of business."

2. Neither the surreptitious use of a telephone extension to record a private telephone conversation nor a general practice of surreptitious monitoring would qualify as a legal exception.[7] You should never tape a call to get "evidence" that a customer agreed to do something. The Direct Mail Marketing Association (DMMA) suggested guidelines for marketing by telephone also discuss the taping of telephone conversations. A copy of these industry self-regulation guidelines is available from the New York City DMMA office—(212) 689-4977.

To play it safe:

   a. State your purpose in writing when you procure the equipment from the common carrier.

   b. Give advance notice to *all* managers and employees involved.

   c. Obtain a release from your employees stating that they are aware of the fact that their supervisor will listen in unannounced and that they agree to this.

d. *Never* tape a call with the intention of using the tape as evidence that a customer agreed to make a purchase.

3. Do not attempt to monitor personal calls to "prove" that there is a violation of a legitimate business policy against such calls without first warning the individuals involved about the violation of a "no-personal-calls" policy.

4. Consult state law as to the permissible time period in which to call (and coordinate the calls according to the time zones).

5. If you reach someone at his or her place of employment, it is a good idea to purge the individual's business number from your marketing files. It may also be unethical to sell or rent it.

6. You should identify the firm and the purpose of the call immediately.

7. We'll discuss automatic dialing and electronic equipment later in this chapter. Review this area as to its specific requirements.

8. Consult the DMMA guidelines for telephone marketers (as to times of day to call, whether Sunday is proper, how many times to ring the phone, and so on). Industry self-regulation is in your own interest.

9. With the increased growth of international business in general and marketing in particular, one final comment is useful. The provisions of the Wire Interception and Interception of Oral Communications Act apply only within the territorial jurisdiction of the United States. The law of the nation where the monitoring takes place (situs) governs the validity of such monitoring. This is true even though a U.S. citizen is involved and/or the intercepted telephone conversation traveled in part over the U.S. communications system. Therefore, a U.S.-based firm physically located in the United States may monitor calls to Canadian customers subject to U.S. law. Likewise, a Canadian-based firm monitoring calls to U.S. customers is bound by Canadian law on point.

Conclusion

The direct marketer, in monitoring any aspect of employee calls, must be careful that he or she does not monitor in a manner which would be considered "intercepting" calls. There is no interception under federal law if the acquisition of the contents of the communication is accomplished through telephone equipment used in the ordinary course of business.

The Toll-Free Number

This can be the key to success. It provides the means for instant customer responses without apparent cost, at the moment of greatest advertising impact. It can be used in conjunction with *any* medium and can, if you wish, make your firm a 24-hour-a-day operation. Blue laws are avoided, and because the customer is calling you, no religious sensitivities are infringed upon.

Unlike any other advertising medium, the telephone allows for certainty, as the delivery of each response message is assured, and each order is quantifiable. Further, you can reach the party you intend to reach. If you are writing to a particular family member, another might discard the piece before the targeted person even comes home! With a call, you can be sure you've reached the person you want. In addition, a toll-free number encourages the audience to act immediately. Without such an immediate response vehicle, even an interested customer may forget to fill in the card, buy a stamp, or mail the envelope—or put off doing these things. Procrastination on the part of the consumer is your worst enemy; a toll-free number can eliminate many obstacles that stand in the way of a successful order completion. The point is obvious. If it is at all practical, get the option of a toll-free number in conjunction with whatever other medium you are using.

Don't forget the telephone's other uses when combined with other media. Cost savings may be considerable, especially with small lists. Here, it may be less expensive to use the phone directly rather than to write a mailing piece, have artwork done, print the pieces, mail them, and wait for letters or responses via the toll-free number. List testing by phone is fast, inexpensive, and self-cleaning. Then reverse the process. Mail after a telephone contact or call after a mail contact. Call even if a toll-free number is available, and if you can't close the sale immediately, emphasize the response via the toll-free number if the customer reconsiders.

Don't forget customer relations. Getting customers is a high-cost operation. You want to treat them properly and not lose them. Train your people to separate a response call from a complaint call. Transfer the latter politely to the proper person.

The customer is then able to voice a complaint to a real interrelating party. Contacting your firm is not a matter of trying to "talk" to a computer. You might have saved an order and a future customer already. If you have a CRT terminal, your customer relations professional can establish instant rapport with immediate access to the caller's account.

Other utilities are legion. You can market-test *and* media-test (make sure you ask what medium was the source of information leading to the call). Each call offers live feedback on your product and promotion. If necessary or desired, you can direct the customer to a nearby retail outlet. Use the phone!

Finally, for purposes of this text, both the toll-free number in particular and the phone in general will enable you to avoid legal problems. (Because nothing is perfect, however, you should be aware that a possible drawback to the otherwise ideal use of a toll-free number is the fact that it could lend itself to some abuse. For example, phony orders might be called in by unethical individuals. This would cause an unordered-merchandise problem. More about telephone solicitation and unordered merchandise later.)

Access to a toll-free number will make it more convenient for a disgruntled customer to call you rather than write to the FTC or the attorney general's office. This is why it is so important to coordinate the selling operation with customer relations. His order is late (30 Day Rule issue). Her billing complaint was not answered on time and dunning continues (Fair Credit Billing issue). Any complaint to the FTC hurts your firm alone. A high volume of complaints hurts your industry. If you don't think that the FTC audits and *adds* all complaints, order a copy of the *Digest of Consumer Complaints and Inquiries*.[8] You can expect similar problems with state attorney generals and the alphabet soup of agencies that spring up at times like this. But a coordinated toll-free-system may well prevent a legal complaint and action and also keep a customer if he or she is properly placated.

Further, use the phone directly if you see a legal (or basic goodwill) issue arising.

1. Is the order late? Call the customer.

2. Is there a need for substitution with regard to the color, the shade, the size, or the product itself? Call the customer.

3. Did an order card arrive in-house incomplete? (Remember the 30 Day Rule discussion of a properly completed order.) If you wish to speed up the order or avoid the chance of losing it, don't write back; call for the missing information.

Each call establishes human interaction and personalizes your firm.

Bait and Switch

When an individual calls your toll-free number, you have a consumer who is already interested in at least the product he or she is calling about. Any additional soft sell will be treated as information. This is a good time to cross-sell. He wants a fishing rod—how about a tackle box? A *well-trained* marketer might also attempt to sell up or trade up. But be careful here. You must not "bait and switch" or even suggest such a tactic.

"Bait" merchandise is often the too-good-to-be-true offer—a good product at a great price. A consumer calls, and the seller disparages the item and "switches" the consumer to a more expensive model that is "well worth" the cost. False or misleading comparisons may be made between the original product desired and the product the seller wishes to switch the consumer to. Finally, the seller may tell the consumer that the bait item is not available but the switch product is.

The FTC Guides Against Bait Advertising[9] should be studied by any marketer attempting to trade up, even when this is done in good faith. A legal issue arises if you violate the Guides. The inference will also present problems, as this issue is familiar to consumers because of a successful education effort by the FTC and other groups.

Again, trading up is not an illegal practice if it is done in conformity with the Guides. Trading up is full-line selling, that is, giving your customers information and the opportunity to learn about the various features available in the product line. In this way, they can make an informed buying decision by matching their individual needs and budgetary requirements with the product and features you are offering in your total line. For example, if a customer calls to purchase an air conditioner, your informed salesperson may ask questions about his or her needs, such as a question about the size of the room. If the original order is inadequate, you may tell the customer this and then attempt to sell a piece of equipment that can fulfill the customer's needs. Not only are you within the law, but the customer might be lost for the future if he or she has reason to blame your firm for the inadequate cooling. Further, your customer service relations will be enhanced, as the customer will appreciate making a buying decision based on personal attention directed to his or her own particular needs.

Here is a checklist to help you avoid bait-and-switch problems.

1. Don't disparage any product you sell.

2. Any comparison must be positively oriented.

3. Stress what each item will do, not what it won't do.

4. No employee should contradict the promotion piece that prompted the call unless there was an objective error (e.g., a typographical error). If such an error exists, switch the caller to customer service.

5. Obviously, no untrue or misrepresenting statements should be made by any personnel.

6. If there is any resistance at all to trading up, you must cease. Don't try to talk the customer into it, even in good faith.

7. Once a customer reviews your trade-up presentation and elects the original item, you must close the sale. The customer should not be asked or in any way encouraged to reconsider.

8. A policy of rain checks would help here whenever an advertised product becomes out of stock before the advertised termination date (or before a "reasonable time" if no date is specified).

9. If for some unavoidable reason you cannot fulfill the order after a failed attempt at trading up, you may contact the customer concerning substitution, that is, offering an equal or better product at the *same price* as the advertised item, or you may cancel the order. You may not look upon this as a fortuitous opportunity to reopen the trade-up negotiations.

Your supervisory personnel must be well trained in spotting the bait-and-switch practice in the monitoring tests. If even a tendency to deceive is found, the supervisor must immediately correct this tendency in the employee. Otherwise, your firm will face both a potential legal problem and a loss of customer goodwill.

The Massive Legislative Battle

The telephone medium helps make sales, promotes customer satisfaction, and is available (potentially through toll-free numbers) 24 hours a day for doing business at a time that is convenient with regard to the customer's schedule or impulse. If it's so good for all parties concerned, why all the flak?

Case Against Unsolicited Commercial Calls

A number of factors jelled to create problems for the industry in the late 1970s.

First there were the varied self-appointed consumer types who raise a ruckus whenever they can find an antibusiness "cause."

Second, the introduction of automatic devices that can prerecord calls, give a sales presentation, and take orders was met with certain resistance. The calls were quickly dubbed "junk calls." Did you ever notice how those media (TV, radio, newspapers, magazines) which are losing advertising dollars to direct-mail and telephone advertising and sales are quick to label their competition as "junk"? Well, the mass media can attack in self-serving exposés with impunity. The direct marketer and the public should realize that it's not concern for the public but concern for competitive revenue which brings on the "junk call/junk mail" chorus.

Finally, there were concerns that were legitimate, though amplified by hysteria. A number of legislatures heard the following testimony. A woman whose mother suffered a heart attack was prevented from calling an ambulance because of a computerized sales tape. The tape was long and would not disconnect even if you hung up. Needing no amplification was the reality that the pretaped calls were somewhat intrusive.

All media attacks[10] focused on the automatic dialers and implied that these accounted for a large percentage of calls. The automatic sequential dialer in particular received bad press because it called unlisted numbers, and some feared that it could intrude on national security numbers (Strategic Bomber Command) or the numbers of the local police and fire departments.

The peak year of legislative activity was (and probably will remain) 1978. Charles Ferris, Chairman of the FCC, began a formal investigation of rule making, citing "widespread public concern."[11] No such concern ever materialized, despite orchestrated attempts to arouse it. After jurisdictional debates as to whether the FCC had the authority to regulate intrastate telephone communication, the FCC eventually dropped all procedures.[12]

Congressman Les Aspin (D—Wisconsin) introduced H.R. 9505 to effectively ban commercial free speech by phone. This led to 54 similar bills in 23 states within a year; they were modeled after H.R. 9505. No broad ban was passed in any state.

The newspapers lost their concern for "junk calls" when informed that they received 50 percent of their subscriptions by phone. With their own dollars at stake, their "public interest" clamor subsided. The antibusiness consumerists don't work in profit-producing jobs and therefore can't appreciate that any channel will die if there is no popular demand for it. The current magnitude of sales made would not be possible without a receptive public. No mailer or telephone solicitor is interested in spending time and money to contact someone who will not purchase anything. The DMMA itself is on record as opposing any calls made without a prior relationship (i.e., the so-called cold calls).

A Powder Keg Remains

Some harm was done to the industry, and the threat of consumerists remains. Each year 15 to 20 varied forms of telephone marketing restrictions are introduced in the state legislatures. Judge John C. Gilman[13] might be attempting to impose his own views by effectively banning cold calls for *many* commercial solicitors—but not for certain solicitors, such as politicians and those employed in the insurance industry. The latter exception would make such restrictions unconstitutional on its face even if the balance of the order somehow survived an impartial court review.

Another requirement found in this order and in many state bills is that utilities must publish a solicitor's list and inform residential subscribers at least once a year of the option to be deleted from the list. The cost of all this preparation and compiling must be borne by the solicitor.

But all of the above may or may not happen. Some adverse laws and some nuisance laws have been enacted, and you must be aware of them to do business.

Note: For purposes of this topic, it might be helpful to clarify jurisdictions. Under the Communications Act, the FCC has jurisdiction to regulate interstate and foreign communications, but it does not have the authority to regulate local and intrastate telephone use unless it substantially affects interstate communications. Intrastate communications (97 percent of all calls) are under the jurisdiction of the public utilities commission of the state.

The FTC Indicates. . . .

A marketer should always keep an eye on the FTC's public statements. They can be a harbinger of trouble to come. For instance, when the FTC submitted its comments to the FCC,[14] it recommended four things in particular and made one observation.

The observation was that it noted a shift away from door-to-door direct selling and toward telephone solicitation as a means of circumventing the FTC's cooling-off period for door-to-door sales.[15] The states immediately began to act on this by incorporating provisions concerning telephone solicitation within their respective home solicitation laws. The FTC recommended:

1. A means to end the obvious problem posed for consumer protection enforcement when sales are consummated without a written document

2. A system of name removal or prior consent to telephone solicitation calls, an expense which must ultimately be borne by the list users

3. The requirement that all solicitors state the purpose of their call before delivering a message

4. A broad curb on misrepresentation

The industry focused on Congress and the FCC very effectively. It was slower to anticipate that the vacuum left by the lack of national standards would be filled by disparate state laws and ad hoc FTC cease and desist orders.

Laws Concerning Automatic Dialing Devices

The states have enacted various laws concerning commercial solicitation calls. The primary areas of regulation involve automatic dialing devices and the incorporation of telephone solicitation within the home solicitation laws.

The best way to review the area of automatic dialing devices is to run through some representative states and discuss impact. This listing may not be exhaustive, and counsel should be consulted.

Alaska   Alaska has banned "junk telephone calls." A "junk" telephone call is "a telephone call made for the purpose of advertising through the use of a recorded advertisement."[16]

California   Because of its large size and history of setting precedents, this is a good state to examine in detail. The law[17] permits the use of an "automatic dialing-announcing device" in the placement of a telephone call *only* with the prior consent of the party called *or* when the caller identifies the nature of the call and the business making the call, states the address and telephone number of the business, and asks the party whether he or she will agree to receive the call.

Before any firm begins telephone marketing employing this kind of device, it must formally apply to the telephone corporation serving the area of the proposed market.

Section 2821 of the California law defines "automatic dialing-announcing device" as follows:

> . . . any automatic equipment which incorporates a storage capability of telephone numbers to be called or a random or sequential number generator capable of producing numbers to be called and the capability, working alone or in conjunction with other equipment, to disseminate a prerecorded message to the telephone number called.

This definition is as well written as any and should be considered the norm for this discussion.

Colorado This state bans the use of automated dialing systems with prerecorded messages asking the person called to purchase goods or services unless there is an *existing* business relationship between the caller and the person called and the person who is called agrees to hear the recorded message.[18]

Florida Section 365.165 reads as follows:

(1) No person shall use a telephone or knowingly allow a telephone to be used for the purpose of offering any goods or services for sale or conveying information regarding any goods or services when such use involves an automated system for the selection and dialing of telephone numbers and the playing of a recorded message when a connection is completed to the called number.[19]

Maryland This state bans utilization of an automated dialing, push-button, or tone-activated address signaling system with a prerecorded message for commercial solicitation *or* requesting survey information where results are used directly or indirectly for the purpose of soliciting persons to purchase goods or services.[20]

Michigan Michigan bans telephone solicitations using recorded messages unless the telephone subscriber has requested or authorized the call.[21]

Nebraska In this state you are required only to obtain a permit from the Public Service Commission before calling begins. The law also allows the Public Service Commission to promulgate rules governing the length of the message and the time of day when the calls are to be made. Therefore, before you begin any telephone marketing in this state, you should review the current rules the commission has issued.[22]

For purposes of state monitoring, always keep in mind that this state is the only one possessing a unicameral legislature. With no second house to check or stop the first, legislation can move quickly in this state. This is important to know if you don't like the legislation that's moving.

North Carolina North Carolina regulates (but does not ban) automatic dialing devices.[23]

Virginia   Virginia requires that any recorded call must terminate as soon as the receiver hangs up.[24]

The marketer should also comply with the voluntary Code of Ethics issued by the Virginia Telephone Solicitation Ethics Council.[25] Self-regulation will help the marketer avoid governmental intrusion.

Wisconsin   Wisconsin requires *prior consent* for prerecorded messages.[26]

Conclusion   Automated dialing systems took a beating during the years 1978 to 1979. (A glance at the Appendix will give you the time of primary legislative activity.) The states remain alert to the use of these systems, and it is important that every telephone marketer consult the laws of each state in which calls are made.

Even if all your calls are placed manually, you may still have varied state problems, as indicated in the next section.

Three-Day Cooling-Off Period

For years you've seen the satirized confrontation between Dagwood Bumstead and his nemesis, the door-to-door salesman. The scenario is familiar—the leg in the door, chases from room to room, physical confrontations, and other exhibitions of the hard sell. The FTC and other consumer groups have argued that a salesperson coming to your door represents an unplanned purchase, often after a less dramatic but no less effective hard sell, than Dagwood was subjected to. The FTC's Rule[27] applies not merely to sales made in your home but also to sales agreements made anywhere other than in the seller's normal place of business (e.g., it applies to that fascinating American institution, the Tupperware party). The social policy behind the Rule was to allow an individual 3 days of nonprejudicial time to reflect after signing a hard-sell personal contract.

When the consumer does sign a contract, the salesperson must inform him or her of the cancellation rights. Within 3 business days after the contract date, the consumer can send in the cancellation form provided. Proof of mailing date and receipt are important, so a certified letter provides the best protection. Finally, no reason is required to cancel.

Within 10 days of receipt of the cancellation form, the seller will:

1. Cancel and return any papers the consumer signed

2. Refund the consumer's money and indicate whether any product left with him or her will be picked up

3. Return any trade-in

Within 20 days, the seller must either pick up the items or, if the consumer agrees to send back the items, reimburse the consumer for mailing expenses.

Exceptions: The FTC exempted sales under $25 or those made totally by mail or phone. The exemption of sales made by mail is obvious. The exemption of sales made by phone should be too, as the high pressure is greatly diminished by the "safety-valve" action of simply hanging up. Further, there is no confrontation presence before you.

Cooling Off the Telephone's Spontaneity

When the FTC commented that it noted a shift away from door-to-door selling and toward telephone solicitation as a means of circumventing the cooling-off requirements, it gave many state legislators an idea. They began to incorporate telephone sales within the scope of their home solicitation laws. This puts a serious damper on the spontaneity and immediacy of the telephone in closing a sale. Now (where applicable) you'll be required to provide a cancellation agreement in writing after soliciting an order via the telephone. You'll have to allow for the 3-day cooling off *plus* enough time for the customer to receive the cancellation form and for you to get it back in the mail. (Figure 10 business days from the time you send the cancellation form to the day you may ship the product to allow for mailing time.)

The following is again an overview. Counsel should be consulted in case other states incorporate telephone sales. This incorporation has been a slow but steady process since 1978. *Each* state varies in its incorporation, so please review the following carefully as to differences between state laws and the FTC's Rule.

Arizona   This state incorporates telephone solicitations for all sales regardless of amount (no $25 threshold).[28]

Arkansas   This state amended its Home Solicitation Law[29] to include telephone sales and thus requires a 3-day cooling-off period for "all telephone sales in which the seller has initiated contact regardless of his location and the consumer's agreement to purchase is made *at the consumer's home.*" It's important to note that this pertains to sales of more than $25.

Indiana   Here you will have problems if the sale is a consumer credit sale of goods.[30] No compliance is required for cash payments but would probably be required for installment payment plans even where no finance charge is imposed.

  If compliance is required, it applies to all telephone sales—there is no $25 cutoff.

Louisiana   The Louisiana law[31] is similar to Indiana's except that it excludes catalog credit sales.

Michigan   The law[32] in Michigan mandates that *all* telephone sales of *more* than $25 must conform to the state's Home Solicitation Law (including the 3-day cooling-off period and confirmed written documents). The law is also quite explicit in stating that "business days" means Monday through Friday *only,* and it further excludes certain specific holidays from "business days."

North Dakota   The law[33] in North Dakota incorporates all telephone sales into the current Personal Solicitation Sales Law.

Oregon   The Oregon law[34] affects all sales of *$25 or more* under the following conditions:

  1. The seller or person acting for the seller engages in a solicitation conducted by telephone to a residence.

  2. The transaction is initiated by the seller or person acting for the seller and *is in no way solicited by the buyer.*

3. The buyer's agreement or offer to purchase is given over the telephone to the seller or person acting for the seller.

4. There is no personal contact between the buyer and the seller or person acting for the seller prior to the delivery of the goods or the performance of the services.

Virginia   This state has established a set of guidelines[35] which are endorsed by the state's Better Business Bureau, Office of Consumer Affairs, Chamber of Commerce, and the like.

They "advise" following the state's Home Solicitation Law. This would require providing the buyer with an agreement form which he or she would sign confirming the date of solicitation, the price, and so on. Upon mailing the form, the buyer would have 3 days to cancel, and *the cancellation would be effective when mailed, not when received* by the seller.

This would apply to all sales of $15 or more if you decide to conform to the suggested guidelines.

Wyoming   The Wyoming law[36] applies to consumer credit sales of $25 or more made by telephone sellers.

Conclusion   These laws will affect your telephone sales promotion if you plan to ship immediately after the telephone order is completed. If you plan on first receiving a signed, written confirmation from the customer, then there should be little adverse effect. (As to the signed confirmation, please review the FTC's cease and desist orders below.)

For the other telephone marketers in these states, you can't effectively consummate a sale over the telephone. You can solicit an order, but:

1. You must follow up with a written confirmation including instructions as to the customer's right to the cooling-off period and a card to exercise such right.

2. You must honor any valid notice of cancellation by the buyer that is received within 10 *business* days after you've mailed the cancellation form.

The above laws are definitely negative ones for the telephone marketer. The spontaneity advantage of telephone marketing is lessened. Further, there is the additional burden and cost of the follow-up mailing and then the delay while awaiting the possible negative response from someone you hoped would be a customer.

Local Ordinances

A number of municipal ordinances may adversely affect your right to do business. A few of the municipalities involved are as follows:

1. Anniston, Alabama (see the court case discussion below)
2. Sheffield, Alabama[37]
3. Carlsbad, New Mexico[38]
4. Bedford, Ohio[39]
5. Bedford Heights, Ohio[40]

Can a municipality declare unwanted telephone solicitations a nuisance? Yes it can, in the opinion of the Supreme Court of Alabama.[41]

Here the Alabama Law Enforcement Officers, Inc., sought to declare a local ordinance (number 2457) void and unconstitutional. In denying an injunction against the order, the court made the following observation (emphasis my own):

> It seems to us reasonable to conclude that if municipal corporations in the State of Alabama are charged with the duty and have the power to adopt ordinances, not inconsistent with the law of the State of Alabama, to provide for the safety, preserve the health, promote the prosperity, and improve the morals, order, comfort and convenience of the inhabitants of said municipalities, then unwanted knocks on the door by day or night can be declared to be a nuisance to peace and quiet by the municipal authorities. Accordingly, *unwanted telephone calls by day or night can be declared to be a nuisance to peace and quiet.* When the telephone rings the person called answers the telephone because there is no way for him or her to determine in advance whether it is an unwanted or a wanted telephone call. There certainly are times when even a person of temperate disposition, when he finds out that the one calling is seeking to get him to purchase an advertisement or to make a donation or

pay money for some tickets, flag, tag, badge, flower, token, or symbol, is outraged or upset by such call.[42]

So, telephone marketer, you must keep an eye on Congress, state
legislatures, and local municipalities. Further, don't forget the FTC—
the Commission hasn't forgotten you.

FTC Opinions of Note

There is no federal law (though, as we've just reviewed, there are
state laws) requiring a 3-day cooling-off period and/or written confirmation of a telephone sale. However, some alleged unethical practices by certain telephone marketers as well as the fact that the area
is fraught with potential unordered-merchandise problems have
resulted in a number of FTC complaints and consent agreements.
These indicate potential future problems for this spontaneous, interactive medium. Examples are discussed below.

1. Commencing in 1980, the FTC began to require certain disclosures of telephone marketers on a case-by-case basis. Neighborhood
Periodical Club, Inc.,[43] advertised, offered for sale, sold, and distributed magazine subscriptions. Among many points, the telephone solic-
itation/unordered-merchandise issue arose. In the future:

a. The firm must orally inform the purchaser during the telephone conversation of his or her right to rescind or cancel the subscription order within 3 business days from the time he or she
receives the subscription order form (*not* 3 days from the call).

b. The subscription order form must disclose clearly and conspicuously the purchaser's right to cancel the entire order within 3
business days from the receipt of the order form.

c. All such cancellations received within 10 business days must
be honored.

This requirement is in the negative option form (that is, if the customer doesn't respond within the time period specified, then the order
is still active). All order fulfillment will in effect be delayed approximately 14 days. The practical effect, however, is that orders will inev-
itably be lost, and the spontaneity associated with rapid telephone
orders and order fulfillment will be severely diminished if not lost.

2. The FTC went further in a subsequent consent agreement[44] involving a commercial transaction. Here the firm agreed to the following:

a. All telephone orders will be confirmed in writing.

b. The form must include a toll-free telephone number that can be called to cancel an order within 10 days.

c. No products may be shipped and no bill may be sent without the prior expressed consent of the recipient.

d. No collection letters may be sent to dun a customer without the customer's prior expressed consent.

This case incorporates all the written requirements of the first and also imposes an order-losing toll-free-number requirement.

3. Another magazine seller[45] agreed:

a. To inform all potential customers, both verbally and in writing, of the full terms of their order and specific cancellation rights.

b. To provide an understandable cancellation form with all follow-up subscription orders.

c. To honor all cancellations received within 10 business days of mailing the order.

d. To make any refunds within 30 days.

e. To allow all customers who did not specifically sign orders (within the period from July 1, 1979, to July 1, 1980) to cancel immediately.

f. Not to fulfill any orders in the future without a signed confirmation. Thus magazines that are received where there is no prior signed confirmation may be treated as unordered merchandise.

This agreement may be an omen to all telephone marketers that while the telephone may be a solicitation medium (or, in the case of a toll-free number, a follow-up medium), the full sale resulting in fulfillment will not be possible through the telephone alone.

4. Two subsequent consent orders requiring the cooling-off period resulted from *United States v. Budget Marketing, Inc.*,[46] and *United States v. Allied Publishers Service*.[47] Of further interest in the latter case is the FTC's term "knowledge fairly implied."[48] This applies to both of the following:

a. Neglecting to be aware of and in compliance with an FTC rule

b. Neglecting to be aware of FTC precedents, that is, consent agreements

For your purposes, you should distinguish this term from "actual knowledge," which applies where (a) awareness of the law was apparent and a conscious intent to ignore the law was demonstrated, or (b) the firm itself signed a prior order on point, or (c) the FTC specifically and formally wrote to a firm concerning the practice and the firm ignored the notification.

The Reader's Digest simulated-check case (see the section in Chapter 5 on the simulated-check promotion) was an example of failing the "actual knowledge" test as to all three situations.

What Should You Do?

Requiring cooling-off periods and written confirmation of orders are methods to prevent customers from becoming hard-sell victims and to avoid billing for unordered merchandise. The former requires careful screening of your script and monitoring of your personnel. Then consult your counsel as to the requirement or lack of same for cooling-off periods in the various states (and localities) you elect to do business in.

As to avoiding the problem of unordered merchandise with regard to telephone orders, there are at least three steps and then four suggestions.

At a minimum:

1. You have the legal right to presume that the person who answers a telephone at an address and identifies himself or herself as the person being called is that person. Make sure your script is written so as to establish this basic identification: call the correct number; ask for the person at a specific address; and if the party you wish to call is called to the phone, again confirm his or her identity.

2. You must train your people to screen "suspicious" voices (e.g., children's voices) at the receiving end of incoming or outgoing calls.

3. Internally your firm (in the customer service department or in other departments involved) *must* have *written* procedures detailing how any unordered-merchandise complaints will be speedily investigated and resolved in-house. Such procedural controls are your defense against isolated complaints.

Then, if you've made the business decision to process call orders (incoming or outgoing) without a prior written contract, the following might be considered for your internal control system.

1. Send all orders COD so unordered merchandise will be rejected up front.

2. Follow up all orders (particularly incoming) with a phone call confirming the name of the caller, the order, and other particulars.

3. Send a postage-paid (not prestamped, so the only postage costs are for legitimate returns) envelope with the order. Anyone who received unordered goods will be encouraged to return them at no cost to himself or herself.

4. Examine any other controls common to your trade which can help assure that people will not receive unordered merchandise.

Conclusion

The first part of this chapter examined laws and rulings of particular interest to telephone marketers. The reader should not view this chapter in isolation. Most of the laws discussed in the previous chapters are necessary to the telephone marketer's grasp of the dynamics of his or her legal environment. Similarly, the laws and rules discussed in this chapter (e.g., those pertaining to bait-and-switch tactics and door-to-door selling) are obviously applicable to other forms of direct marketing.

The telephone is an important direct-marketing device in its own right. However, it is much more important as a support medium. For follow-up calls in direct-mail or door-to-door efforts, it is an invaluable tool. A toll-free number will help increase sales in conjunction with any other medium. Finally, commercial TV, radio, and cable TV are no longer passive media for the viewer. A toll-free number makes all such media actively interactive, and so immediate information feedback and orders are possible. We shall now proceed to discuss the laws you need to know to remain in legal compliance as you exploit the formerly passive electronic media.

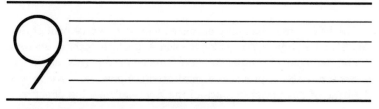

Broadcast Media

Television and radio need little introduction. There is no property right in a broadcast license. Both TV and radio stations are licensed as "scarce resources" by the Federal Communications Commission for a 3-year period.[1] Each has certain FCC-imposed obligations regarding both its programming and its relations with the communities it serves. Each station has a broad mandate to serve the public interest—convenience and necessity.[2]

Through the common interactive device of the telephone, the American home is gaining access to a much greater variety of products and services. The telephone has enabled TV and radio to "sell" directly to the consumer merely by providing a follow-up number (often a toll-free number). These everyday media are, therefore, less passive than they once were.

The interactive utility of these media is enhanced by the electronic transfer of funds. An electronic funds transfer system instantly credit-qualifies a consumer and immediately provides funds for payment.

Legally, all the logical rules we've reviewed apply—the rules concerning sweepstakes, the use of the word "free," negative option, and so on. There are a few twists on others which we'll review shortly. The FCC has few rules which apply directly to the marketer. The key governing impact agency for the direct marketer here as elsewhere is the FTC.

The FTC is the sole entity entrusted with the enforcement of Section 5[3] of the Federal Trade Commission Act, which declares unlawful "unfair methods of competition in or affecting commerce, and unfair or deceptive acts or practices in or affecting commerce."[4] We've seen the hand of this power in much of the law regulating the direct marketer.

Demonstrating Your Product Visually

Television is currently the most important medium used by large national firms to reach potential buyers of consumer goods. At present, its two large drawbacks are the cost for commercial time and the lact of segmentation (in general) of the viewers. One great asset is the opportunity to have your product demonstrated visually. One obvious way to sell many products is to show them in their best light "in action." The mass audience demonstration is unique to television. When demonstrating, you must be truthful as to any "material" statement. The FTC regards any statement as material if it would affect the consumer's decision to purchase. The concept of materiality runs throughout the FTC's decisions on point.

Three other points:

1. The demonstration must actually prove something relating to the quality of the product.

2. The demonstration must accurately reflect the honest experience a user would have.

3. Consumers are entitled to see what they are told they are seeing.

Before reviewing the following discussion, it would be a good idea to refresh your memory concerning the discussion of endorsements in Chapter 5.

Actually Prove Something

Normally, the representation which is relevant in determining the legality of an advertisement is the general impression given by the advertisement when it is read or seen as a whole.[5] However, when you conduct a demonstration on TV, it must actually be relevant to your product's major attribute.

For example, Colgate-Palmolive Company[6] marketed a product called Baggies. It was designed to prevent food from spoiling. Colgate demonstrated on TV the more visually dramatic ability of the product to keep water off the enclosed food. The FTC obtained a consent order stating that the demonstration of the product's capacity to keep water out *(though true)* was irrelevant to its ability to prevent food spoilage.

A similar case was found in *Eversharp, Inc.*[7] As discussed above, the FTC seeks to bar any material untruths in advertising. It considers as "materiality" any practice which would influence the purchase decision. Here, an irrelevant demonstration (though true and accurate in its own right) might result in the purchase of an item because of a factor other than its primary purpose.

Honest Experience of User

Ideal Toy Company[8] marketed its robot commando in various TV commercials. The commercials indicated that this toy would perform acts as directed by the user's vocal command.

The reality was that each act was governed by the manual setting of a control on the toy. The toy would only perform the specific act set on the control. If you wanted a different act, you could use your "vocal command" until you were blue in the face—the robot would ignore you. Only if you manually changed the setting would the robot follow your command.

The FTC did not like this. It was a milder agency in those days (1964) and merely required Ideal to cease and desist from:

> Stating, implying or otherwise representing by words, pictures, depictions, demonstrations or any combination thereof, or otherwise, that any toy performs in any manner not in accordance with fact.[9]

It is important not to exaggerate or mislead in any demonstration. During the early 1970s, many gasoline additives were put on the market in an attempt to capitalize on the post-1973 Arab embargo, and there were gas price hikes as well to cultivate the environment-conscious market.

Sun Oil Company[10] showed a car pulling two boxcars and a caboose— over 100 tons! How could your car do this too (if you really wanted to pull a train)? By using Sunoco 260 blended gasoline. After you heard the pitch, you saw a repeat of the demonstration with the statement "you're seeing Sunoco premium deliver in this car."[11]

The demonstration was visually effective. However, the FTC found that the demonstration implied that "Sunoco 260 Action" was unique or unusual in that it alone provided the power necessary to enable a consumer's car to perform the task depicted.

However, the consumer would find in typical driving that Sunoco 260 did not have unique qualities—that is, qualities not available in competitive brands. Sunoco's blend did not consistently provide more engine power than a gasoline of a comparable octane rating.

There was no intent to deceive. Sun Oil sought to capture consumer attention through its demonstration. However, its demonstration misrepresented realistic consumer experience. Sun Oil agreed to cease and desist from:

1. Representing directly or by implication that it has a unique product when in fact its product is not unique among its competitors

2. Demonstrating any fact or product feature that is material to the purchase decision without providing evidence that actually proves such fact or product feature

In both of the above cases, the demonstration was at best a gross exaggeration. In both cases, the firms sought to enhance a product with a vivid visual demonstration which the viewer could remember. However, no such demonstration is permitted if it states or implies a material untruth, thus affecting the purchase decision.

Seeing Is Believing

As television became the leading entertainment medium, the advertisers developed new dimensions in the use of props and mock-ups to enhance the impact of television demonstrations. Some props were a necessity and acceptable (e.g., mashed potatoes used to simulate ice cream), while others were more questionable.

The crux of the problem came to a head in a landmark Supreme Court decision in 1965.[12] Involved was a television commercial in which Palmolive Rapid Shave cream was applied to a substance that the viewer was told was sandpaper. The intent of the commercial was to give the viewer visual "proof" that Rapid Shave could soften sandpaper. However, the shaving cream the viewer saw on TV did not actually come into contact with sandpaper. Instead, it was applied to a prop or mock-up made of Plexiglas to which sand had been applied.

The FTC held that even fine sandpaper could not have been shaved until "moisturized" for an hour. Thus it held that there had been a clear misrepresentation of a material fact through the use of the demonstration's mock-up. The viewing public had not seen a test, experiment, or demonstration which proved any product claim.

There ensued two Court of Appeals decisions: a clarification of the original order by the Commission and a Supreme Court review. Because of the enormous precedent value of this case to the topic of visual demonstrations, it will be reviewed in detail.

When it came to a philosophy of the "show must go on" or the truth, the Supreme Court held for the latter.

> If however, it becomes impossible or impractical to show simulated demonstrations on television in a truthful manner, this indicates that television is not a medium that lends itself to this type of commercial, not that the commercial must survive at all costs. Similarly unpersuasive is respondents' objection that the Commission's decision discriminates against sellers whose product claims cannot be "verified" on television without the use of simulation. All methods of advertising do not equally favor every seller. If the inherent limitations of a method do not permit its use in the way a seller desires, the seller cannot by material misrepresentation compensate for those limitations.[13]

The Court then went on to distinguish mock-ups which were incidental to objective claims from those which were material.

> In the ice cream case the mashed potato prop is not being used for additional proof of the product claim, while the purpose of the Rapid Shave commercial is to give the viewer *objective proof of the claims made.* If in the ice cream hypothetical the *focus of the commercial* becomes the undisclosed potato prop and the viewer is invited, explicitly or by implication, to see for himself the truth or the claims about the ice cream's rich texture and full color, and perhaps compare it to a "rival product," then the commercial has become similar to the one now before us. Clearly, however, a commercial which depicts happy actors delightedly eating ice cream that is in fact mashed potatoes or drinking a product appearing to be coffee but which is in fact some other substance is not covered by the present order.[14] [Emphasis Added.]

The Court then went on to state that the emphasis should be on the impression the demonstration will have on the viewing public. Here the FTC has broad discretion because of its presumed expertise in this area.

> In commercials where the emphasis is on the seller's word, and not on the viewer's own perception, the respondents need not fear that an undisclosed use of props is prohibited by the present order. On the other hand, *when the commercial not only makes a claim, but also invites the viewer to rely on his own perception for demonstrative proof of the claim,* the respondents will be aware that the use of undisclosed props in strategic places might be a material deception.[15] [Emphasis added.]

In the final analysis, it was decided that consumers are entitled to see what they are told they are seeing. The FTC does not need to prove that there was actual deception or that the advertising actually influenced consumer decisions. To measure deceptiveness, the FTC looks at the total impression. It will reject "literal truth" as a defense if the overall impression is false or deceptive.

This was a tough, drawn-out case. In other cases, the issues are less complicated. For example, an advertiser for the Campbell Soup Company[16] placed marbles at the bottom of a bowl of soup to force the solids up. The visual effect achieved by this demonstration was to show a bowl of piping hot soup jammed with ample vegetables. This technique was found to be deceptive, as the viewers were not seeing an accurate picture of what they could actually consume at mealtime.

Concluding Case

Finally, we all remember the "Wonder Years."[17] If you watched TV during the years 1964 to 1970, particularly certain children's shows, you probably remember the twice-repeated rapid growth of a young boy. He was experiencing his "wonder years—the years from 1 to 12 when a child grows to 90 percent of his or her adult height."

The Court noted:

> Although there is evidence that American consumers do not pay much attention to nutritional content when purchasing bread, for many years the advertisers of Wonder Bread apparently operated on the contrary assumption.[18]

Ironically, Wonder Bread was ahead of its time. In the days before diet and health food were taken seriously, the nutritional qualities of this product were being marketed as a unique selling feature. The only drawback was that the consumer would not experience the claims if he or she ingested Wonder Bread.

A bread enrichment program was undertaken during World War II to combat dietary deficiency diseases prevalent at that time (anemia, beriberi, and pellagra). Wonder Bread conformed to the relevant standards of the federal Food and Drug Administration.

Wonder Bread's demonstration effectively violated two of the three points previously discussed. The demonstration was not irrelevant; however, the experience of the average user would reveal that the nutritional value of Wonder Bread is not significantly different from that of similar breads (recall the case involving the gasoline additive of Sun Oil). Further, the demonstration was not true as seen, and it was employed to demonstrate to the viewer the objective claims made. Wonder Bread was not an extraordinary food for producing dramatic growth or health in children (recall the case involving Colgate's Rapid Shave).

Finally, a new FTC remedy was devised: corrective advertising.

Corrective Advertising

ITT Continental, the Wonder Bread people, did not have to implement this form of disclosure. However, any marketer should be aware of this threat, particularly one employing visual demonstrations.

Corrective ads involve an "unwanted message" (correction of past false claims) which is controlled by someone other than the advertiser (FTC-negotiated or -litigated) and which must be disseminated at the advertiser's expense.

Corrective ads are imposed because of past deceptive claims which have resulted in present lingering beliefs of consumers. If such lingering effects are found, the remedy is imposed for the period necessary to reduce the incorrect or false beliefs to an "acceptable level." Because of their wide impact, television demonstrations have a greater risk (if they are false) of being hit with the corrective-advertising penalty.

The most celebrated case to date has been the Listerine case.[19] Here, Warner-Lambert was required to state the following:

> Contrary to prior advertising, Listerine will not help prevent colds or sore throats or lessen their severity.

This statement had to be added to all Listerine commercials until $10 million was expended. The case was appealed.[20] The FTC's decision was affirmed, except that "contrary to prior advertising" was stricken from the required disclosure. In affirming the FTC's power to impose corrective advertising, the Appeals Court suggested that if advertisements did not have long-lasting effects, then companies everywhere might be "wasting their massive advertising budgets."[21]

The criteria for "lingering beliefs" will probably be developed on a case-by-case basis. This remedy—corrective advertising—is one all marketers, especially those employing visual demonstrations, must reckon with in the future.

Planning a Visual Demonstration?

1. Have you reviewed the section in Chapter 5 on the endorsement promotion issues? Many such issues may come into operation directly or indirectly depending on how the demonstration is being conducted, who is conducting it, and the type of audience.

2. Will there be adequate disclosure of all relevant information so that the consumer can make an *informed* evaluation of the demonstration?

3. Will there be a fair demonstration of the product's merits, *and* will the demonstration actually prove something *material* with regard to such merits?

4. Has the demonstration been carefully screened in order to eliminate any express or implied exaggerations or excessive puffery? If the demonstration asserts a "scientific argument," have objective and well-controlled tests been performed and documented so that *all* statements made and/or visually demonstrated can be verified?

5. Finally—and this is very important—are you demonstrating a product requiring legal disclosures? For example, if the commercial involves "free" being printed across the screen, are there any qualifications in acceptable print size to pass a Flesch readability test? If the presentation is oral but requires disclosures (e.g., Negative Option Rule or Truth-in-Lending), you would be wise to have your demonstration reviewed by one of the agencies which do audio recall tests. The laws on point do not end with print media. The *Colgate* axiom holds: If either the commercial or legal compliance is to survive, you can bet the courts and/or agencies will opt for legal compliance. Consult counsel.

Then for the demonstration area remember some general advertising guidelines that are applicable to all the direct-marketing media vehicles.

1. The statutory ban against false and misleading demonstrations applies to that which is suggested as well as to that which is asserted. Where demonstrations convey more than one meaning, one of which is false, you are liable for the misleading meaning conveyed.

2. A demonstration that contains less than the whole truth may be found deceptive by omission.

3. The product that is demonstrated may not be represented as different from what the consumer will actually receive, even though the product received may be better.

4. Don't expect a better shake from the courts on appeal. In any determination of what impression a demonstration will have on the viewing public or a specific segment of that public, the FTC will be given broad discretion by the courts. On appeal, the courts will generally not interfere with an FTC order so long as a reasonable relationship between the remedy and the unlawful practice is found to exist. If your firm has had the misfortune of having an FTC order, be sure to stay in compliance. If you subsequently violate it, *each* broadcast of the commercial can be a separate violation.[22]

Then, after all the legal hurdles are overcome, there are still consumer groups and individuals engaging in private verification of demonstrations. *Consumer Reports* magazine is one example of a large testing group. Then there are the individuals as personified by David Horowitz, host of the syndicated TV show *Fight Back! With David Horowitz*. This show tests the tests of the advertisers. One article quoted Mr. Horowitz as stating that one out of four ads flunk as to performance claims.[23]

Industry Codes

These are a factor to be considered in planning your promotion on TV and radio. The codes go beyond codified statutes. Most broadcast stations (both radio and television) are members of the National Association of Broadcasters (NAB) and adhere to its code, which provides guidelines for the industry. From time to time they are amended, so you should check with counsel as to the current wording and interpretations. However, in certain limited areas they tend to be stricter than the law we've reviewed up to this point. It would be a good idea to highlight those areas for your future planning.

Advertisements

You may be required to make available to your advertiser and/or the Code Authority documentation that will support the validity and truthfulness of claims, demonstrations, testimonials, and endorsements contained in your commercial messages. This might include (where applicable) scientific tests (unless biased conditions were clearly identified), consumer research, or proof that your endorser is still a satisfied user of your product.

The same disclosure standards may be applied to your contests. The recommendations of the NAB code regarding contests are similar to the guidelines for games of chance discussed in Chapter 5.

Children

The Television Code is very explicit as to solicitations directed at children, especially preschoolers, and at the family in general.

1. No personality or cartoon character on a children's program should deliver a commercial message or endorse a product during his or her (or its!) own program or during the program appearing immediately before or after.

2. Exhortative language should be avoided.

3. Two sections,[24] J and K, are of particular note:

J. The use of real-life authority figures/celebrities as product presenters shall not include their personal testimonials or endorsements.

K. Persons who are recognized as being identified, specifically or generally, with an advertised product's counterpart in real-life may not be used as spokespeople or endorsers. This prohibition also applies to actors representing such persons.

The code also has tight standards as to price, costuming, and premiums. Finally, the code requires that the word "free" be shown in the same type size used for any conditions or qualifications.

As stated, these guidelines are tighter and more narrowly drawn than the FTC's rules and guidelines on point. The FTC does not specifically distinguish between children and adults in either its endorsement guidelines or the free rule. However, it is a good practice to be extra careful when designing an advertisement for children, since the FTC is on record as bringing actions against advertisements which might not deceive an adult but would mislead a child. The FTC will always analyze the advertisement's probable impact on the specific type of person to whom it is addressed.

Similar advertising guidelines have been issued by the Children's Advertising Review Unit of the National Advertising Division of the Council of Better Business Bureaus. These guidelines are worthwhile reading for all marketers involved in children's advertising. Of note in these guidelines is the encouragement to use all possible creative talent in wording or verbalizing disclosures required by law so that the language is appropriate for the maturity level of the segment you are realistically planning to address.

Conclusion

The above codes and guidelines are responsible steps toward self-regulation. They closely parallel existing law and occasionally are constructed more narrowly in an effort to protect certain audience segments, particularly minors. *In general,* compliance with these guidelines will mean total legal compliance. Further, large-scale self-regulation diminishes the justification for mandated government regulation.

Cable TV

Interactive cable TV has the potential to give the audiovisual direct marketer more precise demographic data about the audience. It could make mass commercial TV obsolete similar to the way the seg-mented-audience magazines doomed many of the general-audience magazines (e.g., *Look* and *Life*). Finally, it will radically alter our cul-ture and further strengthen the political trend toward conservatism.

This latter point can't be emphasized too strongly. Increasingly the three major networks recruited from and reflected the values of the eastern seaboard: Boston, New York City, and Washington, D.C. They were more liberal than the nation as a whole and attempted to become the principal arbiters of American opinion.

Cable TV will break the world of homogeneous ideology of the adversary culture (that is, adversary with regard to traditional middle-class values and those in public life embodying them). In order to sur-vive, cable television must reflect the values of the local culture. More programming is devoted to segmented and localized religious and regional groups. The cable stations will reflect at most a diluted liberal bias. On the national level, Ted Turner's Cable News Network is already an alternative for those who believe that the three major net-works should register as lobbyists of the liberal counterculture.

From a political point of view, conservatives will capitalize on this medium the same way Richard Viguerie and other direct-mail wizards have locked onto direct-mail fund raising and candidate promotion. As a result of the no-growth mentality which they have increasingly exhibited, the liberals have failed to "seize the day" with direct mail and other modern media. Consequently, they were unable to make effective use of these tools during the 1980 elections. Failure to make effective use of cable TV to penetrate the grass roots voting popula-tion may further their undoing in 1984, and chances are they will not grasp this opportunity because of the opposition of the three major networks to the expansion of cable TV. Fund raising and other polit-ical promotions are important aspects of direct mail. By 1984, we should expect to see audience-segmented cable TV well utilized by the winning candidates at all levels of government.

From a marketing point of view, these cultural and political aspects will serve to convert television from a mass-audience medium into a segmented-audience medium. Shows run by religious denominations have a narrower focus than a major network's show about such denominations. The market of a locally based ethnic show or of a regional show is a more definite segment than the presumed segments at which advertising is directed over national commercial shows. In short, this medium will in the long run reinforce values rather than oppose them and those attracted to alternative shows for specific audiences will constitute a much more targeted segment in terms of demographic particulars and, upon study, probably in terms of psychographic criteria as well.

Yes, cable TV will be the most revolutionary cultural medium since the birth of commercial television, and politically it will soon become as useful as targeted direct mail. There are great opportunities for marketers who understand where the nation is going.

What Is Cable TV?

Cable television (also called Community Antenna Television, or CATV) is what the name implies—a system for bringing clear television pictures directly into the set by means of a wire (coaxial cable) rather than through the air via an antenna on your roof.

The coaxial cable gives cable television the potential for independence and interaction. Besides transmitting in the usual "downstream" manner (station to subscriber), a coaxial cable can carry information back "upstream" from the subscriber. Each subscriber could have his or her own digital code for rapid computer processing with a computer terminal.

The coaxial cable's bidirectional system is an additional interactive option (as well as the existing telephone) for the marketer in the 1980s. And cable TV will soon take off.

Birth and Evolution of Cable TV

Cable TV was developed in the late 1940s for use in communities that were unable to receive broadcast television signals because of terrain or the distance from major television transmitting stations. It is said that the first town to adopt CATV was Lansford, Pennsylvania (1950). A glance at the map (if it's on your map) shows that Lansford is a small town of 5200 nestled away in Carbon County. It is in a mountainous area not conducive to normal reception. Cable arrived, and this town and hundreds of others were assured "unflaky" access to *I Love Lucy* and *Ozzie and Harriet*.

Over the years, cable TV developed a nonbroadcast entertainment package promotional aspect as well as the clear transmission. Presently, the former asset is its major benefit to consumers. Cable TV can deliver more channels, since signals on the cable are less subject to adjacent-channel interference than signals traveling through the air. Further, there is no problem at present from FCC spectrum policy. Finally, the use of wire provides the option of monitoring and charging for use or simply charging a flat rate.

Why, then, the delay in "universal" household penetration or even in the threshold goal of 30 percent? Three factors significantly delayed cable penetration:

1. Cost
2. FCC restrictions concerning markets
3. FCC restrictions concerning subscription cablecasting

Cost Cable television is a highly capital-intensive industry. The construction costs in urban areas can run from $6500 per mile when cable is laid in sand to over $100,000 per mile in the solid rock of Manhattan Island. Above-ground distribution costs vary from $2500 to $5000 per mile. Then there are the franchise fees paid to local subdivisions. These must be paid because the cables occupy the right-of-way along public streets. State and local governments also regulate pole attachment authority, charges for services, and state revenue provisions.

Even more significant has been the cost of credit. Since 1973, when much of the FCC burden was removed, the borrowing markets have fluctuated, greatly hurting entrepreneurs in this field. There was a shortage of the capital necessary for expansion as well as generally high interest rates. Further, financial institutions had few guidelines by which to judge the financial potential of the cable system. They could judge that the components and techniques they were asked to finance would probably have a high obsolescence rate. Today, the cost problem has abated, but it still lingers to some extent.

FCC Restrictions—Markets The FCC's regulation of cable is more limited than its regulation of over-the-air broadcasting. Cable systems do not use the public's airwaves, and they do not function as common carriers. However, the FCC had assumed control of the importation of distant television signals into urban markets in 1965. The FCC issued rules which discouraged the entry of CATV systems into the top 100 urban markets, which at that time represented 85 percent of the population of the United States! Further supporting the FCC were many local TV stations. These stations objected to the "imported" TV stations; they felt that the "imported" stations would diminish their viewing audience.

The industry found a friend in Dean Burch, who as chairperson of the FCC began efforts at deregulation to permit entry into the top urban markets.

FCC Restrictions—Subscription Cablecasting   The major pay cable services rely on feature films as the primary source of programming, and until recently their access to feature films was restricted by FCC rules regarding subscription cablecasting. These rules specified that most films could be cablecast on premium channels only if they had been in general release for less than 3 years or more than 10 years.

These rules were overturned by the U.S. Court of Appeals in 1977.[25] The court felt that the FCC had exceeded its authority over cable television in promulgating the pay cable rules and because there was no evidence to support the need for such regulations. The court felt that the restraints imposed by the rules were greater than necessary to further any legitimate government interest.

With the FCC's restrictive regulations significantly eased and the capital markets currently improving in the United States, one further situation should be noted. The debate has been resolved as to whether or not cable operators should have copyright liability for the programs they rebroadcast to their subscribers.

The Supreme Court had consistently held that cable systems were not liable under the copyright laws for their use of copyrighted broadcast programs, even though the owner did not consent to such use. The Court had found cable systems to be passive receivers, since they carried without editing the programs they received.[26] As a result, the cable operators were receiving a free ride. The broadcasting industry spent millions to create and purchase programming which the cable operators could then retransmit, without payment to the program suppliers.

In 1976, Congress passed the new Copyright Act (effective January 1, 1978), which requires license fees for all cable systems. Under this act,[27] cable operators are expressly allowed to retransmit programs without having to obtain the consent of or negotiate license fees directly with the copyright owners. In return, the cable operators must pay a statutory royalty fee according to a schedule which is based on the number of distant signals a system carries and its gross revenues. The minimum royalty is 0.675 percent of gross receipts.[28]

Cable will not replace the creative use of copy in the form of letters, catalogs, and other appeals that arrive by mail. Direct mail will also remain the major channel in political and charitable fund raising. But only 25 percent of the public buy merchandise by mail. The marriage of cable and telephone will allow cable to obtain a significant part of the remaining 75 percent primarily from the retail trade and not from other direct-marketing channels.

Advertising Potential

While the typical commercial TV or radio station relies on advertising as its primary source of income, most cable systems continue to rely on subscription charges. This is changing.

Most cable stations accept advertising, though it is of a more local nature. The localism was the result of three factors:

1. The cable audience is more fragmented—it is the nature of the beast.

2. Small firms simply cannot afford prime time in the major media.

3. The market penetration did not offer much of an incentive for the national advertiser.

The local, segmented audiences will remain an asset and become a greater asset. Small firms will continue to maximize their dollars by advertising to a more clearly defined segment. Finally, national firms will pay a premium for the in-place audience segmentation now existing and being defined by market research analysis. Why the sudden attention of national advertisers?

In 1981, cable was available to only 45 percent of the American homes, and less than half of those chose to accept it. At the same time, cable generally lacked reliable data on audiences, penetration, and scheduling. There are dramatic improvements in both of these areas. The 30-percent penetration many pros believe is the critical mass necessary to consistently attract national advertisers is almost a reality and will be by some time in 1984. As to market research, Nielson and other firms are now providing viewer data similar to that available for commercial TV.

The major component contributing to accurate audience segmentation will be the infomercial. Infomercials will run from 120 seconds to 30 minutes or constitute entire programs themselves.[29] When they are combined with interactive technology, a national marketer will be able to reach, inform, and sell directly and immediately.

Infomercials

Instead of passively reviewing a 30-second TV spot, the consumer will be asked to move into a dynamic and often interactive process. This will require:

1. A more motivated and interested viewer

2. New creative approaches to the design of the significantly longer marketing message

The infomercial will allow for more diversity in programming. The expanded variety of programming will then divide the traditionally undefined commercial TV audiences into categories that have identifiable product or service preferences.

The infomercial will provide marketers with the means to present products without the time restrictions inherent in commercial TV. A more leisurely explanation of the product and its warranty and then, perhaps, a demonstration will be feasible. You can then flash a toll-free number on the screen. A credit card payment option will provide the means for electronic funds transfer and credit card billing the same day.

So far there are no new legal issues. To date, we've reviewed warranties, telephone marketing law, demonstration compliance, and other areas which would arise in a "regular" commercial television promotion. The infomercial, by presenting more facts about your product, will probably result in more legal compliance as to disclosures. However, interactive TV by keypad (with its great potential for accumulating viewer market data—see below) may result in a legal backlash which would adversely affect the entire direct-marketing channel, especially the list area.

Qube

The national showcase for fully interactive cable service is Warner Cable's much publicized Qube system in Columbus, Ohio. Why Columbus, Ohio? Columbus is the second-fastest-growing city in America and is fairly representative of the demographic groups that make up the nation. It is a good area of middle America to begin testing one aspect or our interactive future.[30]

The first subscribers in Columbus were offered three tiers of cable service (up to 60 channels), the most interesting of which is Columbus Alive. This is one of ten community channels that give viewers the opportunity to interact with their TV sets. The subscribers are provided with a keypad with five response buttons (in addition to the channel selection buttons) which allow them to answer both yes–no and multiple-choice questions. The viewers are asked to offer their programming preferences for advertising campaigns and issues of the day.

As I write this, I'm watching (4:15 A.M. EST) Ted Turner's Cable News Network (CNN). The Secretary of Education, Mr. Bell, is being interviewed. The Qube viewers are polled as to their opinions about whether or not the Department of Education should be abolished. Ten seconds later:

Yes	64 percent
No	32 percent
No Opinion	4 percent

Regardless of the time when a program is taped, these viewers have impact. If this audience is developed, it could assist opinion molding in all fields. If the system is used in 1984, its polls (simultaneously broadcast in various areas nationwide) might be transformed from a novelty into a more significant event than the New Hampshire primary or other regional primaries! Critics argue that this system presents little time for reflection or meditation.

If the system is adopted and refined on a national scale, the sales potential is mind-boggling! Over a period of time, the interactive connection between the subscriber's set and centrally located computers (which have identified *each* subscriber by shows watched, prior purchase, opinions on issues, and so on) will result in the formation of an individualized audience profile. Advertisers will[31] be able to identify the income, lifestyle, and/or expenditure characteristics of their audiences more accurately than through any other media (offering an opportunity for list renters to tie into their lists). Further, advertisers will receive immediate reactions from the subscribers as to whether they liked or disliked your commercial as well as your product. To either make a purchase or offer a comment, all the viewer has to do is push a button on the TV set! For a purchase, the advertiser's computer can record the order, print the labels, give shipping instructions, and then bill the customer.

Naturally, problems remain. Delivery will not be integrated electronically, and in most cases the carrier will remain the postal service. All issues of channel compliance remain. For example, what if your 5-year-old orders without your knowledge? Unordered merchandise, the 30 Day Rule, and merchandise substitution will remain as potential pitfalls. Now may be a good time for you to return to Chapter 2 for a review. Once you've digested the applicable laws affecting channel compliance, it will be time to move on to the coming privacy debate.[32]

The Coming Privacy Debate?

It all sounds simple. On your little box at home, you push the right sequence of numbers, and as a result, you've ordered a product which human hands never touch until the order gets to the fulfillment house. However, your order, the type of product, the time of day or night you ordered it, and so on, form a very descriptive profile of your life. This is why such data are so valuable to marketers.

Further, in a Qube system, the computer "knows" if you are watching a paid channel. If you are watching a particular movie, it will bill you for that movie. Your viewing selections become part of your profile.

Then, does the consumer want the cost of purchases deducted from his or her bank account? Another profile record grows. People such as Howard Ruff[33] argue against various noncash purchases precisely to avoid having this type of private information wind up in the hands of various government agencies. For example, while banks and credit bureaus fall under federal privacy law regulations, the IRS has access to financial records. The IRS may be very interested in your spending habits and other lifestyle information contained in these files.

As DMMA president, Bob DeLay stated that personal privacy "is probably the most universal area of concern to direct marketers."[34] He was addressing more innocuous areas (e.g., lists), but the principle is especially true here. Will consumers be willing to sacrifice privacy for the convenience of direct electronic ordering? Will they accept a centralized system for recording and storing information on their individual tastes, finances, purchasing behavior, and viewing habits, as well as their answers to opinion polls? If so, will they also add on other devices (such as fire and burglar alarm systems) which can record when you come and go?

Worse than initial nonacceptance would be ignorant acceptance. Then after the consumers think about it, the backlash against this stored reality might result in overbroad legislation hindering the system as well as hurting data compilation in general.

Anyone so naive as to believe a backlash is not in the wings should carefully review the next chapter, which deals with lists. This chapter reviews and discusses list rental in the 1980s. Appellate courts have had to pass on the issue of whether or not a name and address is private information. Could an industry which so carefully (and possibly narrowly) escaped these "privacy" issues really believe there will be no outcry? There will.

The issues will jell when the technology is finally in place on a massive scale (and 30-percent audience penetration is achieved). The cable industry has valuable time to address the privacy issue and other issues such as the potential FTC reaction to the blurring of message identity ("pure" information blurred with marketing and advertising) or obscenity—certain dubious programming readily accessible to children. The industry would be wise to heed the warning of one industry leader: "If cablecasters adopt a public-be-damned, big buck attitude, they may reap 102 years of regulatory woes, just as the utilities and railroads did before them.[35] If certain issues are not addressed early on by responsible industry self-policing, the result will be a mandated cable compliance section (rather than a speculative discussion) in the revised edition of this book.

So much for a look into the future. There's one area of law which should be addressed here, as it is applicable to the infomercial.

Comparative Advertising

This is a method of advertising your product whereby you compare it, directly or indirectly, with another brand. The FTC recommends that you compare material product attributes in concrete and measureable terms. Price, measureable performance, and results of sound objective surveys are all useful means for complying with the FTC's desire to provide information for consumers.

Until fairly recently, self-imposed media industry regulations effectively discouraged comparative advertising. FTC pressure brought about a reversal of policy in 1972. Now one can see the "head-to-head" beer taste tests or firms comparing their lower prices with the prices of the named competitors.[36]

Should you name your competitor? From a legal point of view, yes.[37] There is no greater substantiation required for a comparative advertisement than a standard plug for your product. Further, a claim of superiority over an unidentified competitor's product becomes a claim of superiority over all potential products in the line.[38]

Remember, too, that all other advertising laws come into play. For both legal compliance and communication effectiveness, the base against which a comparison is made must be identified clearly and conspicuously. If a comparative ad can be misread, it is misleading in the eyes of the FTC.

Also, remember the law reviewed in the discussion of demonstrations. If you make a claim of uniqueness or novelty, the attributes must be discernible, relevant, and of *actual* benefit to the consumer.

Finally, if you are comparing brand X with your product, the appearance, size, or shape of brand X in your ad copy or commercial must not be distorted. The impression of brand X that is conveyed should be similar to the way the viewer would see brand X in a store.

Conclusion

Cable TV is an ideal vehicle for briefly complying with the disclosure requirements concerning your competitor. In addition, it offers the opportunity to use minutes rather than seconds to fully sell your product as an item that is not only excellent in its own right but "extra excellent" when compared with your competitor's product.

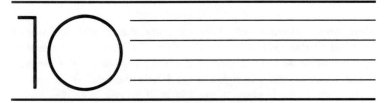

Lists and List Rental

No book concerning the method of business we call direct marketing could be complete without a comprehensive discussion of the list and whether or not the legal or legislation environment will continue to permit generally free access to lists. This chapter will discuss the importance of lists and serve as a warning to direct marketers that things may not be as good as they look at first glance.

Introduction

Independent or public mailings are the lifeline of the direct-marketing channel. Without the list, that lifeline would cease to exist, as there would be no market. The quality of the list determines the success of your promotion; the more refined the list, the better the response. With increasing costs such as the costs of postage, paper, and labor, the direct marketer cannot afford a shotgun approach. The tendency, therefore, has been to seek more efficient methods of targeting one's markets via lists. Direct marketers are relying more heavily on lists of individuals compiled in a sophisticated way in order to effect more positive results from the mailings.

Thus far, the direct-marketing industry has been successful in avoiding the enactment of significant laws at state and federal levels which would severely limit, if not eliminate, the creation and use of such lists on the basis of "privacy" issues. The 1980s could prove to be a crucial decade to the industry if privacy explodes as the "cause" of the 1980s, as did civil rights in the 1950s, the antiwar movement in the 1960s, and ecology in the 1970s. If it does, then direct-marketing businesses will have to evolve new strategies in order to defend and protect their use of compiled lists.[1]

What happens in the courtrooms and legislatures throughout the country in the next decade could spell either disaster or continued success for the industry. Direct marketers should not be lulled into complacency by the Reagan victory (or other conservative victories). Privacy has long been an issue which cuts across the political spectrum, and major privacy legislation has traditionally had conservative Republican co-authorship.[2]

To be forewarned is to be forearmed, and in this case vigilance is essential. If you and other direct marketers are prepared to be involved in some inevitable and tough legal battles over the privacy issue, chances of a favorable outcome for the industry will be greatly enhanced.

The Economics of Direct Advertising

The key to successful direct marketing is knowing what factors influence an individual's decision to buy your product through the medium you have selected. This is particularly true for direct mail and the telephone. How do you make a list tick for you? This is accomplished by defining the characteristics of individuals on a list, mailing (or otherwise communicating) a promotion piece to those individuals, and then reviewing the correlation between the various factors and the buy/no-buy outcome. Finding the best list to use for a promotion, then, involves testing lists and acquiring lists on the basis of test results.

The direct-response industry employs three primary lists in its marketing efforts:

1. *Internal house list*—This is the advertiser's own list of customers. It is obtained through internal compilation or buyer response.

2. *Direct-response list*—This is the list of persons who answered the direct-response offer of another advertiser. It is usually purchased from the firm or through a broker for a one-time-only promotion.

3. *Compiled list*—This list is obtained from public records (e.g., automobile registrations and birth certificates) and other public sources.

The primary objective in selecting a list to rent is to match the characteristics of the individuals on the list with a preselected consumer profile that is expected to be favorably disposed to purchasing. Essentially what is needed is a list of persons who purchase through direct media products that are identical or similar to your own or products which might connote an interest in yours. For example, each magazine has its own readership profile and demographic sketches that make it attractive to various advertisers. Someone who reads a magazine such as *Field and Stream* might purchase items in a related sports line. The more accurate the compiled profile or purchase history, the more likely will be your sale.

What Profiles Are Available?

To target sales, those utilizing lists are increasingly compiling demographic and psychographic information according to zip code and other factors. For example, certain firms are compiling information which will include data such as sex, age, income, marital status, number of children, profession, home ownership, travel history (when and where), and hobbies. It takes no great perception to see that certain credit card firms (perhaps most) could scan an individual's monthly bill and compile profiles on those who travel widely, consistently attend conventions, eat in luxury restaurants, and have other interests. Similar profiles of stay-at-homes exist; they include what stores these individuals shop in or the local restaurants they frequent. Then, of course, a purchase profile regarding goods and services is readily obtainable. The bottom line is that no one simply buys "names and addresses." Firms may purchase sales leads and information about an individual.

In addition, other firms employ zip code or census analysis with penetration analysis techniques to profile zip codes by racial or ethnic percentage, age grouping, income range, car ownership or other favored transportation, home ownership versus rentals, appliances used, amount of personal income spent on food at home or in restaurants, and so on. Such firms not only offer mailers a wide variety of zip code analysis and detailed demographic data on a selected target area but will arrange it all by individual sales category. This information gathering may be enhanced by the nine-digit zip code overlaid with block-level data. Block-level data has been upgraded and made more detailed as a result of the 1980 Census Bureau in-depth reporting.[3] Combining zip code analysis, census tract information, and other demographic data can highlight a buyer profile of your product. Even for lists which are not lucrative, such combined data can make segments of the list profitable. However, the reality is that the more information you retain, the more questions will be asked about the appropriateness of collecting that data. All marketers had best recognize this fact.

Finally, besides the issue of the sophisticated compilation of increasing amounts of data, the industry now has or soon will have the electronic technology which will make possible a day-to-day tracking of media results (particularly with regard to mail) as well as certain individuals (Qube has this potential).

The efforts of direct-mail marketers to more accurately target various markets have already raised the question of privacy rights. Direct mailers claim that lists are not a privacy issue, as they are just "names and addresses." To date, the industry has successfully followed the axiom that the ability to frame the question is the ability to obtain an answer within the frame. However, while the industry has to date been successful in framing the "names and addresses" question, its literature[4] and marketplace reality speak louder than words ("by their deeds ye shall know them"). There is, of course, nothing sinister or unethical in what is being done. However, let's address the issue for what it is. Names and addresses are in a phone book which is usually free. The sophisticated consumer profiles available for sale are expensive because they contain valuable information. The information enables a consumer to receive more personalized service and market choices. He or she should and does want this.

The Victories

No industry in the consumerist 1970s probably escaped so completely unscathed as direct-mail marketing. With some of the most adroit lobbying and educational efforts in history, the industry has focused the privacy debate onto the "names and addresses" argument and away from the increasing development of sophisticated lists. A review of the successes is presented here. This fortunate outcome (at least to date) has primarily been the result of successfully overcoming tort issues and constitutional arguments in the courts as well as stopping adverse legislation before enactment. The direct marketer can look upon these achievements with pride but must remain alert to the fact that as the industry evolves, the precedents may essentially dissolve and new arguments must be created.

Legal Issues

The consumerist constitutional argument was that by merging and purging varied lists, dossier-type data could be compiled on individuals. The list user's arguments against this were greatly assisted by a favorable U.S. Department of Health, Education, and Welfare (HEW) report[5] in 1973. This report found that the small-response factor for direct-marketing promotions negated the financial investment required to compile dossier-type data, while there is a financial incentive to update the accuracy of the information. However, it did distinguish the data retained by credit bureaus as being more sensitive.

A number of plaintiffs then cooperated to initiate actions against direct mail on a limited scope. In *Lamont v. Commissioner of Motor Vehicles*[6] the issue was confined to the privacy status of a public mailbox. In *Shibley v. Time Inc.*[7] the action for privacy was narrowly framed, as it was in another case, *White v. Mobile Oil Corporation,*[8] where the privacy claim was held inadequate as a matter of law.

Similarly, efforts to develop a cause of action as to unwarranted public disclosure (publicity) and appropriation floundered because of a lack of compelling harm.

The mailbox was found to be an essential device for culture, communication, and commerce. Mail is public by nature. It is a public service. There was no intrusion upon "selection or solitude."

1. There is no intrusive means employed. Mail is delivered at a reasonable time in the day.

2. No harassment is involved. The recipient may even elect to rent a box at the post office to avoid even the presence of a postal employee near or on his or her premises. If one lives in an apartment, the mail is delivered in the common-access routes (hallway or lobby), over which the tenant does not exercise a right of control or privacy.

3. There is no nuisance created by mail delivery. A person of ordinary sensibilities, tastes, and habits is not subject to actual physical discomfort.

In short, there is no adverse effect upon the integrity of one's personality, while there are different free speech and legitimate business interests served by permitted direct mail.

Public Relations

The Privacy Act of 1974[9] was a broad enactment of measures to protect from unwarranted disclosure individual records[10] held by federal agencies and offices and by departments of the executive branch, as well as by independent regulatory agencies and government-controlled corporations [as defined in 5 U.S.C. 551(1) and 552(e)]. The act further created the Privacy Protection Study Commission, which can recommend among other things, regulation for private records.

Of immediate alarm to the industry was the House Committee's version of the act, which would have required private organizations engaged in interstate commerce to delete names from mailing lists upon written request.[11] Not to be caught short, firms in the industry— individually and through the Direct Mail Marketing Association (DMMA)—went to work.

An effective education effort was undertaken by the Privacy Protection Study Commission, while simultaneously the DMMA established the Mail Preference Service, which enables a person to remove his or her name from the association's member list. (The list includes approximately 1200 DMMA members participating in the Mail Preference Service.) In a further move demonstrating both élan and savvy, the Mail Preference Service was advertised as a means to also get your name *on* a list. The form enables you to receive advertising mail from approximately 24 different categories of interest (for example, groceries, photography, and stamps). This at once demonstrated a public interest in favor of lists as well as the broad consumer interests served by lists. The numbers also supported the DMMA, as each year since the service was first promoted, the number requesting to be added on was approximately equal to the number requesting to be removed.[12]

Again (as in the courts), the Commission was made to focus on house lists (names and addresses) and the "mere recipient of mail" and not on the compiled lists. The Commission, after a lengthy study, reported to the President and Congress that unsolicited mail was at worst a nuisance but not something that trespasses upon personal privacy. It specifically recommended that legislation not be enacted to require the removal of an individual's name and address from a mailing list, although it did recommend a voluntary program.

The Commission's three final recommendations concerning mailing lists are found in the References.[13]

The Commission had to beg the issue to an extent (assuming that it intended to ignore the privacy concerns with regard to compiled lists). A mandatory system is unworkable.[14] How (and for how long) can a person be accommodated who wishes to be off certain lists? The Commission left the problem unanswered.

Finally, a number of states[15] and at the federal level, Congressman Green (R— 18th District, New York City) introduced legislation in this area. The latter's Section 201 of H.R. 14309 (1978) would have prohibited the sale, rental, or exchange of names for commercial purposes without the prior consent of the individual. Penalties were to be $1000 and/or 30 days in jail for each violation. The practical effect would have been to legislate the industry out of business (with immediate adverse financial effects on the U.S. Postal Service as well as the industry). Again, the industry was fortunate to be presented with overkill legislation rather than finely drafted legislation aimed at banning or limiting the compiled lists themselves.

Compliance for the 1980s—The Adverse Winds

For the immediate future, in-house and direct-response lists are virtually immune from successful court, regulatory, and legislative challenge. Lists can be so lucrative that certain firms operate at an upfront loss simply to create a lucrative list.[16]

The compiled list, however, raises the specter of 1984 to many authorities. Adding in the speed of electronics, the compilers have a profile of a *current* lifestyle, not mere names and addresses of business experience.[17] The real privacy issue raised by the sophisticated data accumulated in lists relates to their actual compilation and storage, not to their rental.[18] The issue for the 1980s may be for the industry to define what is "sensitive" information and to establish self-policing guidelines. Further, new legal defenses must be mustered.

The Mail Preference Service does not address itself to compiled lists or cross-transfers. While it is nice PR and many of its member firms have voluntarily followed the Privacy Study Commission's voluntary-removal recommendations, the DMMA cannot speak for all the individual direct marketers. Many nonprofit associations and fund-raising organizations are refusing to comply.[19] The Mail Preference Service cannot mitigate the compilation of dossier-type information from government records. Finally, even when there is success in removing a name, that success is temporary, for the name will be back on other lists after subsequent purchases.

Those who do not wish the industry well know there is little merit in court or legislative activity directly attacking the sale of names and addresses as a violation of privacy. Representative Green's (18th District, New York City) proposed bill (1978) effectively banning the sale of commercial lists will be the last frontal effort of this nature for a while. The organized constituency against such bills is too great, as Mr. Green has already discovered.

So why the concern? If those opposed to list rental have lost in the courts and legislatures, where do they go? Well, they're not going home. As stressed throughout, never read any chapter in this book in isolation. Even if you and I would disagree that the list area in itself is not a "hot" issue for the 1980s, remember our prior discussion on Qube and other interactive media. The issue of personal data accumulation may begin there and carry over to lists or vice versa. The modern marketer's ability as well as desire for this increased information makes it impossible for this issue to lie dormant. The industry won round one, but it may be losing round two, and this industry can't afford to lose any rounds!

In the 1980s the self-appointed consumerists will borrow a page from Liddell Hart and employ the indirect approach. They will assault the compiled list (i.e., those lists obtained from public records such as automobile and birth registrations and library lists). A win for the opposition here may produce the knockout blow!

Twenty-seven states tried to ban one or more forms of lists, primarily governmental, during the years 1980 to 1981. These lists are not important to you? A parochial attitude will only contribute to your opponent's strategy to slowly dry up the sources of all lists.

Nickel and Dimed to Death

Some bans can be effected for reasons which are beyond the control of the industry. That's what makes your position and the health of future list sales so nebulous beyond 1985. In 1980, Iowa banned the sale of library records which would identify reading habits. Why? Because of a case involving dead livestock found along the roadside. A theory was that the slayings were occult slayings. In the course of the FBI's investigation, an attempt was made to examine the library records to see who might be borrowing books on the occult. The state legislature sought to block information indicating the kind of material checked out by library patrons, and it succeeded![20]

In Arizona, a man made advances to a woman. Not an unusual occurrence! However, he obtained her license plate number, and a check with the vehicle registration office produced her name and address. He followed up on this information and murdered her. This led to legislative activity in Arizona which subsequently had a spillover effect in Texas.[21]

So you don't buy library lists or seek to obtain motor vehicle information. In fact, you don't buy any compiled lists. Well, chances are you do, but indirectly. Do you rent a list from *any source* using public sources? For example, if you rent from a firm which uses compiled lists, you are indirectly, though obviously, benefiting from such lists. If such lists are eliminated, there will be fewer private-sector list names available from varied sources which you currently take for granted.

Every list ban, no matter how innocuous to your immediate marketing effort, helps dry up the universe of names available. So, you are threatened because 27 states have sought to dry up private lists by eliminating access to compiled sources. Any legislative watcher can tell you that it's easier to amend an existing law than to enact a new one. Compiled-list bans on the statute books are potentially amendable, and even if they are never amended, they establish laws in place for adverse court precedents.

Cases to Be Aware of

Two cases on point have compiled-list triggers which, though not controlling, could carry enough weight to ban commercial lists in a worst-case scenario. For example, landmark cases (for list users and compilers) such as *Shibley v. Time Inc.*[22] have potentially fatal flaws. Norman W. Shibley sought to maintain a class action representing those aggrieved by publishers and credit card companies. The object was to prohibit such firms from selling or renting the lists of their subscribers. The claim was a dubious one, but some language of the court is relevant to the issue of compiled-list bans. I've quoted it at length and emphasized areas of particular interest.

> 1. *As defendants have pointed out,* plaintiff and intervenor should look for relief to the legislative branch. The General Assembly has acted in the area of sales of names and addresses to direct mail advertisers in two instances. *One concerns the sale by the state of Ohio of names and addresses of registrants of motor vehicles.* . . .
>
> . . .Ohio R.C. 4503.26 authorizes the sale of lists of names and addresses of registrants of motor vehicles. *In authorizing such sales the Legislature impliedly indicates that sales of lists of names and addresses are not an invasion of the right of privacy.* . . .
>
> 2. As was pointed out in the New York case, Lamont v. Commissioner of Motor Vehicles, such a statute is not subject to attack as being unconstitutional. . . .
>
> 3. Ohio House Bill No. 1056 introduced by Mr. P. Sweeney in January of this year to repeal R.C. 4503.26 *only affirms defendants' contention that the legislative branch should make decisions in this area.* . . .
>
> 4. Ours is a nation of laws and not of men. *This court happens to sympathize with the position of the plaintiffs,* but just as each citizen must obey the law as it exists, whether or not he agrees with it, *so must the court follow the law as it is* and not as the court would wish it to be. Therefore, since *the law as it now exists* prevents the plaintiff from succeeding, for the reasons stated above the court must find that *as the law now is* the plaintiff has failed to state a claim on which relief can be granted.[23]

To Recap

The court clearly favored the plaintiff's position, reflecting an overt bias against the free exchange of governmental lists. It was restrained from deciding in favor of Shibley, however, because of statutes previously enacted by the Ohio Legislature. The message of the decision was clear: Had the Ohio Legislature not previously authorized the sale of state lists (as the defendant, Time Inc., astutely pointed out), the court's decision might well have been different. Similarly, the Ohio Appellate Court in its opinion agreed with the lower court, again giving weight to legislative intent.

The court further pointed out that a bill was introduced to the Ohio General Assembly[24] to repeal the existing statute. Although the bill was not passed, it serves as a warning that existing laws *can* be overturned. (Other bills of similar import were introduced subsequently.) Certainly as times change, laws can and sometimes do change, often by means of the opposition's "whittling away" at an issue—a case here, an amendment there—until the legislature reflects such changes and overturns its previous decision.

Finally, the court cited Lamont as precedent. Here a noncompelling privacy claim was made in the days of long ago (1967) when privacy was not an issue on the front burner. The sale of motor vehicle records was at issue. In its decision, the court (as in Shibley) gave some weight to the state legislature. It also reviewed the laws of the 50 states:

> . . . reports its findings of provisions in every State except Kentucky making public records of vehicle registration information. The substantially uniform state practice *is not decisive,* but *it is another item of some weight* against plaintiff's constitutional theory.[25]

The "item of some weight" is shifting. Other states have joined Kentucky in restricting the use of motor vehicle registration information for commercial mailing lists.[26] (Many others are trying; just review any year's legislative calendar.) Some of the states where the shift is codified and you can expect problems in commercial use include Alaska, Arizona, Arkansas, Connecticut, Hawaii, Massachusetts, Missouri, Nevada, New Jersey, Ohio, Pennsylvania, South Dakota, Virginia, Washington, and Wyoming.

If the government-list bans are successful (and gradually they are being enacted):

1. Will not legislative intent (a weather vane of public opinion) be given great weight where a legislature overrules *prior* practice and bans government lists? Perhaps.

2. As more and more states ban the sale of varied government lists, will not the courts give the quantitative trend "some weight" in their decision to bar? Perhaps.

To review, in 1981 over 20 states sought to bar one or more elements which may be part of compiled lists. This trend will nickel and dime to death commercial lists as commercial list sources are dried up. The trend will set up laws subject to broader ban amendments. Finally, this trend, if allowed to go unchecked, might lead to court challenges overturning favorable precedents "on the books."

You should not assume that all the decisions "on the books" are favorable. Not all are. An interesting case employing the Freedom of Information Act[27] was presented when Wine Hobby USA, Inc.,[28] sought to obtain the names and addresses of all persons who were registered with the U.S. Bureau of Alcohol, Tobacco, and Firearms to produce wine for family use. The decision held that the disclosure of the names of potential customers for commercial business was not sufficient to overcome the purchaser's interest in his or her privacy.

> One consequence of this disclosure is that a registrant will be subject to *unsolicited and possible unwanted mail* from Wine Hobby and perhaps offensive mail from others.
>
> Moreover, information concerning *personal activities* within the home, namely wine-making, is revealed by disclosure. Similarly, disclosure reveals information concerning the *family status* of the registrant, including the fact that he is not living alone and that he exercised family control or responsibility in the household. *Disclosures of these facts concerning the home and private activities within it constitutes an "invasion of personal privacy."*[29] [Emphasis added.]

More ominous clouds for compiled lists and lists in general were presented in note 15 of the above case, where the court stated:

> That Society recognizes the *individual's interest in keeping his address private* is indicated in such practices as non-listing of tele-

phone numbers and the renting of post office boxes.[30] [Emphasis added.]

Finally, another admonition you probably don't want on the books is found in note 17:

> 17. Denial of the lists, moreover, *would impose no private hardship* as Wine Hobby may accomplish its stated purpose, advertising, through the general media *without specific mailings.*[31] [Emphasis added.]

The above precedent is not one that list users will care to quote. Further, when construing the act, courts follow a presumption in favor of disclosure. That presumption was overcome because of the "potential invasion of individual privacy" as a result of the sale of names and addresses.

Note 15 could be an example of how an unfavorable case can set a precedent adversely affecting the industry. The compiled list raises a privacy issue concerning the mailbox that has the potential for affecting the innocuous in-house and direct-response lists. In the 1980s, the compiled list will be assisted and also made *more visible* by the advent of the nine-digit zip code. A combination of this refined zip code and census bloc data will increase the sophistication of compiled lists as well as intrude into areas of privacy.

Finally, these decisions must be viewed against the broader picture. As discussed in preceding chapters, certain types of business lists are becoming highly regulated. A report based upon a firm's business experience with a particular individual is inherently reliable. So long as the information assembled is for the firm's own use, such assembling or evaluating cannot be considered the creation of a "consumer report." The firm may upon request distribute information about a particular individual for the purposes of a particular transaction. It may not disseminate names indiscriminately (e.g., in lists), or it will become a consumer reporting agency.[32]

A firm engaged in the limited exchange of name-and-address information must be careful not to homogenize (i.e., compile) its list with the lists of other firms (or the list of another firm). This is in the realm of sensitive information, as Congress recognized that a consumer's *address* is information bearing not only on creditworthiness but also on credit standing, credit capacity, general reputation, and mode of living. The type of neighborhood in which the consumer lives and the consumer's mental and social status are readily apparent.

The trend toward restricting this type of list information is apparent and should be noted by the industry, especially the large compilers and users of compiled information. We have seen how alert lists of consumers who allegedly passed bad checks are no longer permissible for commercial use. Which lists (if any) are to be banned in the 1980s? The decision is still yours.

To Summarize

As noted above, various factors may conspire to end the insulation of the list from sophisticated consumerist assault in the 1980s. The obvious reason is that the increasing sophistication of data assembly has changed the nature of the lists rented. They may well contain private information. This is not evil in itself (as some might allege) but a fact of the legal and legislative environment that will be addressed by opponents of list compilation, sale, or use. Remember, opponents of lists will have a ready ear with certain media already losing advertising dollars to direct mail and other direct-marketing media employing lists. They may escalate their self-serving crusade against "junk mail."[33] You must accept the following marketplace realities.

1. You can't market successfully in direct marketing—*in any medium*—without a quality list.

2. Public list sources affect your list whether you buy it directly or buy from someone who has already homogenized public-source names into his or her own list.

3. The increasing attempts to ban public lists at the state level might result in a precedent leading to a ban of many, if not all, lists by various courts.

4. If lists are banned, *You're Out Of Business.*

What Can You Do?

You basically have three choices. You can:

1. Act on your own

2. Do nothing

3. Join a concerted group effort[34]

Few firms can afford the time, talent, and general expense involved in choosing the first option beyond a narrow, selected area. As a practical matter, this isn't an option.

Sad to say, too many have elected the second option. You wait for the other person to carry his or her load as well as your own. This "let the other guy do it" attitude is a sad commentary on a marketing channel heavily endowed with the entrepreneurial spirit.

However, maybe you just don't know where to go to get involved or feel your gross profits are too small to make an effective contribution. Well, I'll tell you about two organizations to go to. If you don't contact them, you may have no gross profits left in a few years. (I stress gross profits, as a contribution to either group is a deductible expense.)

1. Call the Direct Mail Marketing Association at (202) 347-1222. Ask for information on GOAL and Freedom to Mail—groups interested in the education of state legislators before a problem and defeating bills which would have an adverse impact on the direct-marketing channel.

2. Call DeHart Associates, Inc., at (202) 659-4000. This group works with the DMMA in defeating list bans. It has particular expertise with regard to which counsel to select in a given state to protect a free distribution of lists. If you are already a DMMA member, it may be in your interest to investigate this group.

Now is a good time to get involved. The long-term effect of doing nothing will be a lot more costly than the incidental business cost of getting involved. Remember, it's your job and business future we're talking about.

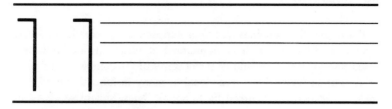

Conclusion

When it comes to government regulations, following a policy of noncompliance (either deliberately or through lack of knowledge) is a bit like playing Russian roulette. If you lose, the penalty can kill you! But at least if you know the rules of the game, the decision as to whether or not to abide by those rules is yours.

Before you make the decision to violate the rules, consider one posture that some business executives take which never ceases to amaze me. On occasion after receiving the advice of counsel, a marketer elects to make a "business decision" to violate the law. There is nothing in the law which insulates the "business decision" from legal sanction, just as there is no justification for a "business decision" to go through a red light in the company car. The marketer may subject both his or her firm and himself or herself to criminal (yes, criminal) as well as civil sanctions. Before electing to make a "business decision" which violates a law, the marketer should consult counsel with regard to both the law and the penalties imposed as a result of violating the law. The marketer should also consider the example he or she is setting by disregarding the law. This "spirit" may be contagious. Employees could make similar "business decisions" to abscond with property, be lax in performance, and otherwise disregard the law.

The marketer who decides not to play by the rules may individually be in an uncomfortable career situation when his or her company is penalized for regulatory noncompliance! As noted throughout the text of this guide, the penalties and fines imposed are generally based on a number of factors, such as the number of infractions involved, previous warnings, the size and financial status of the company, and public deception (even if not intentional in many instances). The $1.75 million civil penalty incurred by *Reader's Digest* should serve as an example and warning to all direct marketers who would rather avoid such punitive penalties. And the fines you read about don't tell the whole story! The greater hardship on a firm may involve not the fine but rather the counsel fees, adverse publicity, loss of goodwill, and special measures which may have to be taken to counteract the "harm" which results from the violation(s). A cogent example is the Book-of-the-Month-Club, which, upon allegedly violating a negative option regulation (shipping and handling disclosure), entered into a consent agreement requiring a settlement of $85,000. In addition, it had to advise all members involved that its advertising did not clearly disclose a material term of membership, and it had to inform those members who had joined under the ad that they would not be required to purchase any other books from the club. Add on to the $85,000, then, the legal costs, the value of the books, the cost of preparing the mailing, and the postage, not to mention the potential loss of members who feel (rightly or wrongly) that the book club will not deal fairly with them in the future, and you're talking about a staggering blow! It should be apparent that the cost in terms of both time and money of having to discontinue an ad or promotion which is not in compliance with federal or state regulations, even when no fine per se is involved, can be monumental. It's essential, therefore, not to dismiss lightly the myriad laws and regulations which affect the industry.

It is my hope that this guide will prove to be a useful tool for direct marketers who wish to protect their direct-marketing campaigns from fates such as these. As stated in the introduction, such a guide by no means precludes the need for legal counsel in most instances, but it should eliminate a great deal of confusion and allow the marketer to more confidently face this decade.

Before we depart, I'd appreciate any comments and opinions you have as to anything contained in this text. Address any correspondence to me in care of McGraw-Hill, or simply write directly to me at 242 Elsie Avenue, Merrick, N. Y. 11566. *All* correspondence will be answered. I look forward to hearing from you.

APPENDIX

USE OF NEGATIVE OPTION PLANS
BY SELLERS IN COMMERCE (Part 425 of Title 16, C.F.R.)

Introduction.

The Federal Trade Commission, pursuant to the Federal Trade Commission Act, as amended, 15 U.S.C. 41, et seq., and the provisions of Subpart B, Part 1 of the Commission's Procedures and Rules of Practice, 16 C.F.R. 1.11, et seq., has conducted a proceeding for the promulgation of a Trade Regulation Rule pertaining to the Use of Negative Option Plans by Sellers in Commerce.

The Commission has now considered all matters of fact, law, policy and discretion, including the data, views and arguments presented on the Record by interested parties in response to the notices, as prescribed by law, and has determined that the adoption of the Trade Regulation Rule and statement of its basis and purpose set forth herein* is in the public interest.

425.1 The Rule

(a) In connection with the sale, offering for sale, or distribution of goods and merchandise in commerce, as "commerce" is defined in the Federal Trade Commission Act, it is an unfair method of competition and an unfair or deceptive act or practice, for a seller in connection with the use of any negative option plan to fail to comply with the following requirements:

(1) Promotional material shall clearly and conspicuously disclose the material terms of the plan, including:

(i) that aspect of the plan under which the subscriber must notify the seller, in the manner provided for by the seller, if he does not wish to purchase the selection;

(ii) any obligation assumed by the subscriber to purchase a minimum quantity of merchandise;

(iii) the right of a contract-complete subscriber to cancel his membership at any time;

(iv) whether billing charges will include an amount for postage and handling;

(v) a disclosure indicating that the subscriber will be provided with at least ten (10) days in which to mail any form, contained in or accompanying an announcement identifying the selection, to the seller;

(vi) a disclosure that the seller will credit the return of any selections sent to a subscriber, and guarantee to the postal service or the subscriber postage to return such selections to the seller when the announcement and form are not received by the subscriber in time to afford him at least ten (10) days in which to mail his form to the seller;

(vii) the frequency with which the announcements and forms will be sent to the

*Statement of Basis and Purpose will be furnished upon request to the Federal Trade Commission, Washington, D.C. 20580.

subscriber, and the maximum number of announcements and forms which will be sent to him during a 12-month period.

(2) Prior to sending any selection, the seller shall mail to its subscribers, within the time specified by subparagraph (3) below:

(i) an announcement identifying the selection;

(ii) a form, contained in or accompanying the announcement, clearly and conspicuously disclosing that the subscriber will receive the selection identified in the announcement unless he instructs the seller that he does not want the selection, designating a procedure by which the form may be used for the purpose of enabling the subscriber so to instruct the seller, and specifying either the return date or the mailing date.

(3) The seller shall mail the announcement and form either at least twenty (20) days prior to the return date or at least fifteen (15) days prior to the mailing date, or provide a mailing date at least ten (10) days after receipt by the subscriber, provided, however, that whichever system the seller chooses for mailing the announcement and form, such system must provide the subscriber with at least ten (10) days in which to mail his form.

(b) In connection with the sale or distribution of goods and merchandise in commerce, as "commerce" is defined in the Federal Trade Commission Act, it shall constitute an unfair method of competition and an unfair or deceptive act or practice for a seller in connection with the use of any negative option plan to:

(1) refuse to credit, for the full invoiced amount thereof, the return of any selection sent to a subscriber, and to guarantee to the postal service or the subscriber postage adequate to return such selection to the seller, when:

(i) the selection is sent to a subscriber whose form indicating that he does not want to receive the selection was received by the seller by the return date or was mailed by the subscriber by the mailing date;

(ii) such form is received by the seller after the return date, but has been mailed by the subscriber and postmarked at least three days prior to the return date;

(iii) prior to the date of shipment of such selection, the seller has received from a contract-complete subscriber, a written notice of cancellation of membership adequately identifying the subscriber; however, this provision is applicable only to the first selection sent to a cancelling contract-complete subscriber after the seller has received written notice of cancellation. After the first selection shipment, all selection shipments thereafter are deemed to be unordered merchandise pursuant to Section 3009 of the Postal Reorganization Act of 1970, as adopted by the Federal Trade Commission in its Public Notice, dated September 11, 1970;

(iv) the announcement and form are not received by the subscriber in time to afford him at least ten (10) days in which to mail his form.

(2) Fail to notify a subscriber known by the seller to be within any of the circumstances set forth in subparagraphs (b)(1)(i) through (b)(1)(iv) above, that if the subscriber elects, the subscriber may return the selection with return postage guaranteed and receive a credit to his account.

(3) Refuse to ship within four weeks after receipt of an order merchandise due subscribers as introductory and bonus merchandise, unless the seller is unable to deliver the merchandise originally offered due to unanticipated circumstances beyond the seller's control and promptly makes a reasonably equivalent alternative offer. However, where the subscriber refuses to accept alternatively offered introductory merchandise, but instead insists upon termination of his membership due to the

seller's failure to provide the subscriber with his originally requested introductory merchandise, *or any portion thereof,* the seller must comply with the subscriber's request for cancellation of membership, provided the subscriber returns to the seller any introductory merchandise which already may have been sent him.

(4) Fail to terminate promptly the membership of a properly identified contract-complete subscriber upon his written request.

(5) Ship, without the express consent of the subscriber, substituted merchandise for that ordered by the subscriber.

(NOTE: The Commission is aware of the fact that many of the consumer complaints received during the course of the proceeding involve allegations of erroneous or unfair billing practices of a type which would be covered by its proposed trade regulation rule involving Billing Practices Arising Out of the Administration of Customer Accounts by Credit Card Issuers and Other Retail Establishments, which proceeding has been postponed indefinitely as a result of and for the reasons stated in the Commission's announcement dated January 7, 1971. In view of the fact that the problems encountered by users of the negative option system of merchandising are no different from those contemplated by the Billing Practices proceeding which was designed to be applicable to all sellers similarly situated, the Commission has not seen fit to include provisions governing such practices in this Rule, but would instead visualize that any subsequent rule or statute on the subject would be equally applicable to the members of this industry. In the meantime, abuses in this area will be dealt with on a case by case basis.)

(c) For the purposes of this Rule:

(1) "Negative option plan" refers to a contractual plan or arrangement under which a seller periodically sends to subscribers an announcement which identifies merchandise (other than annual supplements to previously acquired merchandise) it proposes to send to subscribers to such plan, and the subscribers thereafter receive and are billed for the merchandise identified in each such announcement, unless by a date or within a time specified by the seller with respect to each such announcement the subscribers, in conformity with the provisions of such plan, instruct the seller not to send the identified merchandise.

(2) "Subscriber" means any person who has agreed to receive the benefits of, and assume the obligations entailed in, membership in any negative option plan and whose membership in such negative option plan has been approved and accepted by the seller.

(3) "Contract-complete subscriber" refers to a subscriber who has purchased the minimum quantity of merchandise required by the terms of membership in a negative option plan.

(4) "Promotional material" refers to an advertisement containing or accompanying any device or material which a prospective subscriber sends to the seller to request acceptance or enrollment in a negative option plan.

(5) "Selection" refers to the merchandise identified by a seller under any negative option plan as the merchandise which the subscriber will receive and be billed for, unless by the date, or within the period, specified by the seller the subscriber instructs the seller not to send such merchandise.

(6) "Announcement" refers to any material sent by a seller using a negative option plan in which the selection is identified and offered to subscribers.

(7) "Form" refers to any form which the subscriber returns to the seller to instruct the seller not to send the selection.

(8) "Return date" refers to a date specified by a seller using a negative option plan as the date by which a form must be received by the seller to prevent shipment of the selection.

(9) "Mailing date" refers to the time specified by a seller using a negative option plan as the time by or within which a form must be mailed by a subscriber to prevent shipment of the selection.

Effective: June 7, 1974.
Promulgated: February 15, 1973.
By the Commission.

GAMES OF CHANCE IN THE FOOD RETAILING AND GASOLINE INDUSTRIES (Part 419 of Title 16, C.F.R.)

419.1 The Rule.

The Commission, on the basis of the findings made by it in this proceeding, as set forth in the accompanying Statement of Basis and Purpose, hereby promulgates as a Trade Regulation Rule its determination that in connection with the use of games of chance in the food retailing and gasoline industries, it constitutes an unfair and deceptive act or practice for users, promoters, or manufacturers of such games to:

(a) Engage in advertising or other promotions which misrepresent by any means, directly or indirectly, participants' chances of winning any prize.

(b) Engage in any advertising, including newspaper and broadcast media advertising, or other promotions such as store signs, window streamers, banners, or display materials, or issue any game piece if such game piece refers, on the exposed portion thereof, in any manner to prizes or their number or availability which fail to disclose clearly and conspicuously:

(1) The exact number of prizes in each category or denomination to be made available during the game program and the odds of winning each such prize made available; this disclosure, for prizes in the amount or value of $25 or more, to be revised each week a game extends beyond 30 days to reflect the number of such unredeemed prizes still available and the odds existing of winning each such unredeemed prize; and

(2) The geographic area covered by the game (e.g., "Nation-wide," "Washington, D.C. metropolitan area," etc.); and

(3) The total number of retail outlets participating in the game; and

(4) The scheduled termination date of the game.

(c) Fail to mix, distribute, and disperse all game pieces totally and solely on a random basis throughout the game program and throughout the geographic area covered by the game, and fail to maintain such records as are necessary to demonstrate to the Commission that total randomness was used in such mixing, distribution, and dispersal.

(d) Promote, sell, or use any game which is capable of or susceptible to being solved or "broken" so that winning game pieces or prizes are predetermined or preidentified by such methods rather than by random distribution to the participating public.

(e) Fail to post clearly and conspicuously at the conclusion of each game in each individual retail outlet which used the game:

(1) The names and addresses of all persons who redeemed a prize in the individual participating retail outlet, and the amount of value of each prize;

(2) The total number of game pieces distributed in all participating retail outlets;

(3) The total number of prizes in each category or denomination which were made available in all participating retail outlets; and

(4) The total number of prizes in each category or denomination which were awarded in all participating retail outlets.

The information required by subparagraphs (2), (3) and (4) of this paragraph (e), as well as a complete list of the names and addresses of winners of a game, is required to be retained in the records of the game promoter for a period of not less than three (3) years. Upon reasonable request, such information shall be made immediately available to the Commission and its staff for inspection.

(f) Promote or use any new game without a break in time between the new game and any game previously employed in the same retail establishment equivalent to the duration of the game previously employed, or 30 days, whichever is less.

(g) Terminate any game, regardless of the scheduled termination date, prior to the distribution of all game pieces to the participating public.

(h) Add additional winning game pieces during the course of a game, or in any manner replenish the prize structure of a game in progress.

(38 Stat. 717, as amended; 15 U.S.C. 41–58)

(34 FR 13302, Aug. 16, 1969, as amended at 45 FR 57380, 57383, Aug. 28, 1980.)

EFFECTIVE DATE NOTE: Paragraphs (e) and (f) in 419.1 were revised at 45 FR 57380–57383, Aug. 28, 1980. The Commission intends that these regulations become effective 30 days after the conclusion of congressional review. The Commission shall publish a notice of effective date in the FEDERAL REGISTER.

GUIDES AGAINST BAIT ADVERTISING (Part 238 of Title 16, C.F.R.)

SEC.
238.0   Bait advertising defined.
238.1   Bait advertisement.
238.2   Initial offer.
238.3   Discouragement of purchase of advertised merchandise.
238.4   Switch after sale.
AUTHORITY: Secs. 5, 6, 38 Stat. 719, as amended, 721; 15 U.S.C. 45, 46, unless otherwise noted.
SOURCE: 32 FR 15540, Nov. 8, 1967, unless otherwise noted.

238.0 Bait advertising defined.[1]

Bait advertising is an alluring but insincere offer to sell a product or service which the advertiser in truth does not intend or want to sell. Its purpose is to switch consumers from buying the advertised merchandise, in order to sell something else, usually at a higher price or on a basis more advantageous to the advertiser. The primary aim of a bait advertisement is to obtain leads as to persons interested in buying merchandise of the type so advertised.

238.1 Bait advertisement.

No advertisement containing an offer to sell a product should be published when the offer is not a bona fide effort to sell the advertised product. (Guide 1)

---

[1]For the purpose of this part "advertising" includes any form of public notice however disseminated or utilized.

238.2 Initial offer.

(a) No statement or illustration should be used in any advertisement which creates a false impression of the grade, quality, make, value, currency of model, size, color, usability, or origin of the product offered, or which may otherwise misrepresent the product in such a manner that later, on disclosure of the true facts, the purchaser may be switched from the advertised product to another.

(b) Even though the true facts are subsequently made known to the buyer, the law is violated if the first contact or interview is secured by deception. (Guide 2)

238.3 Discouragement of purchase of advertised merchandise.

No act or practice should be engaged in by an advertiser to discourage the purchase of the advertised merchandise as part of a bait scheme to sell other merchandise. Among acts or practices which will be considered in determining if an advertisement is a bona fide offer are:

(a) The refusal to show, demonstrate, or sell the product offered in accordance with the terms of the offer,

(b) The disparagement by acts or words of the advertised product or the disparagement of the guarantee, credit terms, availability of service, repairs or parts, or in any other respect, in connection with it,

(c) The failure to have available at all outlets listed in the advertisement a sufficient quantity of the advertised product to meet reasonably anticipated demands, unless the advertisement clearly and adequately discloses that supply is limited and/or the merchandise is available only at designated outlets,

(d) The refusal to take orders for the advertised merchandise to be delivered within a reasonable period of time,

(e) The showing or demonstrating of a product which is defective, unusable or impractical for the purpose represented or implied in the advertisement,

(f) Use of a sales plan or method of compensation for salesmen or penalizing salesmen, designed to prevent or discourage them from selling the advertised product. (Guide 3)

238.4 Switch after sale.

No practice should be pursued by an advertiser, in the event of sale of the advertised product, of "unselling" with the intent and purpose of selling other merchandise in its stead. Among acts or practices which will be considered in determining if the initial sale was in good faith, and not a strategem to sell other merchandise, are:

(a) Accepting a deposit for the advertised product, then switching the purchaser to a higher-priced product,

(b) Failure to make delivery of the advertised product within a reasonable time or to make a refund,

(c) Disparagement by acts or words of the advertised product, or the disparagement of the guarantee, credit terms, availability of service, repairs, or in any other respect, in connection with it,

(d) The delivery of the advertised product which is defective, unusable or impractical for the purpose represented or implied in the advertisement. (Guide 4)

NOTE: Sales of advertised merchandise. Sales of the advertised merchandise do not preclude the existence of a bait and switch scheme. It has been determined that, on occasions, this is a mere incidental byproduct of the fundamental plan and is intended to provide an aura of legitimacy to the overall operation.

GUIDES AGAINST DECEPTIVE PRICING (Part 233 of Title 16, C.F.R.)

SEC.
233.1 Former price comparisons.
233.2 Retail price comparisons; comparable value comparisons.
233.3 Advertising retail prices which have been established or suggested by
      manufacturers (or other nonretail distributors).
233.4 Bargain offers based upon the purchase of other merchandise.
233.5 Miscellaneous price comparisons.
AUTHORITY: Secs. 5, 6, 38 Stat. 719, as amended, 721: 15 U.S.C. 45, 46, unless
      otherwise noted.
SOURCE: 32 FR 15534, Nov. 8, 1967, unless otherwise noted.

233.1 Former price comparisons.

(a) One of the most commonly used forms of bargain advertising is to offer a reduction from the advertiser's own former price for an article. If the former price is the actual, bona fide price at which the article was offered to the public on a regular basis for a reasonably substantial period of time, it provides a legitimate basis for the advertising of a price comparison. Where the former price is genuine, the bargain being advertised is a true one. If, on the other hand, the former price being advertised is not bona fide but fictitious—for example, where an artificial, inflated price was established for the purpose of enabling the subsequent offer of a large reduction—the "bargain" being advertised is a false one; the purchaser is not receiving the unusual value he expects. In such a case, the "reduced" price is, in reality, probably just the seller's regular price.

(b) A former price is not necessarily fictitious merely because no sales at the advertised price were made. The advertiser should be especially careful, however, in such a case, that the price is one at which the product was openly and actively offered for sale, for a reasonably substantial period of time, in the recent, regular course of his business, honestly and in good faith—and, of course, not for the purpose of establishing a fictitious higher price on which a deceptive comparison might be based. And the advertiser should scrupulously avoid any implication that a former price is a selling, not an asking price (for example, by use of such language as, "Formerly sold at $---"), unless substantial sales at that price were actually made.

(c) The following is an example of a price comparison based on a fictitious former price. John Doe is a retailer of Brand X fountain pens, which cost him $5 each. His usual markup is 50 percent over cost; that is, his regular retail price is $7.50. In order subsequently to offer an unusual "bargain," Doe begins offering Brand X at $10 per pen. He realizes that he will be able to sell no, or very few, pens at this inflated price. But he doesn't care, for he maintains that price for only a few days. Then he "cuts" the price to its usual level—$7.50—and advertises: "Terrific Bargain: X Pens, Were $10, Now Only $7.50!" This is obviously a false claim. The advertised "bargain" is not genuine.

(d) Other illustrations of fictitious price comparisons could be given. An advertiser might use a price at which he never offered the article at all; he might feature a price which was not used in the regular course of business, or which was not used in the recent past but at some remote period in the past, without making disclosure of that fact; he might use a price that was not openly offered to the public, or that was not maintained for a reasonable length of time, but was immediately reduced.

(e) If the former price is set forth in the advertisement, whether accompanied or not by descriptive terminology such as "Regularly," "Usually," "Formerly," etc., the advertiser should make certain that the former price is not a fictitious one. If the former price, or the amount or percentage of reduction, is not stated in the advertisement, as when the ad merely states, "Sale," the advertiser must take care that the amount of reduction is not so insignificant as to be meaningless. It should be sufficiently large that the consumer, if he knew what it was, would believe that a genuine bargain or saving was being offered. An advertiser who claims that an item has been "Reduced to $9.99," when the former price was $10, is misleading the consumer, who will understand the claim to mean that a much greater, and not merely nominal, reduction was being offered. (Guide I)

233.2 Retail price comparisons; comparable value comparisons.

(a) Another commonly used form of bargain advertising is to offer goods at prices lower than those being charged by others for the same merchandise in the advertiser's trade area (the area in which he does business). This may be done either on a temporary or a permanent basis, but in either case the advertised higher price must be based upon fact, and not be fictitious or misleading. Whenever an advertiser represents that he is selling below the prices being charged in his area for a particular article, he should be reasonably certain that the higher price he advertises does not appreciably exceed the price at which substantial sales of the article are being made in the area—that is, a sufficient number of sales so that a consumer would consider a reduction from the price to represent a genuine bargain or saving. Expressed another way, if a number of the principal retail outlets in the area are regularly selling Brand X fountain pens at $10, it is not dishonest for retailer Doe to advertise: "Brand X Pens, Price Elsewhere $10, Our Price $7.50."

(b) The following example, however, illustrates a misleading use of this advertising technique. Retailer Doe advertises Brand X pens as having a "Retail Value $15.00, My Price $7.50," when the fact is that only a few small suburban outlets in the area charge $15. All of the larger outlets located in and around the main shopping areas charge $7.50, or slightly more or less. The advertisement here would be deceptive, since the price charged by the small suburban outlets would have no real significance to Doe's customers, to whom the advertisement of "Retail Value $15.00" would suggest a prevailing, and not merely an isolated and unrepresentative, price in the area in which they shop.

(c) A closely related form of bargain advertising is to offer a reduction from the prices being charged either by the advertiser or by others in the advertiser's trade area for other merchandise of like grade and quality—in other words, comparable or competing merchandise—to that being advertised. Such advertising can serve a useful and legitimate purpose when it is made clear to the consumer that a comparison is being made with other merchandise and the other merchandise is, in fact, of essentially similar quality and obtainable in the area. The advertiser should, however, be reasonably certain, just as in the case of comparisons involving the same merchandise, that the price advertised as being the price of comparable merchandise does not exceed the price at which such merchandise is being offered by representative retail outlets in the area. For example, retailer Doe advertises Brand X pen as having "Comparable Value $15.00." Unless a reasonable number of the principal outlets in the area are offering Brand Y, an essentially similar pen, for that price, this advertisement would be deceptive. (Guide II)

233.3 Advertising retail prices which have been established or suggested by manufacturers (or other nonretail distributors).

(a) Many members of the purchasing public believe that a manufacturer's list price, or suggested retail price, is the price at which an article is generally sold. Therefore, if a reduction from this price is advertised, many people will believe that they are being offered a genuine bargain. To the extent that list or suggested retail prices do not in fact correspond to prices at which a substantial number of sales of the article in question are made, the advertisement of a reduction may mislead the consumer.

(b) There are many methods by which manufacturers' suggested retail or list prices are advertised: large scale (often nationwide) mass-media advertising by the manufacturer himself; preticketing by the manufacturer; direct mail advertising; distribution of promotional material or price lists designed for display to the public. The mechanics used are not of the essence. This part is concerned with any means employed for placing such prices before the consuming public.

(c) There would be little problem of deception in this area if all products were invariably sold at the retail price set by the manufacturer. However, the widespread failure to observe manufacturers' suggested or list prices, and the advent of retail discounting on a wide scale, have seriously undermined the dependability of list prices as indicators of the exact prices at which articles are in fact generally sold at retail. Changing competitive conditions have created a more acute problem of deception than may have existed previously. Today, only in the rare case are all sales of an article at the manufacturer's suggested retail or list price.

(d) But this does not mean that all list prices are fictitious and all offers of reductions from list, therefore, deceptive. Typically, a list price is a price at which articles are sold, if not everywhere, than at least in the principal retail outlets which do not conduct their business on a discount basis. It will not be deemed fictitious if it is the price at which substantial (that is, not isolated or insignificant) sales are made in the advertiser's trade area (the area in which he does business). Conversely, if the list price is significantly in excess of the highest price at which substantial sales in the trade area are made, there is a clear and serious danger of the consumer being misled by an advertised reduction from this price.

(e) This general principle applies whether the advertiser is a national or regional manufacturer (or other non-retail distributor), a mail-order or catalog distributor who deals directly with the consuming public, or a local retailer. But certain differences in the responsibility of these various types of businessmen should be noted. A retailer competing in a local area has at least a general knowledge of the prices being charged in his area. Therefore, before advertising a manufacturer's list price as a basis for comparison with his own lower price, the retailer should ascertain whether the list price is in fact the price regularly charged by principal outlets in his area.

(f) In other words, a retailer who advertises a manufacturer's or distributor's suggested retail price should be careful to avoid creating a false impression that he is offering a reduction from the price at which the product is generally sold in his trade area. If a number of the principal retail outlets in the area are regularly engaged in making sales at the manufacturer's suggested price, that price may be used in advertising by one who is selling at a lower price. If, however, the list price is being followed only by, for example, small suburban stores, house-to-house canvassers, and credit houses, accounting for only an insubstantial volume of sales in the area, advertising of the list price would be deceptive.

(g) On the other hand, a manufacturer or other distributor who does business on a large regional or national scale cannot be required to police or investigate in detail the prevailing prices of his articles throughout so large a trade area. If he advertises or disseminates a list or preticketed price in good faith (i.e., as an honest estimate of the actual retail price) which does not appreciably exceed the highest price at which substantial sales are made in his trade area, he will not be chargeable with having engaged in a deceptive practice. Consider the following example:

(h) Manufacturer Roe, who makes Brand X pens and sells them throughout the United States, advertises his pen in a national magazine as having a "Suggested Retail Price $10," a price determined on the basis of a market survey. In a substantial number of representative communities, the principal retail outlets are selling the product at this price in the regular course of business and in substantial volume. Roe would not be considered to have advertised a fictitious "suggested retail price." If retailer Doe does business in one of these communities, he would not be guilty of a deceptive practice by advertising, "Brand X Pens, Manufacturer's Suggested Retail Price, $10, Our Price, $7.50."

(i) It bears repeating that the manufacturer, distributor or retailer must in every case act honestly and in good faith in advertising a list price, and not with the intention of establishing a basis, or creating an instrumentality, for deceptive comparison in any local or other trade area. For instance, a manufacturer may not affix price tickets containing inflated prices as an accommodation to particular retailers who intend to use such prices as the basis for advertising fictitious price reductions. (Guide III)

233.4 Bargain offers based upon the purchase of other merchandise.

(a) Frequently, advertisers choose to offer bargains in the form of additional merchandise to be given a customer on the condition that he purchase a particular article at the price usually offered by the advertiser. The forms which such offers may take are numerous and varied, yet all have essentially the same purpose and effect. Representative of the language frequently employed in such offers are "Free," "Buy One—Get One Free," "2-For-1 Sale," "Half Price Sale," "1¢ Sale," "50% Off," etc. Literally, of course, the seller is not offering anything "free" (i.e., an unconditional gift), or ½ free, or for only 1¢, when he makes such an offer, since the purchaser is required to purchase an article in order to receive the "free" or "1¢" item. It is important, therefore, that where such a form of offer is used, care be taken not to mislead the consumer.

(b) Where the seller, in making such an offer, increases his regular price of the article required to be bought, or decreases the quantity and quality of that article, or otherwise attaches strings (other than the basic condition that the article be purchased in order for the purchaser to be entitled to the "free" or "1¢" additional merchandise) to the offer, the consumer may be deceived.

(c) Accordingly, whenever a "free," "2-for-1," "half price sale," "1¢ sale," "50% off" or similar type of offer is made, all the terms and conditions of the offer should be made clear at the outset. (Guide IV)

233.5 Miscellaneous price comparisons.

The practices covered in the provisions set forth above represent the most frequently employed forms of bargain advertising. However, there are many variations which appear from time to time and which are, in the main, controlled by the same general principles. For example, retailers should not advertise a retail price as a "wholesale" price. They should not represent that they are selling at "factory" prices when they are not selling at the prices paid by those purchasing directly from the manufacturer. They should not offer seconds or imperfect or irregular merchandise at a reduced price without disclosing that the higher comparative price refers to the price of the merchandise if perfect. They should not offer an advance sale under circumstances where they do not in good faith expect to increase the price at a later date, or make a "limited" offer which, in fact, is not limited. In all of these situations, as well as in others too numerous to mention, advertisers should make certain that the bargain offer is genuine and truthful. Doing so will serve their own interest as well as that of the public. (Guide V)

GUIDES AGAINST DECEPTIVE ADVERTISING
OF GUARANTEES (Part 239 of Title 16, C.F.R.)

SEC.
239.0 Determining violations.
239.1 Guarantees in general.
239.2 Prorata adjustment of guarantees.
239.3 "Satisfaction or Your Money Back" representations.
239.4 Lifetime guarantees.
239.5 Savings guarantees.
239.6 Guarantees under which the guarantor does not or cannot perform.
239.7 Guarantee as a misrepresentation.
AUTHORITY: Secs. 5, 6, 38 Stat. 719, as amended, 721; 15 U.S.C. 45, 46, unless
             otherwise noted.
SOURCE: 32 FR 15541, Nov. 8, 1967, unless otherwise noted.

239.0 Determining violations.

In determining whether terminology and direct or implied representations concerning guarantees, however made, i.e., in advertising or otherwise, in connection with the sale or offering for sale of a product, may be in violation of the Federal Trade Commission Act, the following general principles will be used.

239.1 Guarantees in general.

In general, any guarantee in advertising shall clearly and conspicuously disclose—
(a) The nature and extent of the guarantee. This includes disclosure of—
(1) What product or part of the product is guaranteed,
(2) What characteristics or properties of the designated product or part thereof are covered by, or excluded from, the guarantee,
(3) What is the duration of the guarantee,
(4) What, if anything, any one claiming under the guarantee must do before the guarantor will fulfill his obligation under the guarantee, such as return of the product and payment of service or labor charges; and
(b) The manner in which the guarantor will perform. This consists primarily of a statement of exactly what the guarantor undertakes to do under the guarantee. Examples of this would be repair, replacement, refund. If the guarantor or the person receiving the guarantee has an option as to what may satisfy the guarantee this should be set out; and
(c) The identity of the guarantor. The identity of the guarantor should be clearly revealed in all advertising, as well as in any documents evidencing the guarantee. Confusion of purchasers often occurs when it is not clear whether the manufacturer or the retailer is the guarantor. (Guide 1)

239.2 Prorata adjustment of guarantees.

(a) Many guarantees are adjusted by the guarantor on a prorata basis. The advertising of these guarantees should clearly disclose this fact, the basis on which they will be prorated, e.g., the time for which the guaranteed product has been used, and the manner in which the guarantor will perform.

(b) If these guarantees are to be adjusted on the basis of a price other than that paid by the purchaser, this price should be clearly and conspicuously disclosed.

Example: "A" sells a tire with list price of $48 to "B" for $24, with a 12 months guarantee. After 6 months use the tire proves defective. If "A" adjusts on the basis of the price "B" paid, $24, "B" will only have to pay one-half of $24, or $12, for a new tire. If "A" instead adjusts on the basis of list price, "B" will owe one-half of $48, or $24, for a new tire. The guarantor would be required to disclose here the following: That this was a 12 months guarantee, that a list price of $48 would be used in the adjustment, that there would be an adjustment on the basis of the time that the tire was used, and that he would not pay the adjusted amount in cash, but would make an adjustment on a new tire.

NOTE: Guarantees which provide for an adjustment based on a fictitious list price should not be used even where adequate disclosure of the price used is made. (Guide 2)

239.3 "Satisfaction or Your Money Back" representations.

(a) "Satisfaction or Your Money Back," "10 Day Free Trial," or similar representations will be construed as a guarantee that the full purchase price will be refunded at the option of the purchaser.

(b) If this guarantee is subject to any conditions or limitations whatsoever, they shall be set forth as provided for in 239.1 of this part.

Example: A rose bush is advertised under the representation "Satisfaction or Your Money Back." The guarantor requires return of the product within 1 year of purchase date before he will make refund. These limitations, i.e., "return" and "time" shall be clearly and conspicuously disclosed in the ad. (Guide 3)

MAILING OF UNORDERED MERCHANDISE (Section 3009 of Title 39, U.S.C.)

(a) Except for (1) free samples clearly and conspicuously marked as such, and (2) merchandise mailed by a charitable organization soliciting contributions, the mailing of unordered merchandise or of communications prohibited by subsection (c) of this section constitutes an unfair method of competition and an unfair trade practice in violation of section 45(a)(1) of title 15 (of the United States Code).

(b) Any merchandise mailed in violation of subsection (a) of this section, or within the exceptions contained therein, may be treated as a gift by the recipient, who shall have the right to retain, use, discard, or dispose of it in any manner he sees fit without any obligation whatsoever to the sender. All such merchandise shall have attached to it a clear and conspicuous statement informing the recipient that he may treat the merchandise as a gift to him and has the right to retain, use, discard, or dispose of it in any manner he sees fit without any obligation whatsoever to the sender.

(c) No mailer of any merchandise mailed in violation of subsection (a) of this section, or within the exceptions contained therein, shall mail to any recipient of such merchandise a bill for such merchandise or any dunning communications.

(d) For the purposes of this section, "unordered merchandise" means merchandise mailed without the prior expressed request or consent of the recipient.

Pub.L. 91–375, Aug. 12, 1970, 84 Stat. 749. (Postal Reorganization Act.)

GUIDE CONCERNING USE OF THE WORD
"FREE" AND SIMILAR REPRESENTATIONS (Part 251 of Title 16, C.F.R.)

251.1 The guide.

(a) General. (1) The offer of "Free" merchandise or service is a promotional device frequently used to attract customers. Providing such merchandise or service with the purchase of some other article or service has often been found to be a useful and valuable marketing tool.

(2) Because the purchasing public continually searches for the best buy, and regards the offer of "Free" merchandise or service to be a special bargain, all such offers must be made with extreme care so as to avoid any possibility that consumers will be misled or deceived. Representative of the language frequently used in such offers are "Free," "Buy 1—Get 1 Free," "2-for-1 Sale," "50% off with purchase of Two," "1¢ Sale," etc.

(b) Meaning of "Free." (1) The public understands that, except in the case of introductory offers in connection with the sale of a product or service (See paragraph (f) of this section), an offer of "Free" merchandise or service is based upon a regular price for the merchandise or service which must be purchased by consumers in order to avail themselves of that which is represented to be "Free." In other words, when the purchaser is told that an article is "Free" to him if another article is purchased, the word "Free" indicates that he is paying nothing for that article and no more than the regular price for the other. Thus, a purchaser has a right to believe that the merchant will not directly and immediately recover, in whole or in part, the cost of the free merchandise or service by marking up the price of the article which must be purchased, by the substitution of inferior merchandise or service, or otherwise.

(2) The term "regular" when used with the term "price" means the price, in the same quantity, quality and with the same service, at which the seller or advertiser of the product or service has openly and actively sold the product or service in the geographic market or trade area in which he is making a "Free" or similar offer in the most recent and regular course of business, for a reasonably substantial period of time, i.e., a 30-day period. For consumer products or services which fluctuate in price, the "regular" price shall be lowest price at which any substantial sales were made during the aforesaid 30-day period. Except in the case of introductory offers, if no substantial sales were made, in fact, at the "regular" price, a "Free" or similar offer would not be proper.

(c) Disclosure of conditions. When making "Free" or similar offers all the terms, conditions and obligations upon which receipt and retention of the "Free" item are contingent should be set forth clearly and conspicuously at the outset of the offer so as to leave no reasonable probability that the terms of the offer might be misunderstood. Stated differently, all of the terms, conditions and obligations should appear in close conjunction with the offer of "Free" merchandise or service. For example, disclosure of the terms of the offer set forth in a footnote of an advertisement to which reference is made by an asterisk or other symbol placed next to the offer, is not regarded as making disclosure at the outset. However, mere notice of the existence of a "Free" offer on the main display panel of a label or package is not precluded provided that (1) the notice does not constitute an offer or identify the item being offered "Free," (2) the notice informs the customer of the location, elsewhere on the package or label, where the disclosure required by this section may be found, (3) no purchase or other such material affirmative act is required in order to discover the terms and conditions of the offer, and (4) the notice and the offer are not otherwise deceptive.

(d) Supplier's responsibilities. Nothing in this section should be construed as authorizing or condoning the illegal setting or policing of retail prices by a supplier. However, if the supplier knows, or should know, that a "Free" offer he is promoting is not being passed on by a reseller, or otherwise is being used by a reseller as an instrumentality for deception, it is improper for the supplier to continue to offer the product as promoted to such reseller. He should take appropriate steps to bring an end to the deception, including the withdrawal of the "Free" offer.

(e) Reseller's participation in supplier's offers. Prior to advertising a "Free" promotion, a supplier should offer the product as promoted to all competing resellers as provided for in the Commission's "Guides for Advertising Allowance and Other Merchandising Payments and Services." In advertising the "Free" promotion, the supplier should identify those areas in which the offer is not available if the advertising is likely to be seen in such areas, and should clearly state that it is available only through participating resellers, indicating the extent of participation by the use of such terms as "some," "all," "a majority," or "a few," as the case may be.

(f) Introductory offers. (1) No "Free" offer should be made in connection with the introduction of a new product or service offered for sale at a specified price unless the offeror expects, in good faith, to discontinue the offer after the limited time and to commence selling the product or service promoted, separately, at the same price at which it was promoted with a "Free" offer.

(2) In such offers, no representation may be made that the price is for one item and that the other is "Free" unless the offeror expects, in good faith, to discontinue the offer after a limited time and to commence selling the product or service promoted, separately, at the same price at which it was promoted with a "Free" offer.

(g) Negotiated sales. If a product or service usually is sold at a price arrived at through bargaining, rather than at a regular price, it is improper to represent that another product or service is being offered "Free" with the sale. The same representation is also improper where there may be a regular price, but where other material factors such as quantity, quality, or size are arrived at through bargaining.

(h) Frequency of offers. So that a "Free" offer will be special and meaningful, a single size of a product or a single kind of service should not be advertised with a "Free" offer in a trade area for more than 6 months in any 12-month period. At least 30 days should elaspe before another such offer is promoted in the same trade area. No more than three such offers should be made in the same area in any 12-month period. In such period, the offeror's sale in that area of the product in the size promoted with a "Free" offer should not exceed 50 percent of the total volume of his sales of the product, in the same size, in the area.

(1) Similar terms. Offers of "Free" merchandise or services which may be deceptive for failure to meet the provisions of this section may not be corrected by the substitution of such similar words and terms as "gift," "given without charge," "bonus," or other words or terms which tend to convey the impression to the consuming public that an article of merchandise or service is "Free."

MAIL ORDER MERCHANDISE (Part 435 of Title 16, C.F.R.)
Promulgation of Trade Regulation Rule

The Federal Trade Commission, pursuant to the Federal Trade Commission Act, as amended, 15 U.S.C. 41, et seq., and the provision of Subpart B, Part I of the Commission's Procedures and Rules of Practice, 16 CFR 1.11, et seq., has conducted a proceeding for the promulgation of a Trade Regulation Rule concerning Undelivered Mail Order Merchandise and Services. Notice of this proceeding, including a proposed Rule, was published in the FEDERAL REGISTER on September 28, 1971 (36 FR

19092 (1971). Interested parties were thereafter afforded opportunity to participate in the proceeding through the submission of written data, views and arguments, and to appear and express their views orally and to suggest amendments, revisions, and additions to the proposed Rule.

After it had considered the suggestions, criticisms, objections, and other pertinent information in the Record, the Commission on March 8, 1974, published a revised proposed rule in a notice in the FEDERAL REGISTER (39 FR 9201 (1974) extending an opportunity to interested parties to submit data, views or arguments regarding the revised proposal. Written comments of the Direct Mail/Marketing Association (DM/MA) were admitted into the Record at a subsequent date and the public was given 30 days to submit written views and comments related to the DM/MA submission (39 FR 40515 (1974).

The Commission has now considered all matters of fact, law, policy and discretion, including the data, views and arguments presented on the Record by interested parties in response to the Notices, as prescribed by law, and has determined that the adoption of the Trade Regulation Rule set forth herein and its Statement of Basis and Purpose[1] is in the public interest.

Accordingly, the Commission hereby amends Subchapter D, Trade Regulation Rules, Chapter I of 16 C.F.R. by adding a new Part 435 as follows:

Sec.

435.1 The Rule.

435.2 Definitions.

AUTHORITY   The provisions of this Part 435 issued under 38 Stat. 717, as amended, 15 U.S.C. 41, et seq.

435.1 The Rule.

In connection with mail order sales in commerce, as "commerce" is defined in the Federal Trade Commission Act, it constitutes an unfair method of competition, and an unfair or deceptive act and practice for a seller:

(a) (1) To solicit any order for the sale of merchandise to be ordered by the buyer through the mails unless, at the time of the solicitation, the seller has a reasonable basis to expect that he will be able to ship any ordered merchandise to the buyer: (i) within that time clearly and conspicuously stated in any such solicitation, or (ii) if no time is clearly and conspicuously stated, within thirty (30) days after receipt of a properly completed order from the buyer.

(2) To provide any buyer with any revised shipping date, as provided in paragraph (b), unless, at the time any such revised shipping date is provided, the seller has a reasonable basis for making such representation regarding a definite revised shipping date.

(3) To inform any buyer that he is unable to make any representation regarding the length of any delay unless (i) the seller has a reasonable basis for so informing the buyer and (ii) the seller informs the buyer of the reason or reasons for the delay.

(4) In any action brought by the Federal Trade Commission, alleging a violation of this part, the failure of a respondent-seller to have records or other documentary proof establishing his use of systems and procedures which assure the shipment of merchandise in the ordinary course of business within any applicable time set forth in this part will create a rebuttable presumption that the seller lacked a reasonable basis for an expectation of shipment within said applicable time.

---

[1]Statement of Basis and Purpose filed as part of the original document.

(b) (1) Where a seller is unable to ship merchandise within the applicable time set forth in paragraph (a)(1), above, to fail to offer to the buyer, clearly and conspicuously and without prior demand, an option either to consent to a delay in shipping or to cancel his order and receive a prompt refund. Said offer shall be made within a reasonable time after the seller first becomes aware of his inability to ship within the applicable time set forth in paragraph (a)(1), but in no event later than said applicable time.

(i) Any offer to the buyer of such an option shall fully inform the buyer regarding his right to cancel the order and to obtain a prompt refund and shall provide a definite revised shipping date, but where the seller lacks a reasonable basis for providing a definite revised shipping date the notice shall inform the buyer that the seller is unable to make any representation regarding the length of the delay.

(ii) Where the seller has provided a definite revised shipping date which is thirty (30) days or less later than the applicable time set forth in paragraph (a)(1), the offer of said option shall expressly inform the buyer that, unless the seller receives, prior to shipment and prior to the expiration of the definite revised shipping date, a response from the buyer rejecting the delay and cancelling the order, the buyer will be deemed to have consented to a delayed shipment on or before the definite revised shipping date.

(iii) Where the seller has provided a definite revised shipping date which is more than thirty (30) days later than the applicable time set forth in paragraph (a)(1) or where the seller is unable to provide a definite revised shipping date and therefore informs the buyer that he is unable to make any representation regarding the length of the delay, the offer of said option shall also expressly inform the buyer that his order will automatically be deemed to have been cancelled unless (A) the seller has shipped the merchandise within thirty (30) days of the applicable time set forth in paragraph (a)(1), and has received no cancellation prior to shipment, or (B) the seller has received from the buyer within thirty (30) days of said applicable time, a response specifically consenting to said shipping delay. Where the seller informs the buyer that he is unable to make any representation regarding the length of the delay, the buyer shall be expressly informed that, should he consent to an indefinite delay, he will have a continuing right to cancel his order at any time after the applicable time set forth in paragraph (a)(1) by so notifying the seller prior to actual shipment.

(iv) Nothing in this paragraph shall prohibit a seller who furnishes a definite revised shipping date pursuant to paragraph (b)(1)(i)above, from requesting, simultaneously with or at any time subsequent to the offer of an option pursuant to paragraph (b)(1), above, the buyer's express consent to a further unanticipated delay beyond the definite revised shipping date in the form of a response from the buyer specifically consenting to said further delay. *Provided, however,* That where the seller solicits consent to an unanticipated indefinite delay the solicitation shall expressly inform the buyer that, should he so consent to an indefinite delay, he shall have a continuing right to cancel his order at any time after the definite revised shipping date by so notifying the seller prior to actual shipment.

(2) Where a seller is unable to ship merchandise on or before the definite revised shipping date provided under paragraph (b)(1)(i) and consented to by the buyer pursuant to paragraph (b)(1)(ii) or (iii), to fail to offer to the buyer, clearly and conspicuously and without prior demand, a renewed option either to consent to a further delay or to cancel the order and to receive a prompt refund. Said offer shall be made within a reasonable time after the seller first becomes aware of his inability to ship before the said definite revised date, but in no event later than the expiration of the definite

revised shipping date. *Provided, however,* That where the seller previously has obtained the buyer's express consent to an unanticipated delay until a specific date beyond the definite revised shipping date, pursuant to paragraph (b)(1)(iv) or to a further delay until a specific date beyond the definite revised shipping date pursuant to this paragraph (b) (2), that date to which the buyer has expressly consented shall supersede the definite revised shipping date for purposes of this paragraph (b)(2).

(i) Any offer to the buyer of said renewed option shall provide the buyer with a new definite revised shipping date, but where the seller lacks a reasonable basis for providing a new definite revised shipping date, the notice shall inform the buyer that the seller is unable to make any representation regarding the length of the further delay.

(ii) The offer of a renewed option shall expressly inform the buyer that, unless the seller receives, prior to the expiration of the old definite revised shipping date or any date superseding the old definite revised shipping date, notification from the buyer specifically consenting to the further delay, the buyer will be deemed to have rejected any further delay, and to have cancelled the order if the seller is in fact unable to ship prior to the expiration of the old definite revised shipping date or any date superseding the old definite revised shipping date.

Provided, however, That where the seller offers the buyer the option to consent to an indefinite delay the offer shall expressly inform the buyer that, should he so consent to an indefinite delay, he shall have a continuing right to cancel his order at any time after the old definite revised shipping date or any date superseding the old definite revised shipping date.

(iii) This paragraph (b)(2) shall not apply to any situation where a seller pursuant to the provisions of paragraph (b)(1)(iv), has previously obtained consent from the buyer to an indefinite extension beyond the first revised shipping date.

(3) Wherever a buyer has the right to exercise any option under this part or to cancel an order by so notifying the seller prior to shipment, to fail to furnish the buyer with adequate means, at the seller's expense, to exercise such option or to notify the seller regarding cancellation. In any action brought by the Federal Trade Commission alleging a violation of this part, the failure of a respondent-seller:

(i) To provide any offer, notice or option required by this part in writing and by first class mail will create a rebuttable presumption that the respondent-seller failed to offer a clear and conspicuous offer, notice or option;

(ii) To provide the buyer with the means in writing (by business reply mail or with postage prepaid by the seller) to exercise any option or to notify the seller regarding a decision to cancel, will create a rebuttable presumption that the respondent-seller did not provide the buyer with adequate means pursuant to this subparagraph (3).

Nothing in paragraph (b) of this part shall prevent a seller, where he is unable to make shipment within the time set forth in paragraph (a)(1) or within a delay period consented to by the buyer, from deciding to consider the order cancelled and providing the buyer with notice of said decision within a reasonable time after he becomes aware of said inability to ship, together with a prompt refund.

(c) To fail to deem an order cancelled and to make a prompt refund to the buyer whenever:

(1) The seller receives, prior to the time of shipment, notification from the buyer cancelling the order pursuant to any option, renewed option or continuing option under this part;

(2) The seller has, pursuant to paragraph (b)(1)(iii), provided the buyer with a definite revised shipping date which is more than thirty (30) days later than the applicable time set forth in paragraph (a)(1) or has notified the buyer that he is unable to

make any representation regarding the length of the delay and the seller (i) has not shipped the merchandise within thirty (30) days of the applicable time set forth in paragraph (a)(1), and (ii) has not received the buyer's express consent to said shipping delay within said thirty (30) days;

(3) The seller is unable to ship within the applicable time set forth in paragraph (b)(2), and has not received, within the said applicable time, the buyer's consent to any further delay;

(4) The seller has notified the buyer of his inability to make shipment and has indicated his decision not to ship the merchandise;

(5) The seller fails to offer the option prescribed in paragraph (b)(1) and has not shipped the merchandise within the applicable time set forth in paragraph (a)(1).

(d) In any action brought by the Federal Trade Commission, alleging a violation of this part, the failure of a respondent-seller to have records or other documentary proof establishing his use of systems and procedures which assure compliance, in the ordinary course of business, with any requirement of paragraphs (b) or (c) of this part will create a rebuttable presumption that the seller failed to comply with said requirements.

NOTE 1: This part shall not apply to subscriptions, such as magazine sales, ordered for serial delivery, after the initial shipment is made in compliance with this part.

NOTE 2: This part shall not apply to orders of seeds and growing plants.

NOTE 3: This part shall not apply to orders made on a collect-on-delivery (C.O.D.) basis.

NOTE 4: This part shall not apply to transactions governed by the Federal Trade Commission's Trade Regulation Rule entitled "Use of Negative Option Plans by Sellers in Commerce," 16 C.F.R. 425.

NOTE 5: By taking action in this area, the Federal Trade Commission does not intend to preempt action in the same area, which is not inconsistent with this part, by any State, municipal, or other local government. This part does not annul or diminish any rights or remedies provided to consumers by any State law, municipal ordinance, or other local regulation, insofar as those rights or remedies are equal to or greater than those provided by this part. In addition, this part does not supersede those provisions of any State law, municipal ordinance, or other local regulation which impose obligations or liabilities upon sellers, when sellers subject to this part are not in compliance therewith. This part does supersede those provisions of any State law, municipal ordinance, or other local regulation which are inconsistent with this part to the extent that those provisions do not provide a buyer with rights which are equal to or greater than those rights granted a buyer by this part. This part also supersedes those provisions of any State law, municipal ordinance, or other local regulation requiring that a buyer be notified of a right which is the same as a right provided by this part but requiring that a buyer be given notice of this right in a language, form, or manner which is different in any way from that required by this part.

In those instances where any State law, municipal ordinance, or other local regulation contains provisions, some but not all of which are partially or completely superseded by this part, the provisions or portions of those provisions which have not been superseded retain their full force and effect.

NOTE 6: If any provision of this part or its application to any person, partnership, corporation, act or practice is held invalid, the remainder of this part or the application of the provision to any other person, partnership, corporation, act or practice shall not be affected thereby.

NOTE 7: Section 435.1(a)(1) of this part governs all solicitations where the time of solicitation is more than 100 days after promulgation of this part. The remainder of this part governs all transactions where receipt of a properly completed order occurs more than 100 days after promulgation of this part.

435.2 Definitions.

For purposes of this part:

(a) "Shipment" shall mean the act by which the merchandise is physically placed in the possession of the carrier.

(b) "Receipt of a properly completed order" shall mean:

(1) Where there is a credit sale and the buyer has not previously tendered partial payment, the time at which the seller charges the buyer's account;

(2) Where the buyer tenders full or partial payment in the proper amount in the form of cash, check or money order, the time at which the seller has received both said payment and an order from the buyer containing all the information needed by the seller to process and ship the order. *Provided, however,* That where the seller receives notice that the check or money order tendered by the buyer has been dishonored or that the buyer does not qualify for a credit sale, "receipt of a properly completed order" shall mean the time at which (i) the seller receives notice that a check or money order for the proper amount tendered by the buyer has been honored, (ii) the buyer tenders cash in the proper amount or (iii) the seller receives notice that the buyer qualified for a credit sale.

(c) "Refund" shall mean:

(1) Where the buyer tendered full payment for the unshipped merchandise in the form of cash, check or money order, a return of the amount tendered in the form of cash, check or money order;

(2) Where there is a credit sale:

(i) And the seller is a creditor, a copy of a credit memorandum or the like or an account statement reflecting the removal or absence of any remaining charge incurred as a result of the sale from the buyer's account;

(ii) And a third party is the creditor, a copy of an appropriate credit memorandum or the like to the third party creditor which will remove the charge from the buyer's account or a statement from the seller acknowledging the cancellation of the order and representing that he has not taken any action regarding the order which will result in a charge to the buyer's account with the third party;

(iii) And the buyer tendered partial payment for the unshipped merchandise in the form of cash, check or money order, a return of the amount tendered in the form of cash, check or money order.

(d) "Prompt refund" shall mean:

(1) Where a refund is made pursuant to Definition (c)(1) or (2)(iii) a refund sent to the buyer by first class mail within seven (7) working days of the date on which the buyer's right to refund vests under the provisions of this part;

(2) Where a refund is made pursuant to Definition (c)(2)(i) or (ii), a refund sent to the buyer by first class mail within one (1) billing cycle from the date on which the buyer's right to refund vests under the provisions of this part.

(e) The "time of solicitation" of an order shall mean that time when the seller has:

(1) Mailed or otherwise disseminated the solicitation to a prospective purchaser.

(2) Made arrangements for an advertisement containing the solicitation to appear in a newspaper, magazine or the like or on radio or television which cannot be changed or cancelled without incurring substantial expense, or

(3) Made arrangements for the printing of a catalog, brochure or the like which

cannot be changed without incurring substantial expense, in which the solicitation in question forms an insubstantial part.

GUIDES CONCERNING USE OF ENDORSEMENTS AND
TESTIMONIALS IN ADVERTISING (Part 255 of Title 16, C.F.R.)

SEC.
255.0 Definitions
255.1 General considerations
255.2 Consumer endorsements
255.3 Expert endorsements
255.4 Endorsements by organizations
255.5 Disclosure of material connections
AUTHORITY: 38 Stat. 717, as amended; 15 U.S.C. 41-58
SOURCE: 40 FR 22128, May 21, 1975; 45 FR 3870, January 18, 1980, unless otherwise noted.

255.0 Definitions.

(a) The Commission intends to treat endorsements and testimonials identically in the context of its enforcements of the Federal Trade Commission Act and for purposes of this part. The term "endorsements" is therefore generally used hereinafter to cover both terms and situations.

(b) For purposes of this part, an "endorsement" means any advertising message (including verbal statements, demonstrations, or depictions of the name, signature, likeness or other identifying personal characteristics of an individual or the name or seal of an organization) which message consumers are likely to believe reflects the opinions, beliefs, findings, or experience of a party other than the sponsoring advertiser. The party whose opinions, beliefs, findings, or experience the message appears to reflect will be called the endorser and may be an individual, group or institution.

(c) For purposes of this part, the term "product" includes any product, service, company or industry.

(d) For purposes of this part, an "expert" is an individual, group or institution possessing, as a result of experience, study or training, knowledge of a particular subject, which knowledge is superior to that generally acquired by ordinary individuals.

Example 1: A film critic's review of a movie is excerpted in an advertisement. When so used, the review meets the definition of an endorsement since it is viewed by readers as a statement of the critic's own opinions and not those of the film producer, distributor or exhibitor. Therefore, any alteration in or quotation from the text of the review which does not fairly reflect its substance would be a violation of the standards set by this part.

Example 2: A TV commercial depicts two women in a supermarket buying a laundry detergent. The women are not identified outside the context of the advertisement. One comments to the other how clean her brand makes her family's clothes, and the other then comments that she will try it because she has not been fully satisfied with her own brand. This obvious fictional dramatization of a real life situation would not be an endorsement.

Example 3: In an advertisement for a pain remedy, an announcer who is not familar to consumers except as a spokesman for the advertising drug company praises the drug's ability to deliver fast and lasting pain relief. He purports to speak, not on the basis of his own opinions, but rather in the place of and on behalf of the drug company. Such an advertisement would not be an endorsement.

Example 4: A manufacturer of automobile tires hires a well-known professional automobile racing driver to deliver its advertising message in television commercials.

In these commercials, the driver speaks of the smooth ride, strength, and long life of the tires. Even though the message is not expressly declared to be the personal opinion of the driver, it may nevertheless constitute an endorsement of the tires. Many consumers will recognize this individual as being primarily a racing driver and not merely a spokesman or announcer for the advertisement. Accordingly, they may well believe the driver would not speak for an automotive product unless he/she actually believed in what he/she was saying and had personal knowledge sufficient to form that belief. Hence they would think that the advertising message reflects the driver's personal views as well as those of the sponsoring advertiser. This attribution of the underlying views to the driver brings the advertisement within the definition of an endorsement for purposes of this art.

Example 5: A television advertisement for golf balls shows a prominent and well-recognized professional golfer hitting the golf balls. This would be an endorsement by the golfer even though he makes no verbal statement in the advertisement.

255.1 General considerations.

(a) Endorsements must always reflect the honest opinions, findings, beliefs, or experiences of the endorser. Furthermore, they may not contain any representations which would be deceptive, or could not be substantiated if made directly for the advertiser. (See Example 2 to Guide 3 (255.3) illustrating that a valid endorsement may constitute all or part of an advertiser's substantiation.)

(b) The endorsement message need not be phrased in the exact words of the endorser, unless the advertisement affirmatively so represents. However, the endorsement may neither be presented out of context nor reworded so as to distort in any way the endorser's opinion or experience with the product. An advertiser may use an endorsement of an expert or celebrity only as long as it has good reason to believe that the endorser continues to subscribe to the views presented. An advertiser may satisfy this obligation by securing the endorser's views at reasonable intervals where reasonableness will be determined by such facts as new information on the performance or effectiveness of the product, a material alteration in the product, changes in the performance of competitors' products, and the advertiser's contract commitments.

(c) In particular, where the advertisement represents that the endorser uses the endorsed product, then the endorser must have been a bona fide user of it at the time the endorsement was given. Additionally, the advertiser may continue to run the advertisement only so long as he has good reason to believe that the endorser remains a bona fide user of the product. (See 255.5 (b) regarding the "good reason to believe" requirement.)

Guide 1, Example 1: A building contractor states in an advertisement that he specifies the advertiser's exterior house paint because of its remarkable quick drying properties and its durability. This endorsement must comply with the pertinent requirements of Guide 3. Subsequently, the advertiser reformulates its paint to enable it to cover exterior surfaces with only one coat. Prior to continued use of the contractor's endorsement, the advertiser must contact the contractor in order to determine whether the contractor would continue to specify the paint and to subscribe to the views presented previously.

Example 2: A television advertisement portrays a woman seated at a desk on which rest five unmarked electric typewriters. An announcer says "We asked Mrs. X, an executive secretary for over ten years, to try these five unmarked typewriters and tell us which one she liked best."

The advertisement portrays the secretary typing on each machine, and then picking the advertiser's brand. The announcer asks her why, and Mrs. X gives her reasons.

Assuming that consumers would perceive this presentation as a "blind" test, this endorsement would probably not represent that Mrs. X actually uses the advertiser's machines in her work. In addition, the endorsement may also be required to meet the standards of Guide 3 on Expert Endorsements. (Guide 1)

255.2 Consumer endorsements.

(a) An advertisement employing an endorsement reflecting the experience of an individual or a group of consumers on a central or key attribute of the product or service will be interpreted as representing that the endorser's experience is representative of what consumers will generally achieve with the advertised product in actual, albeit variable, conditions of use. Therefore, unless the advertiser possesses and relies upon adequate substantiation for this representation, the advertisement should either clearly and conspicuously disclose the limited applicability of the endorser's experience to what consumers may generally expect to achieve. The Commission's position regarding the acceptance of disclaimers or disclosures is described in the preamble to these Guides published in the Federal Register on January 18, 1980.

(b) Advertisements presenting endorsements by what are represented, directly or by implication, to be "actual consumers" should utilize actual consumers, in both the audio and video or clearly and conspicuously disclose that the persons in such advertisements are not actual consumers of the advertised product.

(c) Claims concerning the efficacy of any drug or device as defined in the Federal Trade Commission Act, 15 U.S.C. 55, shall not be made in lay endorsements unless (a) the advertiser has adequate scientific substantiation for such claims and (b) the claims are not inconsistent with any determination that has been made by the Food and Drug Administration with respect to the drug or device that is the subject of the claim.

Guide 2, Example 1: An advertisement presents the endorsement of an owner of one of the advertiser's television sets. The consumer states that she has needed to take the set to the shop for repairs only one time during her 2-year period of ownership and the costs of servicing the set to date have been under $10.00. Unless the advertiser possesses and relied upon adequate substantiation for the implied claim that such performance reflects that which a significant proportion of consumers would be likely to experience, the advertiser should include a disclosure that either states clearly and conspicuously what the generally expectable performance would be or clearly and conspicuously informs consumers that the performance experienced by the endorser is not what they should expect to experience. The mere disclosure that "not all consumers will get this result" is insufficient because it can imply that while all consumers cannot expect the advertised results, a substantial number can expect them. (See the cross reference in Guide 2 (a) regarding the acceptability of disclaimers or disclosures.)

Example 2: An advertiser presents the results of a poll of consumers who have used the advertiser's cake mixes as well as their own recipes. The results purport to show that the majority believed that their families could not tell the difference between the advertised mix and their own cakes baked from scratch. Many of the consumers are actually pictured in the advertisement along with relevant, quoted portions of their statements endorsing the product. This use of the results of a poll or survey of consumers probably represents a promise to consumers that this is the typical result that ordinary customers can expect from the advertiser's cake mix.

Example 3: An advertisement purports to portray a "hidden camera" situation in a crowded cafeteria at breakfast time. A spokesperson for the advertiser asks a series of actual patrons of the cafeteria for their spontaneous, honest opinions of the advertiser's recently introduced breakfast cereal. Even though the words "hidden camera" are not displayed on the screen, and even though none of the actual patrons is specifically identified during the advertisement, the net impression conveyed to consumers may well be that these are actual customers, and not actors. If actors have been employed, this fact should be disclosed. (Guide 2)

255.3 Expert endorsements.

(a) Whenever an advertisement represents, directly or by implication, that the endorser is an expert with respect to the endorsement message, then the endorser's qualifications must in fact give him the expertise that he is represented as possessing with respect to the endorsement.

(b) While the expert may, in endorsing a product, take into account factors not within his expertise (e.g., matters of taste or price), his endorsement must be supported by an actual exercise of his expertise in evaluating product features or characteristics with respect to which he is expert and which are both relevant to an ordinary consumer's use of or experience with the product and also are available to the ordinary consumer. This evaluation must have included an examination or testing of the product at least as extensive as someone with the same degree of expertise would normally need to conduct in order to support the conclusions presented in the endorsement. Where, and to the extent that, the advertisement implies that the endorsement was based upon a comparison such comparison must have been included in his evaluation; and as a result of such comparison, he must have concluded that, with respect to those features on which he is expert and which are relevant and available to an ordinary consumer, the endorsed product is at least equal overall to the competitor's products. Moreover, where the net impression created by the endorsement is that the advertised product is superior to other products with respect to any such feature or features, then the expert must in fact have found such superiority.

Example 1: An endorsement of a particular automobile by one described as an "engineer" implies that the endorser's professional training and experience are such that he is well acquainted with the design and performance of automobiles. If the endorser's field is, for example, chemical engineering, the endorsement would be deceptive.

Example 2: A manufacturer of automobile parts advertises that its products are approved by the "American Institute of Science." From its very name, consumers would infer that the "American Institute of Science" is a bona fide independent testing organization with expertise in judging automobile parts and that, as such, it would not approve any automobile part without first testing its efficacy by means of valid scientific methods. Even if the American Institute of Science is such a bona fide expert testing organization, as consumers would expect, the endorsement may nevertheless be deceptive unless the Institute has conducted valid scientific tests of the advertised products and the test results support the endorsement message.

Example 3: A manufacturer of a non-prescription drug product represents that its product has been selected in preference to competing products by a large metropolitan hospital. The hospital has selected the product because the manufacturer, unlike its competitors, has packaged each dose of the product separately. This package form is not generally available to the public. Under the circumstances, the endorsement would be deceptive because the basis for the choice of the manufacturer's product, convenience of packaging, is neither relevant nor available to consumers.

Example 4: The president of a commercial "home cleaning service" states in a television advertisement that the service uses a particular brand of cleanser in its business. Since the cleaning service's professional success depends largely upon the performance of the cleansers it uses, consumers would expect the service to be expert with respect to judging cleansing ability, and not be satisfied using an inferior cleanser in its business when it knows of a better one available to it. Accordingly, the cleaning service's endorsement must at least conform to those consumer expectations. The service must, of course, actually use the endorsed cleanser. Additionally, on the basis of its expertise, it must have determined that the cleansing ability of the endorsed cleaner is at least equal (or superior, if such is the net impression conveyed by the advertisement) to that of competing products with which the service has had experience and which remain reasonably available to it. Since in this example, the cleaning service's president makes no mention that the endorsed cleanser was "chosen," "selected," or otherwise evaluated in side-by-side comparisons against its competitors, it is sufficient if the service has relied solely upon its accumulated experience in evaluating cleansers without having to have performed side-by-side or scientific comparisons.

Example 5: An association of professional athletes states in an advertisement that it has "selected" a particular brand of beverages as its "Official breakfast drink." As in Example 4, the association would be regarded as expert in the field of nutrition for purposes of this section, because consumers would expect to rely upon the selection of nutritious foods as part of its business needs. Consequently, the association's endorsement must be based upon an expert evaluation of the nutritional value of the endorsed beverage. Furthermore, unlike Example 4, the use of the words "selected" and "official" in this endorsement imply that it was given only after direct comparisons had been performed among competing brands. Hence, the advertisement would be deceptive unless the association has in fact performed such comparisons between the endorsed brand and its leading competitors in terms of nutritional criteria, and the results of such comparisons conform to the net impression created by the advertisement. (Guide 3)

255.4 Endorsement by organizations.

Endorsements by organizations, especially expert ones, are viewed as representing the judgment of a group whose collective experience exceeds that of any individual member, and whose judgments are generally free of the sort of subjective factors which vary from individual to individual. Therefore an organization's endorsement must be reached by a process sufficient to ensure that the endorsement fairly reflects the collective judgment of the organization. Moreover, if an organization is represented as being expert, then in conjunction with a proper exercise of its expertise in evaluating the product under 255.3 of this part (Expert endorsements), it must utilize an expert or experts recognized as such by the organization or standards previously adopted by the organization and suitable for judging the relevant merits of such products.

Example: A mattress seller advertises that its product is endorsed by a chiropractic association. Since the association would be regarded as expert with respect to judging mattresses, its endorsement must be supported by an expert evaluation by an expert or experts recognized as such by the organization, or by compliance with standards previously adopted by the organization and aimed at measuring the performance of mattresses in general and not designed with the particular attributes of the advertised mattress in mind. (See also 255.3, Example 5.) (Guide 4)

255.5 Disclosure of material connections.

When there exists a connection between the endorser and the seller of the advertised product which might materially affect the weight or credibility of the endorsement (i.e., the connection is not reasonably expected by the audience) such connection must be fully disclosed. An example of a connection that is ordinarily expected by viewers and need not be disclosed is the payment or promise of payment to an endorser who is an expert or well-known personality, as long as the advertiser does not represent that the endorsement was given without compensation. However, when the endorser is neither represented in the advertisement as an expert nor is known to a significant portion of the viewing public, then the advertiser should clearly and conspicuously disclose either the payment or promise of compensation prior to and in exchange for the endorsement or the fact that the endorser knew or had reasons to know or to believe that if the endorsement favors the advertised product some benefit, such as an appearance on TV, would be extended to the endorser.

Example 1: A drug company commissions research on its product by a well-known research organization. The drug company pays a substantial share of the expenses of the research project, but the test design is under the control of the research organization. A subsequent advertisement by the drug company mentions the research results as the "findings" of the well-known research organization. The advertiser's payment will not affect the weight or credibility of the endorsement.

Example 2: A film star endorses a particular food product. The endorsement regards only points of taste and individual preference. This endorsement must of course comply with Section 255.1; but even though the compensation paid the endorser is substantial, neither the fact nor the amount of compensation need to be revealed.

Example 3: An actual patron of a restaurant, who is neither known to the public nor presented as an expert, is shown seated at the counter. He is asked for his "spontaneous" opinion of a new food product served in the restaurant. Assume, first, that the advertiser had posted a sign on the door of the restaurant informing all who entered that day that patrons would be interviewed by the advertiser as part of its TV promotion of its new soy protein "steak." This notification would materially affect the weight or credibility of the patron's endorsement, and, therefore, viewers of the advertisement should be clearly and conspicuously informed of the circumstances under which the endorsement was obtained.

Assume, in the alternative, that the advertiser had not posted a sign on the door of the restaurant, but had informed all the interviewed customers of the "hidden camera" only after interviews were completed and the customers had no other reason to know or to believe that their response was being recorded for use in an advertisement. Even if patrons were also told that they would be paid for allowing the use of their opinions in advertising, these facts need not be disclosed. (Guide 5)

FAIR DEBT COLLECTION PRACTICES ACT (15 U.S.C. 1692 *et seq.*)

812. Furnishing certain deceptive forms.
813. Civil liability.
814. Administrative enforcement.
815. Reports to Congress by the Commission.
816. Relation to State laws.
817. Exemption of State regulation.
818. Effective date.

15 USC 1601 note.
801. Short title.

This title may be cited as the "Fair Debt Collection Practices Act."

15 USC 1692.
802. Findings and purpose.

(a) There is abundant evidence of the use of abusive, deceptive, and unfair debt collection practices by many debt collectors. Abusive debt collection practices contribute to the number of personal bankruptcies, to marital instability, to the loss of jobs, and to invasions of individual privacy.

(b) Existing laws and procedures for redressing these injuries are inadequate to protect consumers.

(c) Means other than misrepresentation or other abusive debt collection practices are available for the effective collection of debts.

(d) Abusive debt collection practices are carried on to a substantial extent in interstate commerce and through means and instrumentalities of such commerce. Even where abusive debt collection practices are purely intrastate in character, they nevertheless directly affect interstate commerce.

(e) It is the purpose of this title to eliminate abusive debt collection practices by debt collectors, to insure that those debt collectors who refrain from using abusive debt collection practices are not competitively disadvantaged, and to promote consistent State action to protect consumers against debt collection abuses.

15 USC 1692a.
803. Definitions.

As used in this title —

(1) The term "Commission" means the Federal Trade Commission.

(2) The term "communication" means the conveying of information regarding a debt directly or indirectly to any person through any medium.

(3) The term "consumer" means any natural person obligated or allegedly obligated to pay any debt.

(4) The term "creditor" means any person who offers or extends credit creating a debt or to whom a debt is owed, but such term does not include any person to the extent that he receives an assignment or transfer of a debt in default solely for the purpose of facilitating collection of such debt for another.

(5) The term "debt" means any obligation or alleged obligation of a consumer to pay money arising out of a transaction in which the money, property, insurance, or services which are the subject of the transaction are primarily for personal, family, or household purposes, whether or not such obligation has been reduced to judgment.

(6) The term "debt collector" means any person who uses any instrumentality of interstate commerce or the mails in any business the principal purpose of which is the collection of any debts, or who regularly collects or attempts to collect, directly or indirectly, debts owed or due or asserted to be owed or due another. Notwithstanding the exclusion provided by clause (G) of the last sentence of this paragraph, the term

includes any creditor other than his own which would indicate that a third person is collecting or attempting to collect such debts. For the purpose of section 808 (6), such term also includes any person who uses any instrumentality of interstate commerce or the mails in any business the principal purpose of which is the enforcement of security interests. The term does not include —

(A) any officer or employee of a creditor while, in the name of the creditor, collecting debts for such creditor;

(B) any person while acting as a debt collector for another person, both of whom are related by common ownership or affiliated by corporate control, if the person acting as a debt collector does so only for persons to whom it is so related or affiliated and if the principal business of such person is not the collection of debts;

(C) any officer or employee of the United States or any State to the extent that collecting or attempting to collect any debt is in the performance of his official duties;

(D) any person while serving or attempting to serve legal process on any other person in connection with the judicial enforcement of any debt;

(E) any nonprofit organization which, at the request of consumers, performs bona fide consumer credit counseling and assists consumers in the liquidation of their debts by receiving payments from such consumers and distributing such amounts to creditors;

(F) any attorney-at-law collecting a debt as an attorney on behalf of and in the name of a client; and

(G) any person collecting or attempting to collect any debt owed or due or asserted to be owed or due another to the extent such activity (i) is incidental to a bona fide fiduciary obligation or a bona fide escrow arrangement; (ii) concerns a debt which was originated by such person; (iii) concerns a debt which was not in default at the time it was obtained by such person; or (iv) concerns a debt obtained by such person as a secured party in a commercial credit transaction involving the creditor.

(7) The term "location information" means a consumer's place of abode and his telephone number at such place, or his place of employment.

(8) The term "State" means a State, territory, or possession of the United States, the District of Columbia, the Commonwealth of Puerto Rico, or any political subdivision of any of the foregoing.

15 USC 1692b.

804. Acquisition of location information.

Any debt collector communicating with any person other than the consumer for the purpose of acquiring location information about the consumer shall —

(1) identify himself, state that he is confirming or correcting location information concerning the consumer, and, only if expressly requested, identify his employer;

(2) not state that such consumer owes any debt;

(3) not communicate with any such person more than once unless requested to do so by such person or unless the debt collector reasonably believes that the earlier response of such person is erroneous or incomplete and that such person now has correct or complete location information;

(4) not communicate by post card;

(5) not use any language or symbol on any envelope or in the contents of any communication effected by the mails or telegram that indicates that the debt collector is in the debt collection business or that the communication relates to the collection of a debt; and

(6) after the debt collector knows the consumer is represented by an attorney with regard to the subject debt and has knowledge of, or can readily ascertain, such attor-

ney's name and address, not communicate with any person other than that attorney, unless the attorney fails to respond within a reasonable period of time to communication from the debt collector.

15 USC 1692c.
805. Communication in connection with debt collection.

(a) COMMUNICATION WITH THE CONSUMER GENERALLY — Without the prior consent to the consumer given directly to the debt collector or the express permission of a court of competent jurisdiction, a debt collector may not communicate with a consumer in connection with the collection of any debt —

(1) at any unusual time or place or a time or place known or which should be known to be inconvenient to the consumer. In the absence of knowledge of circumstances to the contrary, a debt collector shall assume that the convenient time for communicating with a consumer is after 8 o'clock antimeridian and before 9 o'clock postmeridian, local time at the consumer's location;

(2) if the debt collector knows the consumer is represented by an attorney with respect to such debt and has knowledge of, or can readily ascertain, such attorney's name and address, unless the attorney fails to respond within a reasonable period of time to a communication from the debt collector or unless the attorney consents to direct communication with the consumer; or

(3) at the consumer's place of employment if the debt collector knows or has reason to know that the consumer's employer prohibits the consumer from receiving such communication.

(b) COMMUNICATION WITH THIRD PARTIES — Except as provided in section 804, without the prior consent of the consumer given directly to the debt collector, or the express permission of a court of competent jurisdiction, or as reasonably necessary to effectuate a postjudgment judicial remedy, a debt collector may not communicate, in connection with the collection of any debt, with any person other than the consumer, his attorney, a consumer reporting agency if otherwise permitted by law, the creditor, the attorney of the creditor, or the attorney of the debt collector.

(c) CEASING COMMUNICATION — If a consumer notifies a debt collector in writing that the consumer refuses to pay a debt or that the consumer wishes the debt collector to cease further communication with the consumer; the debt collector shall not communicate further with the consumer with respect to such debt, except —

(1) to advise the consumer that the debt collector's further efforts are being terminated;

(2) to notify the consumer that the debt collector or creditor may invoke specified remedies which are ordinarily invoked by such debt collector or creditor; or

(3) where applicable, to notify the consumer that the debt collector or creditor intends to invoke a specified remedy.
If such notice from the consumer is made by mail, notification shall be complete upon receipt.

(d) For the purpose of this section, the term "consumer" includes the consumer's spouse, parent (if the consumer is a minor), guardian, executor, or administrator.

15 USC 1692d.
806. Harassment or abuse.

A debt collector may not engage in any conduct the natural consequence of which is to harass, oppress, or abuse any person in connection with the debt. Without limiting the general application of the foregoing, the following conduct is a violation of this section:

(1) The use or threat of use of violence or other criminal means to harm the physical person, reputation, or property of any person.

(2) The use of obscene or profane language or language the natural consequence of which is to abuse the hearer or reader.

(3) The publication of a list of consumers who allegedly refuse to pay debts, except to a consumer reporting agency or to persons meeting the requirements of section 603 (f) or 604 (3) of this Act.

(4) The advertisement of sale of any debt to coerce payment of the debt.

(5) Causing a telephone to ring or engaging any person in telephone conversation repeatedly or continuously with intent to annoy, abuse, or harass any person at the called number.

(6) Except as provided in section 804, the placement of telephone calls without meaningful disclosure of the caller's identity.

15 USC 1692e.
807. False or misleading representations.

A debt collector may not use any false, deceptive, or misleading representation or means in connection with the collection of any debt. Without limiting the general application of the foregoing, the following conduct is a violation of this section:

(1) The false representation or implication that the debt collector is vouched for, bonded by, or affiliated with the United States or any State, including the use of any badge, uniform, or facsimile thereof.

(2) The false representation of—

(A) the character, amount, or legal status of any debt; or

(B) any services rendered or compensation which may be lawfully received by any debt collector for the collection of a debt.

(3) The false representation or implication that any individual is an attorney or that any communication is from an attorney.

(4) The representation or implication that nonpayment of any debt will result in the arrest or imprisonment of any person or the seizure, garnishment, attachment, or sale of any property or wages of any person unless such action is lawful and the debt collector or creditor intends to take such action.

(5) The threat to take any action that cannot legally be taken or that is not intended to be taken.

(6) The false representation or implication that a sale, referral, or other transfer of any interest in a debt shall cause the consumer to—

(A) lose any claim or defense to payment of the debt; or

(B) become subject to any practice prohibited by this title.

(7) The false representation or implication that the consumer committed any crime or other conduct in order to disgrace the consumer.

(8) Communicating or threatening to communicate to any person credit information which is known or which should be known to be false, including the failure to communicate that a disputed debt is disputed.

(9) The use or distribution of any written communication which simulates or is falsely represented to be a document authorized, issued, or approved by any court, official, or agency of the United States or any State, or which creates a false impression as to its source, authorization, or approval.

(10) The use of any false representation or deceptive means to collect or attempt to collect any debt or to obtain information concerning a consumer.

(11) Except as otherwise provided for communications to acquire location information under section 804, the failure to disclose clearly in all communication made

to collect a debt or to obtain information about a consumer, that the debt collector is attempting to collect a debt and that any information obtained will be used for that purpose.

(12) The false representation or implication that accounts have been turned over to innocent purchasers for value.

(13) The false representation or implication that documents are legal process.

(14) The use of any business, company, or organization name other than the true name of the debt collector's business, company, or organization.

(15) The false representation or implication that documents are not legal process forms or do not require action by the consumer.

(16) The false representation or implication that a debt collector operates or is employed by a consumer reporting agency as defined by section 603 (f) of this Act.

15 USC 1681
15 USC 1692f.
808. Unfair practices.

A debt collector may not use unfair or unconscionable means to collect or attempt to collect any debt. Without limiting the general application of the foregoing, the following conduct is a violation of this section:

(1) The collection of any amount (including any interest, fee, charge, or expense incidental to the principal obligation) unless such amount is expressly authorized by the agreement creating the debt or permitted by law.

(2) The acceptance by a debt collector from any person of a check or other payment instrument postdated by more than five days unless such person is notified in writing of the debt collector's intent to deposit such check or instrument not more than ten nor less than three business days prior to such deposit.

(3) The solicitation by a debt collector of any postdated check or other postdated payment instrument for the purpose of threatening or instituting criminal prosecution.

(4) Depositing or threatening to deposit any postdated check or other postdated payment instrument prior to the date on such check or instrument.

(5) Causing charges to be made to any person for communications by concealment of the true purpose of the communication. Such charges include, but are not limited to, collect telephone calls and telegram fees.

(6) Taking or threatening to take any nonjudicial action to effect dispossession or disablement of property if—

(A) there is no present right to possession of the property claimed as collateral through an enforceable security interest;

(B) there is no present intention to take possession of the property; or

(C) the property is exempt by law from such dispossession or disablement.

(7) Communicating with a consumer regarding a debt by post card.

(8) Using any language or symbol, other than the debt collector's address, on any envelope when communicating with a consumer by use of the mails or by telegram, except that a debt collector may use his business name if such name does not indicate that he is in the debt collection business.

15 USC 1692g.
809. Validation of debts.

(a) Within five days after the initial communication with a consumer in connection with the collection of any debt, a debt collector shall, unless the following information is contained in the initial communication or the consumer has paid the debt, send the consumer a written notice containing—

(1) the amount of the debt;

(2) the name of the creditor to whom the debt is owed;

(3) a statement that unless the consumer, within thirty days after receipt of the notice, disputes the validity of the debt, or any portion thereof, the debt will be assumed to be valid by the debt collector;

(4) a statement that if the consumer notifies the debt collector in writing within the thirty-day period that the debt, or any portion thereof, is disputed, the debt collector will obtain verification of the debt or a copy of a judgment against the consumer and a copy of such verification or judgment will be mailed to the consumer by the debt collector; and

(5) a statement that, upon the consumer's written request within the thirty-day period, the debt collector will provide the consumer with the name and address of the original creditor, if different from the current creditor.

(b) If the consumer notifies the debt collector in writing within the thirty-day period described in subsection (a) that the debt, or any portion thereof, is disputed, or that the consumer requests the name and address of the original creditor, the debt collector shall cease collection of the debt, or any disputed portion thereof, until the debt collector obtains verification of the debt or a copy of a judgment, or the name and address of the original creditor, and a copy of such verification or judgment, or name and address of the original creditor, is mailed to the consumer by the debt collector.

(c) The failure of a consumer to dispute the validity of a debt under this section may not be construed by any court as an admission of liability by the consumer.

15 USC 1692h.

810. Multiple debts.

If any consumer owes multiple debts and makes any single payment to any debt collector with respect to such debts, such debt collector may not apply such payment to any debt which is disputed by the consumer and, where applicable, shall apply such payment in accordance with the consumer's directions.

15 USC 1692i.

811. Legal actions by debt collectors.

(a) Any debt collector who brings any legal action on a debt against any consumer shall —

(1) in the case of an action to enforce an interest in real property securing the consumer's obligation, bring such action only in a judicial district or similar legal entity in which such real property is located; or

(2) in the case of an action not described in paragraph (1), bring such action only in the judicial district or similar legal entity —

(A) in which such consumer signed the contract sued upon; or

(B) in which such consumer resides at the commencement of the action.

(b) Nothing in this title shall be construed to authorize the bringing of legal actions by debt collectors.

15 USC 1692j.

812. Furnishing certain deceptive forms.

(a) It is unlawful to design, compile, and furnish any form knowing that such form would be used to create the false belief in a consumer that a person other than the creditor of such consumer is participating in the collection of or in an attempt to collect a debt such consumer allegedly owes such creditor, when in fact such person is not so participating.

(b) Any person who violates this section shall be liable to the same extent and in the same manner as a debt collector is liable under section 813 for failure to comply with a provision of this title.

15 USC 1692k.

813. Civil liability.

(a) Except as otherwise provided by this section, any debt collector who fails to comply with any provision of this title with respect to any person is liable to such person in any amount equal to the sum of—

(1) any actual damage sustained by such person as a result of such failure;

(2) (A) in the case of any action by an individual, such additional damages as the court may allow, but not exceeding $1,000; or

(B) in the case of a class action, (i) such amount for each named plaintiff as could be recovered under subparagraph (A), and (ii) such amount as the court may allow for all other class members, without regard to a minimum individual recovery, not to exceed the lesser of $500,000 or 1 per centum of the net worth of the debt collector; and

(3) in the case of any successful action to enforce the foregoing liability, the costs of the action, together with a reasonable attorney's fee as determined by the court. On a finding by the court that an action under this section was brought in bad faith and for the purpose of harassment, the court may award to the defendant, attorney's fee reasonable in relation to the work expended and costs.

(b) In determining the amount of liability in any action under subsection (a), the court shall consider, among other relevant factors—

(1) in any individual action under subsection (a)(2)(A), the frequency and persistence of noncompliance by the debt collector, the nature of such noncompliance, and the extent to which such noncompliance was intentional; or

(2) in any class action under subsection (a)(2)(B), the frequency and persistence of noncompliance by the debt collector, the nature of such noncompliance, the resources of the debt collector, the number of persons adversely affected, and the extent to which the debt collector's noncompliance was intentional.

(c) A debt collector may not be held liable in any action brought under this title if the debt collector shows by a preponderance of evidence that the violation was not intentional and resulted from a bona fide error notwithstanding the maintenance of procedures reasonably adapted to avoid any such error.

(d) An action to enforce any liability created by this title may be brought in any appropriate United States district court without regard to the amount in controversy, or in any other court of competent jurisdiction, within one year from the date on which the violation occurs.

(e) No provision of this section imposing any liability shall apply to any act done or omitted in good faith in conformity with any advisory opinion of the Commission, notwithstanding that after such act or omission has occurred, such opinion is amended, rescinded, or determined by judicial or other authority to be invalid for any reason.

15 USC 1692l.   814. Administrative enforcement.

(a) Compliance with this title shall be enforced by the Commission, except to the extent that enforcement of the requirements imposed under this title is specifically committed to another agency under subsection (b). For purpose of the exercise by the

Commission of its functions and powers under the Federal Trade Commission Act, a violation of this title shall be deemed an unfair or deceptive act or practice in violation of that Act. All of the functions and powers of the Commission under the Federal Trade Commission Act are available to the Commission to enforce compliance by any person with this title, irrespective of whether that person is engaged in commerce or meets any other jurisdictional tests in the Federal Trade Commission Act, including the power to enforce the provisions of this title in the same manner as if the violation had been a violation of a Federal Trade Commission trade regulation rule.

15 USC 58. (b) Compliance with any requirements imposed under this title shall be enforced under—

12 USC 1818. (1) section 8 of the Federal Deposit Insurance Act, in the case of—

(A) national banks, by the Comptroller of the Currency;

(B) member banks of the Federal Reserve System (other than national banks), by the Federal Reserve Board; and

(C) banks the deposits or accounts of which are insured by the Federal Deposit Insurance Corporation (other than members of the Federal Reserve System), by the Board of Directors of the Federal Deposit Insurance Corporation;

12 USC 1464.
12 USC 1730.
12 USC 1426.
1437.
(2) section 5(d) of the Home Owners Loan Act of 1933, section 407 of the National Housing Act, and sections 6(i) and 17 of the Federal Home Loan Bank Act, by the Federal Home Loan Bank Board (acting directly or through the Federal Savings and Loan Insurance Corporation), in case of any institution subject to any of those provisions;

12 USC 1751. (3) the Federal Credit Union Act, by the Administrator of the National Credit Union Administration with respect to any Federal credit union;

(4) the Acts to regulate commerce, by the Interstate Commerce Commission with respect to any common carrier subject to that Act; and

49 USC 1301 note. (5) the Federal Aviation Act of 1958, by the Civil Aeronautics Board with respect to any air carrier or any foreign air carrier subject to that Act; and

7 USC 181.
7 USC 266–227.
(6) the Packers and Stockyards Act, 1921 (except as provided in section 406 of that Act), by the Secretary of Agriculture with respect to any activities subject to that Act.

(c) For the purpose of the exercise by any agency referred to in subsection (b) of its powers under any Act referred to in that subsection, a violation of any requirement imposed under this title shall be deemed to be a violation of a requirement imposed under that Act. In addition to its powers under any provision of law specifically referred to in subsection (b), each of the agencies referred to in that subsection may exercise, for the purpose of enforcing compliance with any requirement imposed under this title any other authority conferred on it by law, except as provided in subsection (d).

(d) Neither the Commission nor any other agency referred to in subsection (b) may promulgate trade regulation rules or other regulations with respect to the collection of debts by debt collectors as defined in this title.

15 USC 1692m.

815. Reports to Congress by the Commission.

(a) Not later than one year after the effective date of this title and at one-year intervals thereafter, the Commission shall make reports to the Congress concerning the administration of its functions under this title, including such recommendations as the Commission deems necessary or appropriate. In addition, each report of the Commission shall include its assessment of the extent to which compliance with this title is being achieved and a summary of the enforcement actions taken by the Commission under section 814 of this title.

(b) In the exercise of its functions under this title, the Commission may obtain upon request the views of any other Federal agency which exercises enforcement functions under section 814 of this title.

15 USC 1692n.

816. Relation to State laws.

This title does not annul, alter, or affect, or exempt any person subject to the provisions of this title from complying with the laws of any State with respect to debt collection practices, except to the extent that those laws are inconsistent with any provision of this title, and then only to the extent of the inconsistency. For purposes of this section, a State law is not inconsistent with this title if the protection such law affords any consumer is greater than the protection provided by this title.

15 USC 1692o.

817. Exemption for State regulation.

The Commission shall by regulation exempt from the requirements of this title any class of debt collection practices within any State if the Commission determines that under the law of that State that class of debt collection practices is subject to requirements substantially similar to those imposed by this title, and that there is adequate provision for enforcement.

15 USC 1692 note.

818. Effective date.

This title takes effect upon the expiration of six months after the date of its enactment, but section 809 shall apply only with respect to debts for which the initial attempt to collect occurs after such effective date.

Approved September 20, 1977.

LEGISLATIVE HISTORY:
HOUSE REPORT No. 95-131 (Comm. on Banking, Finance, and Urban Affairs).
SENATE REPORT No. 95-382 (Comm. on Banking, Housing, and Urban Affairs).
CONGRESSIONAL RECORD, Vol. 123 (1977):
    Apr. 4, considered and passed House.
    Aug. 5, considered and passed Senate, amended.
    Sept. 8, House agreed to Senate amendment.
WEEKLY COMPILATION OF PRESIDENTIAL DOCUMENTS, Vol. 13, No. 39:
    Sept. 20, Presidential statement.

References

Chapter 1. Introduction

[1]Throughout this book much reference will be made to Federal Trade Commission (FTC) decisions as well as to codified law and case law. Because of their precedent value, you should review these FTC decisions carefully.

Under Section 5(m) of the FTC Act, you and your firm are bound by any cease and desist order regardless of your firm's lack of involvement so long as you or your firm had *actual* knowledge that such act or practice was unfair *or* deceptive and is unlawful under Section 5(a)(1). Specifically, the FTC is authorized to commence a civil action in federal district court against any person, partner, and/or corporation which engages in an act or practice which the Commission has determined in a cease and desist proceeding to be unfair or deceptive and prohibited by the FTC's decision. A violation of any such order may result in a civil penalty of up to $10,000 as well as the FTC's monitoring and access to internal records in matters pertaining to the order. The practical effect is that cease and desist orders are elevated to the level of trade regulation rules once you have actual knowledge. In order to establish such actual knowledge, the FTC will send copies of the order to industry members who may be engaging in the prohibited practice.

This may not afford you or your firm sufficient time to change policy. A more efficient way to do this is to routinely monitor all orders through an internal profit preservation center (see Chapter 2). This will keep you up to date as to compliance as well as assist you in planning for trends coming "down the road."

At a minimum, get yourself on a mailing list, the FTC's. Request that your name be added by writing to the Federal Trade Commission's Press Office, Washington, D.C. 20580.

Chapter 2. Channel Compliance

[1]16 C.F.R. 435.1(a)(1).
See also Robert J. Posch, Jr., "Clouds on the Horizon," *Direct Marketing,*December 1981 pp. 84–87.

[2]Civil Action No. 11, N.J. District Court (1980).

[3]16 C.F.R. 435, n. 4. However, you should note that the Negative Option Rule requires delivery within 4 weeks of introductory or bonus merchandise ordered.

[4]16 C.F.R. 435, ns. 1, 2, and 3.

[5]New York State General Business Law 396(m).

[6]39 U.S.C.S. 3009. New York marketers might review the General Obligations Law, Article 5-332. See also Robert J. Posch, Jr., "Avoiding the Pitfalls of Unordered Merchandise," *Direct Marketing,* January 1982, pp. 98–101.

[7]FTC press release, May 24, 1979.

[8]The marketer should obtain the FTC pamphlet *Shopping by Mail* (government publication N-01-1) to review what information education the consumer is receiving as to these laws.

[9]39 U.S.C.S. 3009(d).

[10]For example, see New York State's General Obligations Law 396-m(e)(z)(i) and (ii).

[11]16 C.F.R. 425 ("Use of Negative Option Plans by Sellers in Commerce"). The FTC Rule is the model for the trade, but the state laws must be consulted (e.g., Kentucky has adopted the FTC Rule, while Hawaii at present is the only state to effectively *ban* the use of negative option plans).

[12]Verlon Industries, Inc., was fined $25,000 (concerning lack of disclosures by its Camera Arts Book Club) and had to comply with various notification requirements. Book-of-the-Month Club, Inc. (78 Civ. 4093) in its consent judgment was fined $85,000, and it incurred mailing costs and a potential loss of membership by agreeing to notify members who joined in response to the challenged ads that it would cancel the minimum-purchase obligations.
Conservative Book Club went through a similar ordeal. Its violations included (1) no notice of the 10-day right to cancel, (2) no indication of the advance announcement or how often it was sent, and (3) no indication that there would be an additional charge for shipping and handling.

[13](a) In the Matter of Alter & Co., 14 F.T.C. 232 (1930).
(b) In the Matter of Barnes, 15 F.T.C. 398 (1931).
(c) In the Matter of Falcon Camera Company, 22 F.T.C. 668 (1936).
(d) Bronzed Baby Shoe Co., 49 F.T.C. 1647 (1953).

(e) Another decision of interest was the more recent Bill Crouch Foreign Imports, Inc., Docket No. C-3030 (1980).

[14]Besides the FTC, many states and other organizations publish consumer information guides concerning these plans. Here are three examples:
- (a) The Minnesota attorney general's pamphlet *How to Complain About Negative Option Sellers*
- (b) The Pennsylvania Department of Justice's Bureau of Consumer Protection, *Be an Open-Eyed Consumer*—guideline no. 50 as to book and record clubs
- (c) Credit Card Service Corporation of Virginia's pamphlet *Negative Option Can Mislead Consumers*

[15]*Note:* Not all firms may recover under this act—only parties meeting size and financial restrictions may recover fees and expenses. Eligible parties include individuals whose net worth does not exceed $1 million and sole owners of unincorporated businesses, partnerships, corporations, and associations of public and private organizations whose net worth does not exceed $5 million. Finally, no business employing more than 500 employees may recover under the act regardless of net worth.

[16]DeHart Associates
1505 22d Street, N.W.
Washington, D.C. 20037
(202) 659-4000

The Martin Ryan Haley Companies
40 Central Park South
New York, N.Y. 10019
(212) 688-0771

Both these services will conduct full information, monitoring, issue analysis, and lobbying campaigns. If you wish to monitor solely for compliance and trends, both these firms are of assistance, as is Federal State Reports, 5203 Leesburg Pike, Suite 1201, Falls Church, Virginia 22041 [(703) 379-0222].

Finally, the obvious. Call the Direct Mail Marketing Association (DMMA) at (202) 347-1222, and ask for the director of government affairs. Ask how *you* can assist and be assisted by the association's many services to the direct marketers (mail, telephone, cable, and so on). Freedom to Mail and Legislator Education are just two worthy operations.

The above organizations are both known to me and personally recommended.

[17]16 C.F.R. 435.1(4) (1981).

[18]For example, New York State's General Business Law 396(m), Section 1(g).

Chapter 3. Comparative Pricing

[1]FTC Guides Against Deceptive Advertising of Guarantees, 16 C.F.R. 233.

[2]United States v. Home Centers, Inc., File No. 762, 3119, July 19, 1978.

[3]United States v. The Kroger Company, Docket No. 9102, June 1, 1979.

⁴*Id.,* p. 80.

⁵*Id.,* p. 75.

⁶*Id.,* p. 80.

⁷*Id.,* p. 76.

Also of note and interest to the marketer concerning the price comparison analysis:

    a. Firestone Tire & Rubber v. FTC, 481 F. 2d 246 (6th Cir. 1973), *cert. denied,* 414 U.S. 1112 (1973).

    b. FTC v. Sperry & Hutchinson Co., 405 U.S. 233 (1972).

    c. Jay Norris Corp. v. FTC (2d Cir. No. 78-4151, 1979).

    d. National Dynamics Corporation, 82 F.T.C. 488 (1973), *aff'd,* 492 F. 2d 1333 (2d Cir. 1974), *cert. denied,* 419 U.S. 993 (1974).

    e. Pfizer, Inc., 81 F.T.C. 23 (1972).

Chapter 4. Copy Headliners

¹Chapter I, Title 16, Part 233 of the Federal Trade Commission Guides Against Deceptive Pricing, 1980.

²See the recent language in Paragraph 5, page 3, of the FTC's complaint issue in *United States v. Keystone Readers' Service, Inc.* (1980). As to significant sales at a stated price, see In the Matter of Encyclopædia Brittanica, Inc., 87 F.T.C. 421, 425.

³City of New York, Department of Consumer Affairs, news release, Nov. 6, 1978.

⁴See FTC Advisory Opinions 120, 246, and 325.

⁵For example, see New Jersey P.R. 5684, especially Section 13:45 A-9.2(7) and (8).

⁶Chapter I, Title 16, Part 251, Section 251.1 of the FTC Guide Concerning Use of the Word "Free" and Similar Representations.

⁷*Id.,* Section 251.1(2)(i).

⁸For example, New York. See "Application of Ford Motor Co.," 99-9906, *New York Tax Reports,* Commerce Clearing House, Inc., 1977.

⁹The FTC has been very vigilant in this area. Some recent discussions of "free" may be found in the following:

    a. United States v. Allied Publishers' Service, Inc. [complaint—p. 13, Paragraph (c)].

    b. United States v. Budget Marketing, Inc. (consent decree), p. 6, Paragraph (c).

    c. In the Matter of Commercial Lighting Products, Inc. (Docket No. C-3018, Decision and Order), Section II, Paragraph 2.

d. See also In the Matter of Encyclopædia Brittanica, Inc., 87 F.T.C. 421, 425. This decision is a model of "what not to do" in many compliance areas.

[10]15 U.S.C. 2301 *et seq.,* 16 C.F.R. 701.

[11]16 C.F.R. 702.3(c)(i) and (ii). See also 16 C.F.R. 702 in general as to the Presale Availability of Written Warranty Terms as well as 16 C.F.R. 701 as to the Disclosure of Written Consumer Product Warranty Terms and Conditions.

[12]For example, a state law might require certain further disclosures, for example, whether the model is the most current.

[13]16 C.F.R. 702(d)(2). The reader would be well advised to write to the FTC for its excellent manual entitled *Warranties: Making Business Sense Out of Warranty Law.*

[14]*a.* California Civil Code 1793.1 and 1795.6 extend the warranty period by the number of days a product is out of the consumer's hands for repairs. Other disclosure requirements must be in 10-point boldface type.
   b. Two recent FTC decisions are "must" reading: United States v. Korvette's, Inc. (1979), Docket No.C-2987, and United States v. Montgomery Ward & Company, Inc. (1979), Docket No. 9117.

[15]Tennessee Acts (from H.B. 1554), Chapter 718 (1980).

[16]Interstate Brands Corp. v. Celestial Seasonings, 576 F.2d 926 (1978). Here, the presence of "red" in front of "zinger" distinguished the mark from any other "zingers."

[17]Du Pont Cellophane Co., Inc. v. Waxed Products Co., Inc., 85 F.2d 75 (2d Cir.), *cert. denied,* 299 U.S. 601 (1936).

[18]Bayer Co., Inc. v. United Drug Co., 272 F. 505 (S.D.N.Y. 1921).

[19]Interstate Brands Corp. v. Way Baking Company, 403 Mich. 479, 270 N.W. 2d 103 (1978). Intermittent periods of nonuse and reduced use do not constitute "abandonment" of a trademark.

[20]"Book-of-the-Month Loses Use of Name in Australia," *The New York Times,* July 18, 1974.
Any attorney or marketer interested in a general but informative short article on registration might review "When Should a Mark Be Registered?," by D. D. Evenson and R. L. Osborne, in *The Practical Lawyer,* Apr. 15, 1980.

Chapter 5. Key Specific Promotions

[1]See 16 C.F.R. 255.0, 255.3, 255.4. Note 255.0:
   "(a) The Commission intends to treat endorsements and testimonials identically in the context of its enforcement of the Federal Trade Commission Act and for

purposes of this part. The term 'endorsements' is therefore generally used here-inafter to cover both terms and situations."

This text will likewise use both terms interchangeably throughout.

[2]15 U.S.C. 45(a)(1) (1976). For a general discussion, see Millstein, "The Federal Trade Commission and False Advertising," appearing in *Symposium: The Fiftieth Anniversary of the FTC*, 67 Colum. L. Rev. 385, 439 (1964); *Symposium: Federal Trade Commission Regulation of Deceptive Advertising*, 17 Kansas L. Rev. 551 (1969); *Comment, False Advertising: The Expanding Presence of the FTC*, 25 Baylor L. Rev. 650 (1973). But see Thompson, *Government Regulation of Deceptive Advertising: Killing the Consumer in Order to "Save" Him*, 8 Antitrust Law & Economic Rev. 81 (1976).

[3]*In re* Pfizer, 81 F.T.C. 23 (1972).

Note: The deception need not deal with the substantive qualities of the product; any extrinsic fact that may influence the purchasing decision may be material. See FTC v. Colgate Palmolive Co., 380 U.S. 344, 386 (1965).

[4]Magnuson-Moss Warranty—FTC Improvement Act, 15 U.S.C. 45(a)(1) (1976). This effectively eliminated the uncertainty created by FTC v. Bunte Bros., Inc., 312 U.S. 349 (1941), which held that the "in commerce" language of the Wheeler-Lea Amendment was held to preclude FTC jurisdiction over completely intrastate activities.

[5]16 C.F.R. 255, 255.0(b)

"(b) For purposes of this part, an 'endorsement' means any advertising message (including verbal statements, demonstrations, or depictions of the name, signature, likeness or other identifying personal characteristics of an individual or the name or seal of an organization) which message consumers are likely to believe reflect the opinions, beliefs, findings, or experience of a party other than the sponsoring advertiser. The party whose opinions, beliefs, findings or experience the message appears to reflect will be called the endorser and may be an individual, group or institution."

[6]FTC, 16 C.F.R. 255, Promulgation of Final Guides Concerning Use of Endorsements and Testimonials in Advertising, M-5.

[7]Coogo Moogo, Inc., 3 Trade Reg. Rep. (CCH) 21, 417 (Consent Order 1978). See also "Let the Stellar Seller Beware," Pat Boone case, *Time*, vol. 111, no. 66, May 22, 1978.

[8]Guides Concerning Use of Endorsements and Testimonials in Advertising, 4 Trade Reg. Rep. (CCH) 39,038, 255.2(a) and (b) and as amended Jan. 18, 1980. (The amendments to the guides supplement the guides adopted by the FTC in 1975.)

[9]3 Trade Reg. Rep. (CCH) 21,380 (FTC, 1977).

[10]87 F.T.C. 756 (1976).

[11]82 F.T.C. 488 (1973), *modified in part*, 442 F.2d 1333 (2d Cir. 1974); *cert. denied*, 419 U.S. 993 (1974), *order modified*, 85 F.T.C. 404 (1975); *order further modified*, 85 F.T.C. 1952 (1975).

[12]16 C.F.R. 255.1. However, Section 255.5 (final guide 5) requires the advertiser to disclose any connection between the advertiser and the endorser that might materially affect the weight or credibility of the endorsement. Further, the payment of any compensation *should* be disclosed when the endorser is neither a celebrity nor an expert. Compensation would not include a minor consideration given in exchange for a release.

[13]Beatrice Foods [1970–1973 Transfer Binder] Trade Reg. Rep. (CCH) 20,107 (Consent Order 1972).

[14]In the Matter of Mattel and Topper, Inc. [1970–1973 Transfer Binder] Trade Reg. Rep. (CCH) 19,735 (Consent Orders 1971).

[15]Steiner, W.: "Producing & Selling Qualified Inquiries," *ZIP Magazine,* March 1981, p. 52.

[16]Blumenthal, Ralph: "Sweepstakes: Some Do Hit the Jackpot," *The New York Times,* July 25, 1979. See also "Will Promotion Sprees Backfire on Business?" *U.S. News & World Report,* July 21, 1980.

[17]Four reputable agencies to investigate for such assistance:

Weston Group, Inc.
44 Post Road West
Westport, Conn. 06880
(203) 226-6933

D. L. Blair Corporation
185 Great Neck Road
Great Neck, N.Y. 11021
(516) 487-9230

Ventura Associates, Inc.
200 Madison Avenue
New York, N.Y. 10016
(212) 689-0011

Marden-Kane, Inc.
666 Fifth Avenue
New York, N.Y. 10103
(212) 582-6600

[18]The body of law which should be studied by the marketer desiring an indepth knowledge of this area is as follows:

Mail fraud law	18 U.S.C. 1341
Fraud by wire, radio, TV	18 U.S.C. 1343
Federal Communications Act	47 U.S.C. 509
Federal Alcohol Administration Act	27 U.S.C. 205c
Federal Food, Drug, and Cosmetic Act	21 U.S.C. 342
Fair Packaging and Labeling Act	15 U.S.C. 1451
FTC guide on the use of the word "free"*	16 C.F.R. 251
Robinson-Patman Act	15 U.S.C. 13
FTC guides on advertising allowances	16 C.F.R. 240
FTC guide on deceptive pricing*	16 C.F.R. 233
Hazardous Substances Act	15 U.S.C. 1261
Consumer Product Safety Act	15 U.S.C. 2051
Federal bank regulations	12 C.F.R. 526

Note: As demonstrated above, the laws affecting this area are quite comprehensive. Do not be misguided into believing that the FTC rules will *only*

*Generally applicable to all promotions. The others will vary by reason of the nature of the product being promoted or the article being awarded as a prize.

apply to games of chance in the food retailing and gasoline industries. Voluntarily comply. The FTC has indicated that it expects other firms running similar promotions to carefully consider the guidelines. I confirmed this with Mr. James Sneed, Director of the FTC's Bureau of Consumer Protection, at a DMMA conference (April 1981). Between January 1970 and March 1977 the FTC was involved with nine cases involving sweepstakes:

D'Arcy Advertising Company, C-1898 (Apr. 12, 1971), 78 F.T.C. 616
McDonald's Corporation, C-1897 (Apr. 12, 1971), 78 F.T.C. 606
The Reuben H. Donnelley Corporation, C-2060 (Oct. 8, 1971), 79 F.T.C. 599
The Proctor & Gamble Company, C-2059 (Oct. 8, 1971), 79 F.T.C. 589
Reader's Digest Association, Inc., C-2075 (Nov. 2, 1971), 79 F.T.C. 696
Longines-Wittnauer, Inc., C-2138 (Dec. 21, 1971), 79 F.T.C. 964
Revere Chemical Corporation, C-2138 (Jan. 24, 1972), 80 F.T.C. 85
Lee Rogers d/b/a American Holiday Association, C-2312 (Nov. 1, 1972), 81 F.T.C. 738
The Coca-Cola Company, D-8824 (Oct. 26, 1976), 88 F.T.C. 656

Conclusion: If you follow the FTC guidelines, you'll avoid complaints from entrants and be within almost all provisions of state law. Compliance follows the old axiom of "do thy patient no harm."

[19]Consult 18 U.S.C. 8, pp. 15, 474, 475, 481, 489, 504.

[20]Formerly, Missouri did not recognize federal preemption of control over mailed offers (Missouri v. Reader's Digest Association, Inc., 527 S.W.2d 355). Subsequently, the people of the state endorsed sweepstakes promotions by popular referendum (1978). This was a demonstrative endorsement that people *want* these promotions and don't regard the mailings as "junk mail." Self-appointed consumer "representatives" should take note.

[21]A door-to-door seller offering a prize for listening to a sales presentation should consult North Carolina Chapter 806 6.5.75-33 (H.B. 1041). North Carolina has seen a lot of legislative activity in this area recently, and it should be closely monitored.

[22]Section 849.094(4)(a)—the Games Registration Law requires a 30-day advance registration of a sweepstakes promotion with the attorney general. Effective July 1, 1981, this was amended to permit the Department of Legal Affairs to waive the bond or trust account requirement for operators who have conducted game promotions in the state of Florida for not less than 5 *consecutive* years and who have stayed within the law during this period. Prior to 1967, Florida banned sweepstakes altogether.

[23]United States v. Reader's Digest Association, Inc., Civil Action No. 75-184, U.S.D.C. Delaware (July 2, 1980).

[24]*Id.*, p. 1.

[25]*Id.*, p. 15.

[26]*Id.*, pp. 2–3.

[27]An excellent article on point (his articles always are) is L. Brock, "Make Sure Your Direct Mail Is Believable," *Direct Marketing,* October 1980, pp. 208–209. The author stresses the need for believability and specifically discusses the checklike insert.

Chapter 6. Implications of the Credit Disclosure Laws for the Direct Marketer

[1]United States v. Montgomery Ward & Co. (D.D.C.), No. 79-140 (1979).

[2]*Id.,* p. 9, paragraph 15.

[3]Pub. L. No. 90-321 as amended. 12 C.F.R. 226; effective July 1, 1969, amended to April 1, 1981 (Regulation Z), 15 U.S.C. 1601 *et seq.*

[4]12 C.F.R. 226.1(c)(1).

[5]12 C.F.R. 226.2(a)(14).

[6]12 C.F.R. 226.2(a)(12).

[7]12 C.F.R. 226.1(c)(1) (iii).

[8]12 C.F.R. 226.4.

[9]12 C.F.R. 226.2(a)(3) and (17).

[10]12 C.F.R. 226.28, 226.29, and Appendixes A, B, and C.

[11]Annotated California Codes 1801.1 *et seq.* See 1802.6.

[12]Rogers Mortuary, Inc. v. White, 594 P.2d 351 (1979). See also 12 C.F.R. 226.4(c)(2).

[13]12 C.F.R. 17(iii).

[14]Chapman v. Miller, 575 S.W.2d 581 (1978), and Charles v. Krauss Co., 572 F.2d 544 (1978). For information as to what information the consumer may receive, contact the Director, Division of Consumer Affairs, Federal Reserve System, Washington, D.C. 20551, and ask for the pamphlet *How to File a Consumer Credit Complaint.*

[15]15 U.S.C. 1681 *et seq.* (1974).

[16]15 U.S.C. 1681(m). *Note:* There is a tighter law in California concerning notification (Civil Code 1785.10–1785.20). An agency must *automatically* advise a consumer of its obligation to provide a written disclosure for each consumer. This disclosure should be made each time the agency gives information to a client. The law further increases a consumer's access to his or her file, though I personally have privacy reservations because it permits a consumer to contact an agency by phone—a potentially improper way to gain access to confidential information about another individual.

[17]15 U.S.C. 1681(i).

[18]15 U.S.C. 1681(c).

[19]15 U.S.C. 1681(a)(a).

[20]15 U.S.C. 1681(a)(d).

[21]15 U.S.C. 1681(b).

[22]A number of states have sought to ban the use of any geographic or residential factors in credit evaluation. To date, none have passed laws affecting direct marketers. However, precedents abound—for example, Annotated Code of Maryland, Chapter 304, Commercial Article 12-503(b)(1) and 12-603, from House Bill 30, effective July 1, 1978. This law amended the retail credit accounts and retail installment laws to prohibit discrimination (solely in these types of transactions) in the granting of credit solely on the basis of the geographic area or neighborhood.

[23]See FTC informal staff opinions letters (Apr. 1, 1971; Apr. 15, 1971; and July 1971).

[24]15 U.S.C. 1681(a)(d)(A).

[25]*Hearings on S.B. 823 before the Subcommittee on Financial Institutions of the Senate Banking and Currency Committee,* 91st Cong., 1st Sess., 1969, p. 62.

[26]New York State General Business Law 380(j)(l)(f)(ii) from Assembly Bill 6051-A (effective Jan. 1, 1980).

[27]New York State General Business Law 380(z) from Assembly Bill 5619 (effective Sept. 1, 1981).

[28]In the Matter of Howard Enterprises, Inc., Docket No. 9096, June 12, 1979, overturning a Jan. 16, 1978, decision by FTC Administrative Judge Parker, 93 F.T.C. 901 (1979).

[29]*Id.,* p. 18.

[30]In the Matter of Hooper Holmes, Inc., Docket No. C-3020 (1980) (respondent furnished information concerning individuals other than those being investigated—an allegation which, if true, means that there was a clear violation of the Fair Credit Reporting Act), and *in re* Equifax, Docket No. 8954 (1981).

[31]15 U.S.C. 1871(a)(c).

[32]*In re* Hooper Holmes, Inc., FTC Docket No. C-3020 (1980).

[33]*Id.,* p. 2.

[34]12 C.F.R. 226.13, 15 U.S.C. 1601 *et seq.*

[35]12 C.F.R. 226.2(14).

[36]12 C.F.R. 226.2(17).

[37]12 C.F.R. 226.2(12).

[38]12 C.F.R. 226.2(20). "Open-end credit" means consumer credit.

[39]12 C.F.R. 226.2(15).

[40]12 C.F.R. 226.2(17)(i–v) and 226.12.

[41]For example, New York General Business Law §§ 701–707.

[42]12 C.F.R. 226.5, 226.6, 226.7, 226.8, and 226.9 should be reviewed.

[43]12 C.F.R. 226.13.

[44]12 C.F.R. 226.14(a)(1)(iii).

[45]15 U.S.C. 1691 *et seq.,* 12 C.F.R. 202 *et seq.*

[46]15 U.S.C. 1691(e)(a–c).

[47]15 U.S.C. 1691(d).

[48]12 C.F.R. 202.6(a) and note 16 above (as well as the legislative history of the act). The so-called effects test is derived from the decision of the U.S. Supreme Court rendered in Griggs v. Duke Power Company, 401 U.S. 424, 91 S. Ct. 849, 28 L. Ed. 2d 158 (1971). Here a high school diploma was required for employment—the effect being to exclude a significantly greater percentage of black applicants. The Supreme Court stated that Title VII (42 U.S.C. 2000 *et seq.*) not only proscribes intentionally discriminatory conduct but also looks to the consequences of conduct, whether the intent to discriminate is present or not. If the *effect* was also discriminatory, it became the employer's burden to show that the job requirement was related to job performance.
Note: Of all the credit statutes enforced by the FTC, the Equal Credit Opportunity Act is taken the most seriously and enforced the most vigorously precisely because of its civil rights background (e.g., with regard to the effects test and the clauses concerning credit rejection).

[49]Cherry v. Amoco Oil Co., 490 F. Supp. 1026 (1980).

[50]12 C.F.R. 202.3(d). This shall be read with 12 C.F.R. 202.3(a)(3).

[51]12 C.F.R. 202.3(a)(1) and (b).

[52]12 C.F.R. 202.3(a)(2) and (c).

[53]12 C.F.R. 202.3(a)(4) and (e).

[54]12 C.F.R. 202.3(a)(5) and (f).

[55]12 C.F.R. 202.3(a)(3) and (d).

[56]12 C.F.R. 202.3(h).

[57]12 C.F.R. 202.3(j).

[58]12 C.F.R. 202.3(e).

[59]12 C.F.R. 202.3(q).

[60]12 C.F.R. 226.2(17).

[61]12 C.F.R. 202.3(d) (1-8) after amendments.

[62]12 C.F.R. 202.4.

[63]12 C.F.R. 202.6(b)(4).

[64]Two good articles on point are N. Capon, "Discrimination in Screening Credit Applicants," *Harvard Business Review,* May-June 1978, and N. Capon, "Credit Ratings and Rights," *The Washington Post,* Dec. 17, 1977.

[65]12 C.F.R. 202.11 and 202.11(a).

[66]15 U.S.C. 1671(d), 12 C.F.R. 704(c).

[67]In the Matter of Aldens, Inc., 92 F.T.C. 901 (1978).

[68]No. C-1-78-730 (S.D. Ohio, Nov. 16, 1978).

[69]No. 79-1412 (D.D.C.).

[70]This area may be getting too farfetched. See "Credit Without Benefit of Clergy," *Consumer Credit and Truth-in-Lending Compliance Report,* vol. 10, no. 3, January 1979, p. 1. The article discusses an unofficial FRB ECOA staff interpretation possibly indicating that credit card issuers must give equal dignity to marriage and living-together arrangements.

[71]12 C.F.R. 202.11(a).

[72]For example, U.S. H.R. 8451 (banning credit discrimination on the basis of geographic location) and U.S. H.R. 8580 (both 1977). For related laws in this area, see California Civil Code, Chapter 1303, Section 51.8 (enacted 1980), and Section 14 of Act 224 of the Michigan Public Acts of 1966, Section 445.864.

[73]German, B.: "Using Zip Codes to Set Credit Applicants' Ratings," *Washington Star,* Nov. 1, 1979.

[74]United States v. Amoco Oil Company, Civ. No. 80-1071 (D.D.C. Apr. 29, 1980).

[75]In the Matter of Hooper Holmes, C-3020 (June 11, 1980).

[76]Sept. 17, 1980.

[77]Maryland H.B. 30, approved May 2, 1978, effective July 1, 1978, enacted in Chapter 304 of laws concerning retail credit accounts and retail

installment sales. For some interesting commentary, see "Legislator Wants Red-Lining Outlawed," *Wisconsin State Journal,* March 5, 1981.

Chapter 7. *Your Complete Guide to Dunning Compliance*

[1]Alabama, Arkansas, Connecticut, Massachusetts, Michigan, Nevada, Ohio, Oklahoma, Pennsylvania, South Carolina, and West Virginia.

[2]For example, Pennsylvania, whose law on point may be amended in 1982 or 1983.

[3]15 U.S.C. 1692 *et seq.*

[4]Regulation 10.1(4) of the New York City Consumer Protection Law provides for certain exclusions, but *not* the exclusion of in-house collectors. It became effective on February 27, 1979. Applies to creditors located *within* the 5 boroughs but protects consumers outside New York City.

[5]37 Pa. Code Chapter 303, Debt Collection Practices, adopted July 27, 1979. This regulation requires your outside agency to include the name, mailing address, and telephone number of the debt collector *and* the creditor.

[6]165 Ohio St. 35, 133 N.E.2d 340 (1956).
Note: Keep your eye on the FTC here. According to Section 815(a) of the Fair Debt Collection Practices Act, the FTC is required to submit an annual report as to the administration and enforcement of the act. The FTC is on record as seeking to include *all* creditors within the scope of the act. (See, e.g., the March 20, 1980, report to Congress, page 11.)

[7]Consumer Credit Counseling Services
National Foundation for Consumer Credit
1819 H Street, N.W.
Washington, D.C. 20006

[8]FTC News Summary
Federal Trade Commission
Washington, D.C. 20580
You can then call the general information number—(202) 523-3598—and order any cease and desist order from the FTC merely by indicating the firm name and docket number.

[9]Capax, Inc. 91 FTC 1048 (1978). A dunning letter series in compliance with Capax would more than pass muster with the FTC's enforcement of the Fair Debt Collection Practices Act. See also a prior consent order agreed to by United Computered Collections Inc., 87 F.T.C. 541, 542 (Docket No. CO2806, 1976). Here speedgrams were prohibited. It was noted that a speedgram "by its color and appearance, styling, printing and format simu-

lates a telegraphic message and . . . by virtue of said simulation, misleads the recipient as to its nature, import, purpose and urgency."

Finally, review Trans World Accounts, Inc. v. F.T.C., 594 F. Supp. 2d 212 (1979), for a more updated discussion of immediacy and urgency in communications.

[10]United States v. Universal Collection Bureau, Inc. (U.S.C.C. S.D.N.Y., 81 Civ. 575), complaint no. 793066, p. 4.

[11]United States v. Credit Rating Bureau, Inc. (U.S.D.C. E.D.N.Y., 81 Civ. 0303).

[12]United States v. Credit Assistance Programs, Inc. (1981). See Exhibit 1.

[13]165 Ohio St. 35, 133 N.E.2d 340 (1956). See also Carrigan v. Central Adjustment Bureau, Inc., 502 F. Supp. 468 (N.D. Ga. 1980). Increasingly, a debt collector must be alert as to tort issues such as invasion of privacy and the intentional infliction of emotional distress.

[14]The Fair Debt Collection Practices Act (Section 816) also allows for broader state laws regulating debt collection practices:

"This title does not annul, alter, or affect, or exempt any person subject to the provisions of this title from complying with the laws of any State with respect to debt collection practices, except to the extent that those laws are inconsistent with any provision of this title, and then only to the extent of the inconsistency. For purposes of this section, a State law is not inconsistent with this title if the protection such law affords any consumer is greater than the protection provided by this title."

[15]Article 56, Annotated Code of Maryland (licenses), Sections 329 B and 329 C.

[16]Connecticut Public Act 78-226 (from S.B. 186—1978), Section 2(b). See also Arizona Revised Statutes, Sections 32-1001 2(b) and 32-1021-32-1022.

[17]California Civil Code, Sections 1788.13 and 1788.16; California Business and Professions Codes 6871, 6886, 6915.4, 6902.5, and 6927 (from S.B. 1463—1980).

[18]If you wnat to see the type of advice that complicates a collector's job, see Jery Giles, *Moneylove*, M. Evans and Company, Inc., New York, 1978, p. 121, n. 4, as to his opinion of dunning efforts.

[19]*a*. Associated Dry Goods Corp., C-2674, 85 F.T.C. C-1096 (1975).
 b. Gimbel Brothers, Inc., C-2675, 85 F.T.C. 1102 (1975).
 c. McCrory Corporation, C-2676, 85 F.T.C. 1109 (1975).
 d. Carter Hawley Hale Stores, Inc., C-2677, 85 F.T.C. 1116 (1975).
 e. Carte Blanche Corporation, C-2870, 89 F.T.C. 305 (1977).
 f. Federated Department Stores, Inc., C-2880, 89 F.T.C. 313 (1977).
 g. Atlantic Richfield Company, C-2882, 89 F.T.C. 330 (1977).

h. Genesco Inc., D-9019, 89 F.T.C. 451 (1977).

i. *In re* Hertz Corporation, D-2945, 92 F.T.C. 980 (1978). See also 12 C.F.R. 266.11.

Chapter 8. The Future Is Now

[1]*The Third Wave* is an interesting book by Alvin Toffler that discusses postindustrial society and the possible social trauma posed if his thesis is correct. It was published in 1980 by William Morrow and Company, Inc., and should be read by anyone interested in the future of literally anything! *Mediacracy,* by Kevin P. Phillips, is the best book you can read on where the postindustrial voter is headed. You guessed it — Reagan. Since the political climate may be the key marketing variable in the United States, *read this book.* It was published by Doubleday & Company, Inc., in 1975, but don't let the date throw you — it's the political book of prophecy for this decade.

[2]Congress's legislation aimed at providing consumer protection for electronic funds transfer will increase public acceptance. See The Financial Institutions Regulatory and Interest Rate Control Act of 1978, 15 U.S.C. § 1692 (also known as the Electronic Fund Transfer Act).

[3]An excellent book for the professional in this area is *Telephone Marketing: How to Build Your Business by Telephone,* by Murray Roman (McGraw-Hill Book Company, New York, 1976).

[4]The marketer should know that the DMMA opposes taping and states so clearly in its Guidelines for Telephone Marketing and Article 37 of its Guidelines for Ethical Business Practices. See also Robert J. Posch, Jr., "Can You Monitor Your Employees' Telephone Performance," *Direct Marketing,* November 1981.

Finally, counsel should review applicable state *and* municipal law. Many states specifically permit it (with qualifications) — for example, Chapter 67, Title 18, Idaho Code; see Section 18-6701(4)(a).

[5]James v. Newspaper Agency Corporation, 591 F.2d 579 (1979). Here the telephone company installed telephone monitoring equipment on phones in the defendant's departments dealing with the general public. The purpose of the monitoring was to allow supervisory personnel to give employees more training in making business calls and also to protect employees from abusive calls. The exception to the definition of "electronic, mechanical or other device" found in 18 U.S.C.S. 2510(5) applied.

[6]The following are discussions on point:

a. Commonwealth v. Look, 402 N.E.2d 470 (1980).

b. Cox v. State, 263 S.E.2d 238 (1979).

c. State v. Hanley, 605 P.2d 1087 (1979).

d. Warden v. Kahn, 160 California Reporter 471 (1979).

[7]State v. Harpel, 493 F.2d 346 (10th Cir. 1974).
Note: The DMMA's Suggested Guidelines for Marketing by Telephone (1978) take a strong position against taping. See Guidelines for Outgoing Telephone Calls, Paragraph 2.

[8]The FTC publishes this every 3 months, and it is available by calling the Public Reference Branch at (202) 523-3598 or writing to the Public Reference Branch, Room 130, Federal Trade Commission, Washington, D.C. 20580.

[9]Title 16, Part 238 (1981).

[10]A few examples include:
  a. Lou Cottin, "Junk Calls Leave Us on the Hook," *Newsday,* Oct. 23, 1978, p. 2A. This biased article stressed harm done to senior citizens without any discussion of how older citizens can benefit (e.g., access to products, employment).
  b. Eisenberg and Orwin, "And Now, Junk Mail by Telephone," *The Washington Post,* Aug. 16, 1977 (reprinted from *Newsday*).
  c. "Foes of Junk Calls Go Into Action," *U.S. News & World Report,* Mar. 27, 1978, p. 67.
  d. WCBS Radio (June 29–30, 1978)—editorial at six intervals condemning "junk phone calls." Interesting how the media argue for free speech for themselves but manage to overcome such concerns through fear of the loss of advertising revenue.

[11]FCC Report No. 13862, Mar. 16, 1978. Eventually the FCC received a grand total of 4500 informal comments during the entire period of the inquiry.

[12]FCC Docket No. 78-100; RM 2955; FCC 80-235 citing page 37740 of the *Federal Register,* vol. 45, no. 109, June 4, 1980.
  "Under the present circumstances our jurisdiction is limited to regulation of interstate unsolicited telephone calls which appear to constitute approximately three percent of all unsolicited calls. Interstate use of the automatic dialer recorded message player also appears to be very limited at present. A general ban on telephone solicitation would raise serious constitutional difficulties, affect only the small percentage of calls which are interstate, and is questionable as a matter of policy. A ban on calls to subscribers who have indicated that they do not want to be called or time, place and manner restrictions at the Federal level are not warranted because of the small percentage of calls affected, the incentives for industry self-regulation, the present tariff language prohibiting abusive solicitation, the difficulty of effective enforcement and the cost of regulation."
Note: The FTC ended its own inquiry into telephone calls as of April 1, 1980. Various states began to follow the lead of the two federal commissions. For example, the Texas Public Utilities Commission ceased its review in June 1981.

[13]See Proposed PUC Report of Administrative Law Judge John C. Gilman.

[14]*Comments of the Federal Trade Commission on Unsolicited Telephone Calls,* RM 2955 (May 31, 1978).

[15]Title 16, Part 429 (1981).

[16]Laws of Alaska, Section 45.50.472(a), (b), and (c) (effective 1978).

[17]Annotated California Codes, Chapter 10, Public Utilities Code, Article 2871-2875.

[18]Colorado Revised Statutes, Title 18, Article 9, Part 3 (effective 1979).

[19]Florida Statutes Annotated, Section 365.165 (effective 1978).

[20]Annotated Code of Maryland, Section 55c, Article 78 (effective July 1979).

[21]Michigan Compiled Laws Annotated, Article 445.111(a) (effective 1980).

[22]Revised Statutes of Nebraska, Section 87-302 (effective 1979).

[23]North Carolina General Statutes, Section 75-30, Chapter 75, Section 1, Article 1 (effective 1979).
Note: See also Chapter 14 of the General Statutes, Section 14/401-.12, which makes it unlawful for professional solicitors to solicit charitable contributions by telephone (effective 1981).

[24]Code of Virginia, Article 6, "Unlawful Use of Telephone," Section 18.2-425.1.

[25]Virginia Telephone Solicitation Ethics Council
P.O. Box 10111
Richmond, Va. 23240

[26]Wisconsin Statutes Annotated, Regulation of Trade, Section 134.72.

[27]See note 15. Noncompliance can be painful. For example, see United States v. Atlantic Industries, Inc. (U.S.D.C.—Southern District of Florida), Civil Action No. 73-956 SMA (1979). Here a firm was forced to refund $40,000 and acknowledge its deception in each customer refund letter. Further, the firm had to pay a $10,000 fine.

[28]Arizona Revised Statutes, Chapter 80 amending Sections 44-5002 and 44-5004 (effective 1978).

[29]Arkansas Statutes 70-914 *et seq.* (effective 1981).

[30]Section 501 1C 24-4.5-2-501 (effective 1979).

[31]Louisiana Revised Statutes, Louisiana Consumer Credit Law, Title 9, Section 3516, Paragraph (17) (effective 1978).

[32]Michigan Compiled Laws of 1970, Section 445.111 (effective 1980).

[33]North Dakota Century Code, Sections 51-18-01 to 51-18-07 (effective 1979).

[34]Oregon Revised Statutes 83.710 and 646.608 (effective 1979).

[35]See note 25.

[36]Section 40194-251 (effective 1979).

[37]Ordinance of Aug. 31, 1965, Section 18-51.1 of the Sheffield Code (1965).

[38]Ordinance No. 727 (1972).

[39]Ordinance No. 4788-78, Section 719.01(b)(1)(c) (1978).

[40]Ordinance No. 76-45, Section 1, Paragraph 733.02 (1976).

[41]Alabama Law Enforcement Officers, Inc. v. City of Anniston, 131 So. 897 (1961).

[42]*Id.,* p. 900.

[43]United States v. Neighborhood Periodical Club, Inc. (U.S.D.C.—Southern District of Ohio), Civil Action No. C-2246 (1980). For various reasons stated, the defendant, *inter alia,* was fined $150,000.

[44]*In re* Commercial Lighting Products, Inc., File No. 792 3053 (1980).

[45]*In re* Perfect Film & Chemical Corporation, Perfect Subscription Company, and Keystone Readers' Service, Inc., Docket No. C-1918 (1980).

[46]Southern District Court—Iowa (1980).

[47]FTC Docket No. 7823035 (1981).

[48]*Id.,* p. 17.

Chapter 9. Broadcast Media

[1]47 U.S.C. § 307(d).

[2]47 U.S.C. § 307.

[3]15 U.S.C. § 45.

[4]15 U.S.C. § 45(a)(1).

[5]Charles of the Ritz Distributors Corp. v. F.T.C., 143 F.2d 676 (1944).

[6][1967–1970 Transfer Binder] Trade Reg. Rep. (CCH), paragraph 19,074 (Consent Order 1970).

[7][1967–1970 Transfer Binder] Trade Reg. Rep. (CCH), paragraph 19,219 (1971).

[8]In the Matter of Ideal Toy Company, 64 F.T.C. 297 (1964).

[9]*Id.,* p. 316.

[10]In the Matter of Sun Oil Co., 84 F.T.C. 247 (1974).

[11]*Id.*, p. 249. The year 1974 was a bad year for additive claimants. See also In the Matter of Standard Oil Company of California, 84 F.T.C. 1401 (1974)—misrepresentation as to its F-310 gasoline additive—and In the Matter of Crown Central Petroleum Corp., 84 F.T.C. 1493 (1974)—misrepresentation of gasoline additive.

[12]F.T.C. v. Colgate-Palmolive Co., 380 U.S. 374 (1964).

[13]*Id.*, pp. 390–391.

[14]*Id.*, p. 393 (emphasis my own).

[15]*Id.*, p. 393 (emphasis my own).

[16][1967–1970 Transfer Binder] Trade Reg. Rep. (CCH), paragraph 18,897 (Consent Order 1970).

[17]ITT Continental Baking Company, Inc. v. F.T.C., 532 F.2d 207 (1976).

[18]*Id.*, p. 210. See also the FTC cases which exhaustively review the facts in issue:
a. In the Matter of ITT Continental Baking Company, 83 F.T.C. 865 (1973).

b. In the Matter of ITT Continental Baking Company, 83 F.T.C. 1105 (1973).

[19]In the Matter of Warner-Lambert Co., 86 F.T.C. 1938 (1975).

[20]Warner-Lambert Company v. F.T.C., 562 F.2d 749, 762 (D.C. Cir. 1977); *cert. denied*, 46 U.S.L.W. 3613 (Apr. 4, 1978).

[21]*Id.*, p. 762.

[22]United States v. J. B. Williams Co., Inc., 498 F.2d 414 (1974).

[23]Marich, Bob: "Consumerist Earns Grudging Respect," *Advertising Age,* Mar. 16, 1981, p. 12. Another article in this area that is well worth reading is *Comment, Illusion or Deception: The Use of "Props" and "Mock-Ups" in Television Advertising,* 72 Yale L.J. 145 (1962).

[24]National Association of Broadcasters Code Authority: *Children's Television Advertising Guidelines,* 2d ed., 1977, Section I: "General."

[25]Home Box Office, Inc. v. FCC, 567 F.2d 9 (1977); *cert. denied*, 434 U.S. 829 (1977).

[26]C.B.S., Inc. v. Teleprompter Corp., 476 F.2d 338, 410 (1973).

[27]17 U.S.C. § 111 (1976).

[28]17 U.S.C. § 111(d)(a)(B) (Supp. I 1977).

[29]*The Home Shopping Show* might be considered an example of an entire-show commercial. In the 30-minute open format the guest appears live solely for the purpose of showcasing his or her product. The advertiser describes

the product in detail and maybe gives a demonstration citing benefits and information on how the viewer can purchase without leaving home. (A toll-free number is employed for taking orders and providing additional information, and a special address for ordering is provided on the air.) Unlike the 30-second jingle of commercial TV, the 30-minute infomercial makes it possible for the buyer to get enough information to make an intelligent purchase decision immediately.

[30]Columbus, Ohio, is not the only Qube service area. Qube is available in many cities across the nation, including Dallas, Houston, Pittsburgh, and St. Louis.

[31]Warner Annex's Qube contracts to date contain statements that the customers' records will be kept confidential. The record of buying tastes, political preferences, shows watched, and so on, *is* in existence.

[32]Another legal area of some potential (though not affecting the marketer directly) is obscenity. Uncut blue movies on *Escapade* or the hard-core programs found on *Midnight Blue* could prompt laws restricting programs. (Legislation to bar or restrict cable porn has already been introduced in Florida, Massachusetts, and New York.) The obscenity law generally observes the "contemporary community" standard. As communities vary, so might the laws. This restrictive legal impact may have programming implications in the 1980s that a marketer might consider, especially because as of 1981 only some blue-movie stations and Home Box Office were showing a profit.

On the positive side, as of 1981 writing talent may improve. One of the criticisms of cable has been that while superior "hardware" exists, the programming or "software" has lagged in quality. The Writers Guild is now permitted to work in cable, and this infusion of talent might improve the programming.

[33]Ruff, Howard: *How to Prosper During the Coming Bad Years*, Time Books, 1979. Anyone reading, *inter alia* pages 91 to 92 and 115, would think twice about getting involved in electronic funds transfer and many banking transactions in general.

[34]DeLay, Robert: "The 1980s: A Time for International Cooperation," *Direct Marketing*, May 1981, p. 35.

[35]Christopher, Maurine: "Ritchie Casts Vote for Strict Cable Rules," *Advertising Age*, Mar. 16, 1981, p. 48, Videotech Update. See also Fred Graham's commentary "Cable TV Could Be the Peeping Tom of the '80s," *TV Guide*, July 4, 1981, pp. 30–31.

[36]Morner: "It Pays to Knock Your Competitor," *Fortune*, Vol. 97, no. 111, Feb. 13, 1978.

[37]There is some debate over exactly who benefits the most—you or your competitor, who obtains free air time. See "Jack v. Mac," *Time*, May 5,

1975, pp. 71–72, and Shimp and Dyer, "The Effects of Comparative Advertising Mediated by Market Position of Sponsoring Brand," *Journal of Advertising,* vol. 13, no. 19, summer 1978.

[38]Firestone Tire and Rubber Co. v. F.T.C., 481 F.2d 246 (1973), *cert. denied,* 414 U.S. 112 (1972).

Chapter 10. Lists and List Rental

[1]See also Robert J. Posch, Jr., "Will Quality Lists Be Available in the 1990s?" *Direct Marketing,* October 1981, p. 202.

[2]For example, U.S. H.R. 1984—the Comprehensive Right to Privacy Act introduced in 1976 by Representative Barry Goldwater Jr. and Ed Koch. The former, bearing a distinctively Conservative name and voting record, has been very active in the field of privacy.

[3]For an excellent article on point, see Alan Magill, "The 9-Digit Zip Code: Will It Fit Into Marketers' Plans to Unlock Census Data?" *ZIP,* March 1981, p. 31.

[4]For example, see Marvin Monsky, "Motivation Demographics: The Dynamics of the Direct Mail Buying Decision," *ZIP,* September 1978, p. 81, and "Future of Compiled Lists," *ZIP,* December 1978, p. 48 (interesting discussion of the potential of the Freedom of Information Act to list compilers).

[5]U.S. Department of Health, Education, and Welfare, *Records, Computers and the Rights of Citizens* (1973), copyright 1973 by the Massachusetts Institute of Technology. See especially pages 71 to 73.

[6]219 F. Supp. 880 (S.D.N.Y. 1967).

[7]40 Ohio Misc. 51, 321 N.E.2d 791 (C.P. 1974), *aff'd,* 45 Ohio App.2d 69, 341 N.E.2d 337 (1975).

[8]Superior Court of California (1977).

[9]15 U.S.C. 552 *et seq.*

[10]These individual records were defined as "any item, collection, or grouping of information about an individual that is maintained by an agency in a system of records, defined as a group of any records under the control of an agency from which information is retrieved by the name of the individual or by some identifying number, symbol, or other identifying particular assigned to the individual" [5 U.S.C. § 552a(a)].

[11]S. Rep. No. 1183, 93d Cong., 2d Sess. 78, reprinted in (1974) U.S. Code of Congress & Ad. News, 6916, 6992.

[12]For more information, write:

DMMA Mail Preference Service
6 East 43d Street
New York, N.Y. 10017

Or call (212) 689-4977.

Two federal statutes also assist an individual trying to eliminate certain specific classes of mail. One of them, 39 U.S.C. 3008, concerns itself with pandering, while 39 U.S.C. 3010 is directed at unsolicited sexually oriented material. Neither affects the normal commercial mailer.

[13]Privacy Protection Study Commission, *Personal Privacy in an Information Society*, 1977, pp. 125–154. The recommendations are found on pages 147 to 153.

Recommendation 1

"That a person engaged in interstate commerce who maintains a mailing list should NOT be required by law to remove an individual's name and address from such a list upon request of that individual, except as already provided by law."

Recommendation 2

"That a private-sector organization which rents, sells, exchanges, or otherwise makes the addresses, or names and addresses, of its customers, members, or donors available to any other person for use in direct-mail marketing and solicitation, should adopt a procedure whereby each customer, member, or donor is informed of the organization's practice in that respect,* including a description of the selection criteria that might be used in selling, renting or exchanging lists, such as ZIP codes, interest, buying patterns, and level of activity, and, in addition, is given an opportunity to indicate to the organization that he does not wish to have his address, or name and address, made available for such purposes. Further, when a private-sector organization is informed by one of its customers, members, or donors that he does not want his address, or name and address, made available to another person for use in direct-mail marketing or solicitation, the organization should promptly take whatever steps are necessary to assure that the name and address is not so used, including notifying a multiple-response compiler or a credit bureau to whom the name and address has been disclosed with the prospect that it may be used to screen or otherwise prepare lists of names and addresses for use in direct mail marketing or solicitation."

Recommendation 3

"That each State review the direct-mail marketing and solicitation uses that are made of State agency records about individuals and for those that are used for such purposes, direct the State agency maintaining them to devise a procedure

*The rationale for this is found throughout this report. The most lucid statement (I believe) is on page 134:

" . . . the fact that so many mailing list users are of the one-way variety is one of several justifications for holding the record keeper in whose files the name originates, rather than the users of lists derived from these files, responsible for removing a name from a list."

whereby an individual can inform the agency that he does not want a record pertaining to himself to be used for such purposes and have that fact noted in the record in a manner that will assure that the individual's preference will be communicated to any user of the record for direct-mail marketing or solicitation. Special attention should be paid to Department of Motor Vehicle records and the practices of agencies who prepare mailing lists for the express purpose of selling, renting or exchanging them with others."

A full text of the entire 651-page report from the Privacy Protection Study Commission might still be obtainable at a nominal charge. Please write to the Superintendent of Documents, U.S. Government Printing Office, Washington, D.C. 20402, and ask about stock number 052-003-00395-3.

See also A. Drey, "Are You Working to Comply with the Privacy Commission?" *Direct Marketing,* March 1978, p. 24.

[14]"Getting It and Getting Rid of It," *Consumer Reports,* 1976, pp. 540 and 542.

[15]For example, California A.B. 150 (1976–1977).

[16]Birnbaum, Jeffrey H.: "After Eros: Ginzburg Pushes Tabloids to Compile Lucrative Mail-Order Lists," *Wall Street Journal,* Mar. 18, 1980.

[17]For a solid review of lists in general, read Robert E. Smith, *PRIVACY— How to Protect What's Left of It,* Anchor Press, Doubleday & Company, Inc., 1979.

[18]Ballard, David P.: "Privacy and Direct Mail Advertising," *Fordham Law Review,* vol. 47, 1979, pp. 495 and 526.

[19]*Privacy Journal,* vol. VI, no. 10, August 1980, p. 1.

[20]Iowa Code, Section 68A.7, Subsection 2.

[21]Arizona Law, Chapter 183 (1981—formerly H.B. 2097). The version in Texas (1981—H.B. 2378) died as of the adjournment of the session in that state.

[22]40 Ohio Misc. 51, 321 N.E.2d 791 (C.P. 1974), *aff'd,* 45 Ohio App.2d 69, 341 N.E.2d 337 (1975).

[23]*Id.,* p. 795.

[24]Another one was subsequently introduced: Ohio S.B. 79 (1979).

[25]Lamont v. Commissioner of Motor Vehicles (D.C., S.D.N.Y. 1967), 269 F. Supp. 880, 884, *aff'd,* 2 Civ. 386 F.2d 449 (1968).

[26]This reverse trend was acknowledged by the report of the Privacy Protection Study Commission, *Personal Privacy in an Information Society,* July 1977, page 127, note 10: that "at this publication there are 36 states that permit motor vehicle records to be used in the manner described." Three less since 1977. We are seeing a steady erosion from the period of 49 states quoted in *Lamont.*

[27]5 U.S.C. 552.

[28]Wine Hobby USA, Inc. v. U.S. Internal Revenue Service, 502 F.2d 133 (3d Cir. 1974).

[29]*Id.,* p. 137 (emphasis my own).

[30]*Id.,* p. 137 (emphasis my own).

[31]*Id.,* p. 138 (emphasis my own).

[32]Refer back to our discussion in Chapter 6 of the Fair Credit Reporting Act (15 U.S.C.S. 1681).

[33]For a well-articulated discussion of the subtle issue, see Ray Lewis, "Speaking Out," *ZIP,* July–August 1980, p. 25.

[34]For a good commentary and call to action, see Ray Lewis, "All Mailers Must Respond to the Challenges Coming in the Individual State Legislatures," *ZIP,* November–December 1980, p. 26.

Glossary

Advertising Medium: The vehicle (e.g., direct mail) used to carry the advertising message from the sender to the intended receiver.

Automated Telephone Services: Machines capable of placing a series of telephone calls, delivering a prerecorded message, and recording the recipient's response. They are the subject of much debate and have been banned or strictly regulated in many states.

Bait and Switch: A bait offer is an attractive but insincere offer to sell a product or service which the seller does not intend to sell. The primary goal of the seller is to switch consumers from the advertised bait product or service in order to sell something else, usually at a higher price or on a basis more advantageous to the seller. The secondary goal is to increase store traffic.

Bona Fide Prices: Prices which must exist and which must actually be paid for goods or services over a reasonable period of time in the same geographic area before they can be referred to in sale advertisements that include price comparisons.

Cable Television: A system in which large antennae are positioned to receive television broadcasts, amplify the signals, and deliver them via coaxial cable to subscribers. Originally it was designed to be a service to those unable to obtain adequate television reception. Increasingly cable systems are being used to deliver a wide selection of channels, features, and services. (Also referred to as CATV—Community Antenna Television.)

Cooling Off: The seller must give oral and written notification of the buyer's right to cancel within 3 business days. In addition, the buyer must receive a copy of the contract or sales receipt.

Copy Segmentation: Adapting the advertising message or its media to the unique needs of each market segment.

Coupon: A sales promotion certificate that entitles the holder to either a specified saving on a product or service or a cash refund.

Credit: Time that is given for paying a debt. Finance charges and/or installment payments may or may not be involved. Whenever a specific credit term is offered, it must be available to all unless the offer clearly discloses any restrictions or qualifications.

Credit Bureau: An organization that collects credit information for dissemination to members or subscribers upon request. Credit bureaus are sometimes cooperatives, owned by the users of the service.

Decoy: A name inserted in a mailing list for verification of its proper usage. This deliberate placement is referred to as "salting."

Demographic Segmentation: Selecting target markets on the basis of statistical information such as age, sex, income, or a geographic unit such as a zip code.

Direct Mail: The mailing of advertising solicitations directly to consumers by means of the Postal Service or private direct-delivery service. The term may refer to a mail-order firm selling only by mail with no retail outlets and a retail store that sells by mail.

Direct-Response List: A list of persons who answered a direct-response offer of another firm. It is purchased from the firm or through a broker for a one-time-only promotion.

Distribution Channel: The route taken by a product as it passes from the original owner or maker to the ultimate consumer.

Drop Shipper: A limited-function merchant wholesaler who sells merchandise to a customer and then arranges for the producer or manufacturer to deliver it directly (drop-ship) to the buyer.

Dual Distribution: Using two channels to market a product.

Effective Cost per Thousand: Obtained by dividing the cost of the medium by the number of persons in the target audience reached by the medium.

Endorsement: A recommendation for a product or service, usually paid for, given by a prominent celebrity or someone who would be expected to have specific experiences to relate concerning the product or service.

Exotic Media: Atypical direct-response vehicles. Examples include door-to-door circulars, coupons, package inserts, catalog bind-ins, and statement stuffers.

Free: This word is used to indicate that a product or service is an unconditional gift. It is also used when a purchase is required. In which case, all the conditions concerning the receipt and retention of the product or service offered must be clearly and conspicuously set forth in immediate conjunction with the first use of the word "free" so that there is no reasonable probability that the terms of the offer will be misunderstood.

Game: A sales-promotion device that requires no skill on the part of the participants, since pure chance determines the winner.

Infomercial: A 5-to-15-minute hybrid cable program having informational and entertainment components similar to those of a typical television program. However, it is designed as an extended advertisement for a particular product or for specific products.

Installment Buyer: One who orders goods or services and pays for them in two or more periodic payments after they are delivered.

Interactive: Refers to a two-way information system whereby the information receiver can communicate directly with the information supplier.

Internal Data: Operational data such as sales figures, credit figures, and lists generated within a firm.

Internal House List: The advertiser's own list of customers obtained through internal compilation or buyer response.

Interstate: Refers to operations crossing state lines. For trademark registration you must place your product in interstate commerce. Interstate telephone services come under the jurisdiction of the Federal Communications Commission.

Intrastate: Refers to operations that remain within the boundaries of a specific state. Telephone services within a particular state are under the jurisdiction of that state's Public Service Commission or Board of Public Utilities.

List Broker: An individual who makes all the necessary arrangements for one company to make use of the list of another company. Services may include research, selection, recommendation, and follow-up analysis and evaluation.

List Cleaning: The process of correcting a name and address on a mailing list and/or removing a name and address because it is no longer accurate.

List Price Comparison: A list price may be advertised as comparable to the advertised sale price only if it is the actual selling price currently charged in the market area where the claim is made and the products in the comparison are of at least like grade and quality, demonstrable by objective evidence.

List Rental: An arrangement in which a list owner furnishes names and addresses on his or her list to a mailer, together with the privilege of using the list one time only (unless otherwise are specified). A list can be selected from a mass list compiled on the basis of geographic, demographic, or psychographic factors, or it can be rented from a firm whose clientele closely resembles the type of audience desired. The list owner is paid a royalty by the mailer, usually a specific fee per name. The list owner will establish a specific date or specific dates on which the user has the obligation to mail to those on a specific list.

Lottery: A sales-promotion device requiring a contest containing the elements of chance, consideration, and prize.

Material Statement: Any statement in a promotion which is capable of affecting the decision to purchase.

Member: One who has paid a fee or has committed himself or herself for a minimum number of purchases during a specified period of time.

Member Get a Member: A term indicating a broad range of referral promotions by various firms whereby a current customer is offered free merchandise for soliciting other customers.

Merge/Purge: Combining two or more lists and simultaneously eliminating duplication.

Microwave: A very short (high-frequency) electromagnetic wave typically used in communications to carry the signals of distant television stations.

Negative Option: A buying plan in which a customer or club member agrees to accept and pay for merchandise announced in advance at regular intervals unless the individual formally notifies the company not to send the merchandise within the time period specified with the announcement.

Out-of-Stock: Refers to merchandise that is not presently available but will be available at some future date.

Pandering Complaint: A formal complaint to the U.S. Postal Service that an individual signs to avoid receiving "obscene" advertising mail from a particular firm or firms.

Place Utility: Value added to a product as a result of making it available to the consumer at a convenient location, that is, his or her home.

Premium: A product offered free or at less than its usual price to encourage the consumer to buy another product or make a commitment to a membership.

Purge: Refers to the deletion or cleaning out of names and addresses in house files.

Rules and Guidelines: The FTC adopts both, but the terms are not synonymous. Trade regulation rules define with specificity acts or practices which are unfair or deceptive. Industry guides do *not* have the force of substantive law. However, the guides do advise the industry of how the FTC will interpret the law. A violation of a guide may lead the FTC to issue a complaint.

Sale: Refers to a significant reduction from the usual and customary price of a product or service offered and may continue for a reasonable period of time not to exceed 30 days.

Shipping and Handling: The cost to the seller of fulfilling and delivering orders. If an extra charge is required for the delivery of an advertised product, it must be clearly and conspicuously stated in the offer.

Sweepstakes: A sales-promotion device that offers prizes to participants but, unlike contests, requires no analytical thinking. Consumers need only to enter their names, numbers, or other identification symbols to qualify for the random drawing. No purchase is necessary.

Target Market: The people who are most likely to purchase a product.

Unique Selling Proposition: An advertising claim concerning a product which is thought to be strong enough to cause customers to buy the product rather than a rival product. To be unique, the proposition must be one that the competition either cannot or does not offer.

Warranty: A subsidiary promise or collateral agreement, the breach of which entitles the buyer to make certain claims for damages, replacement, or repair against the warrantor. The warranty may be full or limited (depending upon the express agreement) or implied in law.

WATS: Wide Area Telephone Service. This is a long-distance service offered to business customers that enables them to get a discount for a high volume of long-distance calls of short duration. It is an excellent service for any telephone marketing program.

Zip Code: A group of five digits (expanding to nine by 1983) used by the U.S. Postal Service to designate specific post offices, stations, branches, buildings, or large firms.

Index

Address hits, 76, 82, 85
Advertising:
  bait and switch, 112–114
  cable TV, 144, 145, 148, 149
  children's, 47, 138, 139
  comparative, 148, 149
  comparative pricing, 15–18
  corrective, 135, 136
  demonstrations, 130–139
  depictions of United States currency
    in, 25, 54
  documentation of claims, demon-
    strations, testimonials, and en-
    dorsements, 138
  endorsements or testimonials in, 39–
    49, 138
  "free" offers, 23–27
  FTC standards, 42, 43
  general guidelines, 137
  infomercials, 145
  sales promotions, 20–22
  simulated checks, 60–63
  sweepstakes, 50–60
  use of term "new," 22
  warranties, 27–30
Advertising medium, definition of, 227
Advisory opinions, FTC, 22
Alabama:
  municipal ordinances affecting tele-
    phone sales in, 123, 124

Alabama (*Cont.*):
  sales tax on bad debts in, 88, 215
Alaska:
  law concerning telephone sales and
    prerecorded messages in, 117
  restrictions affecting commercial lists
    in, 161
Aldens, Inc., 82
Amoco Motor Club, 62
Amoco Oil Company, 80, 84, 85
Arizona:
  legislative activity affecting lists in,
    159, 161
  telephone sales in, cooling-off period
    for, 121
Arkansas:
  restrictions affecting lists in, 161
  sales tax on bad debts in, 88, 215
  telephone sales in, cooling-off period
    for, 121
Artistic property, substitution of, 8
Aspin, Les, 115
Automated telephone services, defini-
    tion of, 227
Automatic dialing devices, 114–119

Bait and switch:
  compliance checklist, 113
  definition of, 227

233